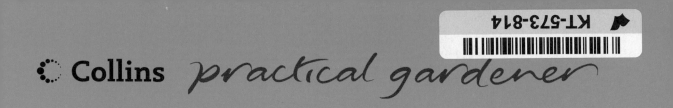

Collins *practical gardener*

BAMBOOS & GRASSES

JON ARDLE

First published in 2005 by HarperCollins*Publishers*

77–85 Fulham Palace Road, London, W6 8JB

The Collins website address is:

www.collins.co.uk

Text by Jon Ardle; copyright © HarperCollins*Publishers*

Artworks and design © HarperCollins*Publishers*

The majority of photographs in this book were taken by
Tim Sandall. A number of other images were supplied
by David Sarton

Cover photography by Tim Sandall

Photographic props: Coolings Nurseries, Rushmore Hill,
Knockholt, Kent, TN14 7NN, www.coolings.co.uk

Design and editorial: Focus Publishing, Sevenoaks, Kent

Project editor: Guy Croton

Editor: Vanessa Townsend

Project co-ordinator: Caroline Watson

Design & illustration: David Etherington

Editorial assistant: Katie Lovell

For HarperCollins

Senior managing editor: Angela Newton

Editor: Alastair Laing

Assistant editor: Lisa John

Design manager: Luke Griffin

Production: Chris Gurney

A CIP catalogue record for this book is available from the
British Library

ISBN 0-00-718299-6

Colour reproduction by Colourscan

Printed and bound in Great Britain by The Bath Press Ltd

Contents

Introduction

Twenty years ago, mention 'grasses' to the average gardener and they would immediately think 'lawn'. Today, the diversity of grasses in size, form and colour available to the adventurous gardener has never been greater. Add in bamboos (also in the grass family) and plants with similarly narrow-leaved, clump-forming growth forms such as sedges, rushes, woodrushes and horsetails, and there are plants to suit every size and style of garden, from the ultra-modern to the most traditional.

Grasses may not produce the showy, scented flowers of insect-pollinated plants – they are pollinated by the wind – but this does not mean they lack interest. Many produce beautiful flowers that stir in the slightest of breezes, introducing movement and often a gentle rustling sound that add a whole new dimension to the garden. Bamboos and some grasses are evergreen, but even the bleached brown leaves of non-evergreen types can stand up to the worst winter weather, adding style and structure to the garden in its quietest season, and looking particularly magnificent rimmed with frost.

There are also grasses and grass-like plants to suit every soil type. Many stand up well to the most exposed

Bamboos are among the most exotic and striking of garden plants, yet are easy to care for

Grass flowers may not have the colours of insect-pollinated plants but the range is amazing

conditions and the thinnest of soils, while others thrive in the boggiest of ground and deep shade. A large proportion make excellent container plants – a group of pots of grasses in contrasting leaf colours can look quite magnificent.

Provided their basic needs for water, light and nutrients are met, most grasses and bamboos require very little looking after; indeed, they are quite happy left largely to their own devices, and as some of the most low-maintenance plants available, are an excellent choice for the busy gardener. There are a wide range of bamboos, grasses and grass-like plants profiled in this book.

How to Use This Book

This book is divided into three parts. The opening section guides you through the practical stages, explaining the various types of plants you can use, where to buy them, when and how to plant them, and finally care and maintenance. A comprehensive plant directory follows, with individual entries on over 80 of the most commonly available genera of bamboos, grasses, sedges, horse tails and rushes. These are listed in alphabetical order in a separate chapter devoted to these groups of plants. The final section of the book covers plant problems. Troubleshooting pages allow you to diagnose the likely cause of any problems, and a directory of pests and diseases offers advice on how to solve them.

latin name of the plant genus, followed by its **common name**

detailed descriptions give specific advice on care for each plant, including pruning and pests and diseases

alphabetical tabs on the side of the page, colour-coded to help you quickly find the plant you want

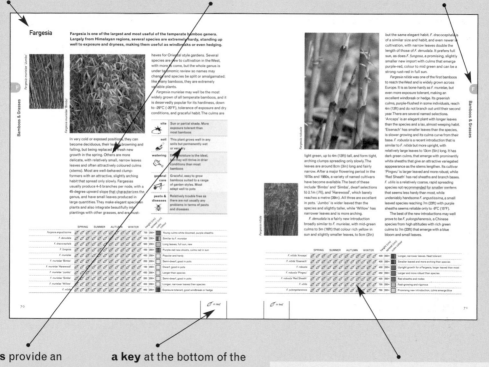

care charts provide an at-a-glance summary of the specific needs of the plant or genus

a key at the bottom of the page explains what each symbol means

variety charts list recommended selections of genera of bamboos, grasses, sedges, horse tails and rushes that feature more than one species or cultivated variety. These display key information to help you choose your ideal plant, showing:

• when (or if) the plant is in leaf during the year
• when (or if) the plant is in flower during the year
• the height and spread of a mature plant
• the principal colour of the flowers (or foliage)
• additional comments from the author

Assessing Your Garden

All gardens contain different microclimates – some areas are more exposed than others, others may be shadier and wetter. Whatever your garden's conditions, and whatever the type of plants you wish to grow, matching species to the conditions where you want to grow them is one of the secrets of gardening success. Give a plant an approximation of the conditions in which it grows in the wild, and it will usually give of its best.

Aspect, exposure & soil

Take time to assess your garden's conditions, particularly the aspect, soil type and degree of shelter, shade or exposure: it will pay dividends and make your chances of success much greater. A garden's aspect affects its degree of exposure to wind and cold, and the amount of light it receives. Some gardens get more sun than others; and some are more shady and cooler.

The degree of exposure of a garden depends largely on the openness of its immediate surroundings. Wind can cause physical damage, and strip plants of moisture to the point of wilting. Many bamboos and grasses, with their small, narrow leaves, stand up extremely well to exposure, and larger species can be used around a garden's boundaries to create more sheltered conditions for plants in their lee.

Knowing your soil is vital in choosing plants appropriate for your conditions. Many grasses, bamboos and grass-like plants are in fact relatively unfussy when it comes to pH, soil type and the amount of light they receive, but there are species that require acid or alkaline conditions and full sun or shade.

KEY

This symbol denotes shade, typically to be found wherever there is a tree or building casting a shadow.

The yellow line denotes sunshine. On one side the sun will shine in the morning, on the other, in the afternoon.

This blue arrow denotes the direction of wind. In this case, the wind swirls over the fence at the end of the garden.

some bamboos make good hedges and windbreaks

many grasses thrive in full sun and go well with herbaceous perennials in mixed borders

rushes, sedges and horsetails like boggy ground, and many will grow well in ponds

larger bamboos make bold specimen plants in lawn

shady areas suit the majority of sedges

Using Grasses, Bamboos and Grass-like Plants in the Garden

As a glance through the A–Z section of this book makes clear, there is a huge range of plants of these types already available to gardeners. More species are coming into cultivation all the time, and a host of new cultivars are being selected and introduced from species that are already well known. There is such a diversity of size, form, leaf colour, vigour and habit that it is difficult to generalize. Where to use each plant is covered in its individual profile, and what plants are best suited to specific gardening styles is covered in detailed notes. This section briefly defines the different plants covered, and gives a broad overview of where in the garden the different groups are likely to perform at their best.

True grasses

Both grasses and bamboos are classified as members of the Poaceae, the grass family. They are characterized by their narrow leaves and wind-pollinated flowers. They are some of the most highly-evolved and widely-distributed plants on earth, and members of the grass family are some of mankind's most important food crops – grains such as wheat, barley, oats and rice. Where conditions are unsuitable for most trees, grasses form the dominant plants of ecosystems like the African savannah, North American Prairies and Russian Steppes.

One of the grasses' secrets of success is the fact that their growing points, instead of being at the tip of their shoots like most plants, are at the base of their leaves, close to the stems. Their leaves can therefore survive the constant trimming of grazing herbivores (and the lawnmower). In the tropics particularly, several genera of bamboos have literally risen to compete with trees. Thanks to the support of their woody stems or culms, they have been able to grow to a great height. Unlike the single trunk of a tree that gradually expands in size as it grows, bamboos grow by sending up many 'trunks' in an ever-widening clump. Many grasses grow in a similar way, spreading by underground stems known as rhizomes that send up new shoots.

Grasses vary tremendously in size and shape. Some form tight clumps or tussocks, while others spread by rhizomes and can make good ground cover. Most flower regularly, adding an extra dimension, and the dynamics added to a garden by the way their leaves stir in the

Grasses of different heights, colours and forms work particularly well planted en masse

slightest of breezes is an under-appreciated aspect. One of the most noticeable differences is in colour – not all grasses are green (and there are many shades of green, from dull olive to bright apple-green). Blues, greys, yellow, bronze, purple and even red-leaved grasses are all available. Leaves can vary from thin, soft and needle-like to relatively broad and leathery, in a few cases even armoured with spines along the edges.

Large, statuesque grasses such as many *Miscanthus sinensis* cultivars, *Stipa gigantea* and *Cortaderia selloana* (pampas grass), all of which are capable of topping 1.8m (6ft), make excellent specimen plants placed by themselves so that their full form can be appreciated. The ubiquitous pampas grass in splendid isolation in the front garden (particularly the hideous pink-flowered forms) has however become a real gardening cliché, so is probably best avoided. The taller Miscanthus cultivars can even make an unusual and attractive 'hedge' – this may not be evergreen, but the bleached straw leaves and flowers have as much winter presence as hornbeam or beech hedges, which also hold onto their brown leaves.

These 'bruisers' of the grass world have the vigour to hold their own with the tallest of herbaceous perennials, whether in traditional borders or the expansive, naturalistic 'Prairie' style of planting.

A characteristic of many species of grass, such as smaller Miscanthus and Stipa cultivars, Eragrostis, *Holcus mollis*, and many of the tussock (clump-forming) species like Pennisetum and Festuca and their selections, is their drought tolerance. Most cope extremely well in gardens with dry, thin and sandy soils, and are adapted to the most exposed of conditions. These more modestly-sized grasses associate well with each other, particularly where a mix of leaf colour and growth forms are placed together, and also with herbaceous perennials and shrubs. They act as perfect foils to more showy, large-flowered plants, and the grasses will still be there long after the flowers of these have faded.

Species adapted to more shady, woodland conditions include Deschampsia, Milium and Phalaris. Variegated selections for shade that can really brighten up dark, dull areas include *Hakonechloa macra* 'Alboaurea', *Holcus mollis* 'Albovariegatus' and yellow-leaved *Milium effusum* 'Aureum'. Most grass species will cope well with partial shade for some of the day, provided they receive a few hours of more direct sunlight.

Small and delicate-looking grass species such as blue-leaved *Festuca glauca*, and smaller Mollinia and Pennisetum cultivars make excellent container plants, either alone, in combination with each other or with herbaceous plants such as the smaller hosta cultivars. Blood-grass, *Imperata cylindrica* 'Rubra', which has scarlet leaf tips is a favourite for container culture, as it is not the hardiest and can be moved to provide it with winter protection.

Few true grasses relish really wet conditions, but fortunately this is where many grass-like species positively thrive. Shady areas that are more moist are the preserve of most sedges, particularly those in the Carex genus. Very wet areas that receive at least some sun, such as bog gardens or the fringes of ponds, also suit sedges, along with rushes, reed mace, Acorus and horsetails.

Sedges

Sedges are primarily evergreen and tend to be found in boggy ground; indeed some species are true emergents, growing in shallow water around the fringes of ponds and lakes, making them particularly useful in boggy conditions and water gardens. Although also wind pollinated, their flower structures are different to those of true grasses and though they look grass-like, they are not close relatives of the grasses and bamboos.

As a group, sedges are mostly found in moist or downright boggy areas, or in standing water. They tend to prefer partial or full shade, and are nearly all evergreen. Relatively low growing, most form dense, arching tufts. Many variegated forms have been selected that keep their striping well even in fairly dense shade, and there are blue, bronze, yellow and brown-leaved species and cultivars available. Like the grasses, sedges are

Reed maces, bullrushes or cat-tails (Typha) are placed in their own family, and while undeniably handsome, with upright leaves to well over 1.8m (6ft), can be similarly thuggish. *Typha latifolia*, another British native, is perhaps best grown in a pond in a container. Smaller species and less vigorous variegated selections are available.

The true rushes, Juncus, are perhaps best described as 'interesting' plants for boggy areas and ponds, though there are a few that have genuine appeal. Members of the genus Acorus are often tagged as 'rushes' but are in fact members of the arum family. Small, neat, clump-forming, evergreen and often variegated, they are ideal for use in and around smaller ponds and make good pot plants.

Horse tails and others

Horse tails are primitive plants that are closer to mosses and ferns than grasses, reproducing by spores rather than seeds. Species of Equisetum, horse tails are the surviving members of an ancient plant lineage and closer to ferns and mosses than any of the other plants in this book. Some species can be invasive (*Equisetum hyemalis* is a native species and the curse of many an allotment holder), but several have real ornamental merit in their ramrod-straight, often brown-banded stems and are again evergreen. Other grass-like plants include several species with strap-shaped, grass-like leaves such as Acorus, lily turf (Liriope), woodrushes (Luzula) and 'black grass' (*Ophiopogon planiscapus* 'Nigrescens'). All are evergreen, useful in shaded areas and adapt well to pot culture.

wind-pollinated, but their flowers are even more demure than those of the grasses. A few New Zealand sedges such as the many forms of *Carex comans* are atypical and will cope with drier, more exposed conditions, and the bronzy leaves of many of these selections complement grasses with coloured leaves. Most sedges make undemanding, attractive container plants, providing they get enough water. Moisture requirements vary from species to species in sedges; this issue is covered in the A–Z section of this book.

Rushes

What tend to be lumped together as 'rushes' belong to several genera that are not particularly closely related, but because they produce strap-shaped or quill-like leaves and are usually found growing in water, have earned the catch-all name 'rush'. The British native common reed, *Phragmites australis*, is actually a grass, but is an aggressive colonizer that can reach 2.4m (8ft) in height. It is not suited to anything but the largest of wildlife ponds, but some of its variegated selections and smaller species are more ornamental and less vigorous grown away from water.

Bamboos

Bamboos are undeniably exotic, and their grace, movement and evergreen structure are finally beginning to be used to their full potential in British gardens, particularly those with an oriental or modern, contemporary feel. Unfortunately, bamboos were long characterized as rampantly invasive: this is not actually true, as controlling their size is no more difficult than keeping a vigorous shrub in check or pruning a fruit tree to maximize its flowering. However, in order to understand where and how to use bamboos successfully in the garden, it is important to know something about their form and growth habits.

All bamboos reproduce largely vegetatively (flowering is extremely rare), by sending up new shoots from below-ground stems called rhizomes, but many form tight clumps and only spread relatively slowly. Keeping them in check can be simply a matter of snapping-off newly emerging shoots (culms) as they appear, either by hand or by lawnmower. There are more invasive or 'running' species, but among the temperate, hardy bamboos, these are relatively few, and there are a few garden situations where this characteristic is of positive benefit. Running bamboos will rapidly colonize large areas of dry shade under trees or close to buildings, for example, and such species can also make excellent hedges or screens.

Clump-formers

Clump-forming bamboos such as Phyllostachys and Fargesia species are characterized by their root systems or rhizomes as pachymorphic. In essence, this means that their rhizomes are relatively short and thick, and each terminates in a new shoot that will produce a single stem or culm. Because unlike trees, for example, a bamboo culm cannot expand sideways, it emerges at its final diameter, growing up rather than out. The number, thickness and final height of new culms tends to increase over time. Culms often emerge and grow to their full height in one year and only produce branches with leaves the following year. All bamboo plants will benefit from regularly thinning out old, thin and leafless dead culms.

> **TIP**
> Most temperate bamboos are nowhere near as invasive as popular myth would have us believe, expanding only slowly over time. Many are no more difficult to keep in check by annual pruning than the majority of ornamental shrubs.

Phyllostachys nigra is a quintessential clump-forming bamboo

the short, unbranched rhizomes of clump-forming or 'pachymorphic' bamboos

There is a growing range of clump-forming species and cultivars available, including several with variegated leaves, and others with vividly-coloured culms. Few other plants can add such an exotic, architectural look to a garden as instantly as a specimen bamboo. Planted alone in lawns or gravel where the beauty of their structure and movement can be appreciated with no distractions, they can look magnificent. They are obvious choices for oriental gardens, and also for the modern 'hardy exotic' style, married with subtropical-looking species such as bananas (Musa), cannas and tree ferns (Dicksonia).

However, bamboos also associate well with a wider range of other plants than is generally appreciated. They make good plants for the backs of borders, demure enough to complement more flamboyant herbaceous perennials in the summer foreground, but coming into their own in winter with their height and evergreen structure. Rounded, broadleaved evergreens such as viburnums, rhododendrons and camellias make an excellent contrast to the upright culms and smaller leaves of bamboos, and even a simple underplanting of ferns or ivy (Hedera) can look extremely effective.

Many clump-formers such as bushy *Shibataea kumasaca* and many of the Phyllostachys genus (perhaps the most varied and useful temperate bamboo genus) make excellent container plants, but it is important to keep them well watered and they will need repotting on a regular basis.

Running bamboos

Running species of bamboo are adapted to rapidly colonizing areas of suitable ground. Rather than forming tight clumps, their culms are more widely separated from each other and the structure of their rhizomes differs from the pachymorphic type. Running rhizomes are termed 'leptomorphic'. Essentially, these grow much longer than those of clump-formers, usually in straight lines, and each forms buds that throw up new culms at regular intervals.

Growth rates can vary considerably with particular conditions, especially the amount of moisture and nutrients a bamboo is getting. Estimating the ultimate height and spread of a bamboo is an inexact science as a result.

Smaller running species such as *Sasa palmata* and Indocalamus species are relatively short, usually 60cm–1m (2–3ft), but broad-leaved, making good ground

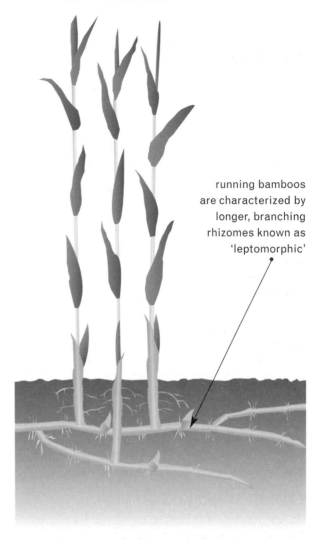

running bamboos are characterized by longer, branching rhizomes known as 'leptomorphic'

Sasa palmata f. *nebulosa* is a typical running bamboo

cover plants. However, unless their growth is restricted by physical barriers such as paving stones or landscape fabric sunk well into the ground all around them, their use in smaller gardens is not to be recommended. An alternative is to grow them in a large pot, where they can look stunning, but their vigour means they may need repotting annually. Slower-growing and smaller running bamboos such as white variegated *Pleioblastus variegatus* or yellow-striped *P. auricomus* (syn. *P. viridistriatus*) make excellent pot plants.

Bamboos for hedging

One of the most exposure-tolerant of bamboos is *Pseudosasa japonica*, making it an excellent hedging plant. *Fargesia nitida* and *Fargesia murielae* are also good choices for hedging and screening bamboos. All three will cope with drier conditions than most bamboo species, which means that they are not as subject to the vagaries of drying winds.

Choosing & Buying Plants

The majority of plants profiled in this book are relatively freely available from nurseries and garden centres, and the remainder are all stocked by at least some specialist nurseries. There are various advantages and disadvantages in buying plants from different sources.

Garden centres

Probably the most convenient of sources, few areas of the country are far from at least one garden centre, and in many areas there is a choice of several. Their major advantages are the ability to select plants yourself, choosing the largest or best individual, and as the majority of their stock is container grown, it can be planted at any time of the year. Spring is the traditional time for garden centre attendance, but providing a container-grown plant is kept well watered after planting out, it should establish successfully at virtually any time of the year.

Individual plants vary, so examine each and look for the largest and most vigorous specimens. Try to ensure that you are choosing from the most recently-acquired stock: tell-tale signs of older plants are faded or

Specialist nurseries normally offer the best selection of bamboos and grasses

missing labels, mosses and lichens colonizing the surface of the compost and a general lack of vigour and colour to the plants.

With so many grasses and sedges growing in distinct clumps, it can often pay to look out for pots with two or three smaller clumps rather than a single large one. These can be carefully split once you get them home (see propagation, pages 23–5), giving you more (albeit smaller) plants for your money. Most smaller sedges and grasses look better planted in threes or more in number rather than as single specimens anyway, particularly in borders.

The main drawback of most garden centres is that they tend to stock only a relatively limited range of the most popular species and cultivars of a broad range of plant types. Also, staff often do not have either the time or knowledge to give specialist plants such as bamboos the tailored care that they need. As non-specialists, their ability to give advice is limited. Garden centres can also be relatively expensive compared to other sources.

Specialist nurseries

Nurseries specializing in grasses, bamboos and sedges are becoming more common. They offer several advantages over garden centres if you are able to visit in person. Most of the plants will have been grown on-site by the staff selling them, who are usually more than happy to pass on their knowledge and experience. The range of plants offered by these nurseries is likely to far exceed that of the average garden centre, and plants may be available in a range of sizes.

Grasses and sedges will most probably have been container grown, but bamboos are often available either as bare-rooted plants (usually in the autumn and winter), often newly divided from mother plants on site whose mature characteristics you can examine, or as 'containerized' plants. They are grown in the ground, then lifted and put into a pot. The advantage of this growing system is that containerized plants tend to retain the vigour of a field-grown plant, which is usually higher than that of a similar plant grown in a pot. Nurseries tend to be cheaper than garden centres for

plants of comparable size, particularly for those grown in the field and most containerized stock.

Mail order

The quality of stock from mail order suppliers can be extremely variable, and if you are trying to source an unusual bamboo or grass, it is advisable to buy from a specialist nursery that offers mail order. Even with the costs of postage, this is often the cheapest way of obtaining particular cultivars, and avoids a long round trip if a nursery is distant. Most mail order specialists pack and prepare their stock extremely well and, for large plants particularly, tend to use couriers rather than the post. Peak mail order times tend to be spring and autumn, with many nurseries only offering the service at these times of year.

If you receive plants by mail order, unpack them immediately and ensure that none are damaged or missing. Either plant them out into their final positions as quickly as possible, or 'heel in' the plants, digging a hole large enough to take their roots comfortably and covering with soil firmed down lightly with the sole of your foot. Roots exposed to the wind can dry out and become damaged extremely quickly, reducing the plants' chances of establishing successfully. Move heeled-in plants to their final position as soon as possible.

TIP

Although there is the disadvantage that you cannot inspect mail order plants before purchase, the specialist nurseries that sell plants by post often have the best ranges, and are produced by growers who really know their plants.

Most mail order suppliers can be relied upon to pack plants properly

Planting

Once you have chosen your plants and decided where in the garden you want to place them, careful planting gives them the best chance of establishing successfully. If you are planting up an area for the first time, take the opportunity to improve the soil, if necessary, by adding bulky organic matter such as well-rotted farmyard manure, compost, and on heavy soils, plenty of sand or grit to improve drainage. It is usually best to have at least a rough idea of how you want a newly planted area to look; even an outline design for an area is better than none. Place the plants roughly where you want them while still in their pots, leaving enough space between them for growth, adjusting where necessary until you are happy with the juxtapositions of colours and forms.

Planting a pot grown grass or bamboo

First decide where you want to position the plant, trying out various arrangements until you are completely happy [A]. Water the plant well while still in its pot, immersing it in a bucket of water if it is really dry. Dig a hole deep enough to comfortably accommodate the size of pot [B]. Opinion is divided on whether to improve the soil by adding organic matter such as compost or well-rotted manure (or a granular fertilizer) to the planting hole – one school of thought says this merely encourages the existing rootball to stay within the environs of the hole rather than having to grow out in search of nutrients. The other argues that because most pot grown plants are raised in peat or compost-based growing media, digging in a quantity of similar material into the hole provides them with a 'half-and-half' mix to establish into.

Ease the plant gently out of its pot. Gently tease out some of the roots from the sides and base of the rootball. Do not worry if you break a few – the idea is to encourage the roots to grow outwards, not continue growing in circles. Sit the plant in the hole and check it is not placed too deep, or proud of the soil surface, adjusting if necessary, then gently feed the excavated soil around the rootball, firming with the fingers and avoiding air pockets. Firm gently around the plant with your foot [C]. Finally, water in well (this is to settle the soil into close contact with the roots, not provide the plant with even more water) [D], and apply an organic or inorganic mulch if necessary.

Planting a bare-root bamboo

Bamboo divisions often arrive bare rooted. Keep the roots well wrapped in damp material or polythene until you are ready to plant, and immerse the root system in a large container of water for a couple of hours immediately prior to planting. Tease out the main roots at the base of the rootball, but do not allow the entire rootball to fall apart [A]. Dig a hole deep enough to comfortably take the root system. Some bamboo nurserymen advocate not improving the soil at all to encourage the root system to grow out into the surrounding soil; others insist that it is best to improve both the excavated soil and soil in the base of the planting hole. Sit the bamboo in the hole [B], and do not be afraid to plant it a little bit deeper than it was previously growing – bamboo rhizomes tend to work their way towards

A

B

C

D

A

B

C

the surface as they grow. Keeping the plant upright, carefully fill around the root system with soil, working it into all the nooks and crannies formed by the tangle of rhizomes and firming it down lightly [C]. Water in well and apply a mulch over the whole area, ideally of its own leaves or those of another bamboo which are full of the silica the plant needs to form its culms, otherwise of organic material, such as composted bark, leafmould or garden compost.

Planting in pots

Many of the grasses and bamboos covered in this book adapt extremely well to pot culture. Although this means more frequent watering, you can tailor the compost to the soil conditions that the particular plant prefers. For

A

B

C

example, a moisture-loving shade tolerant species can be grown in a pot under a tree when planting into the ground may be too dry for it, or an acid-lover can be grown in a pot of ericaceous compost in the chalkiest of gardens. For permanent pot planting, a loam-based, John Innes type compost is always preferable to a peat or peat substitute based organic compost, as the latter tends to break down relatively quickly. Whatever the type of plant, repotting every two or three years into fresh compost will keep them healthy and looking their best.

To contain the growth of a bamboo, you can plant a container-grown specimen directly into the ground. Ideally, pot on the plant into a slightly larger container than the one it is growing in. Place the pot where you wish to install it [A]. Dig the hole to the required dimensions [B]. Ensure the pot sits at the right height, then backfill and firm the surrounding soil [C].

Care & Maintenance

Newly-established plants

Although grasses, bamboos and most other grass-like plants are relatively undemanding in cultivation and need relatively little care and maintenance, like most garden plants to grow them well means becoming familiar with their particular needs, likes and dislikes. Newly-planted plants in particular are vulnerable to adverse conditions such as drought and strong winds, as their root systems have been disturbed, reducing their ability to absorb moisture, and have yet to get firmly anchored. In dry and windy conditions, make sure they are kept well irrigated, particularly with moisture-lovers like many sedges.

In exposed sites, temporary windbreaks of sacking or plastic mesh attached to secured posts may make the difference between a plant surviving or failing to establish and then dying. This is particularly true with plants planted in autumn, when many bare-rooted bamboos are sent out by nurseries. Although bamboos are evergreens, they often lose some of their leaves in winter, and these may brown but be retained on the plant. Do not despair of a newly planted bamboo that browns off over winter, as the chances are it may well leaf out again in spring: it is establishment of the below-ground part of a bamboo that is important to its long term survival. Shortening all the culms of a newly-planted bamboo to reduce its demand for water is often a prudent measure to take on exposed sites.

A temporary plastic windbreak is a good idea for protecting new plants

> **TIP**
>
> If grass seedlings are popping up around the garden, keep the ones colonizing areas where they will look good and weed out the rest. If numbers are becoming a nuisance, prune off the mature seedheads before they begin shedding seeds.

Seasonal care and tidying

Grasses and sedges Many grass species are deciduous, but unlike plants like trees and shrubs, most do not readily shed their leaves. Their dried buff and brown leaves and flowers can be beautiful additions to the autumn and winter garden, but beauty is in the eye of the beholder, and while some gardeners leave their grasses dead and brown over winter, others prefer to shear them to ground level as soon as they bleach of colour. Either way, dead leaves should be removed by early spring before the plants start back into growth, to avoid damaging the delicate emerging new shoots.

A proportion of the leaves of evergreen sedges and grasses also tend to die off and brown over the winter, particularly towards their tips. Dead tips can be cut off relatively easily, and dead leaves are often only loosely attached to the base of the clump so can be teased out by combing through the clumps with the fingers. A word of warning: some grasses and sedges in particular have rows of teeth along the edges of their leaves that can easily cut through skin, so wear stout gloves when combing them out.

It is important to keep newly planted bamboos well watered

Regular combing out keeps grasses healthy and looking their best

Removing discoloured and tired leaves keeps bamboos fresh and neat

Bamboos Brown bamboo leaves can be picked off individually, but the fact that they retain their dead leaves is a characteristic of most species and, providing they are not too numerous, looks entirely natural. Many growers prune off the lowest branches of all the culms to both emphasize their beauty, and allow more light to reach any underplantings. The black culms of *Phyllostachys nigra*, purple stems of *P. violascens* or butter-yellow canes of *P. bambusoides* 'Castilloni', for example, can be polished to a gleam with a soft cloth, and are in fact much better appreciated bare of lower branches.

It is not generally acknowledged that bamboo culms can be shortened drastically to reduce their overall height without ill-effect to the plant, as with most shrubs. Wait until late spring or summer to do this, when

Use secateurs to trim old brown leaf tips from grasses and sedges

Simply snapping off the tips of emerging culms can keep a bamboo in check

A B

C D

plants can brown off completely and their growth be checked so heavily that they take months to recover, and in extreme cases can die off completely. Regularly repotting a container-grown bamboo is extremely important as the vigour of most species is such that they can completely fill a pot with rhizomes and roots in two years. Such pots are not only packed full of roots with a high demand for water, there is also very little soil remaining to store what water they are given, making droughting almost inevitable. This is also true of bamboos grown in pots sunk into the ground, which is a good method of controlling their spread where space is limited.

Generally, slower growing and smaller species of bamboo are the easiest to manage in pots. *Shibataea kumasaca*, Sasaella and smaller Phyllostachys species and cultivars can all be quite happy containerized. Pot growing is also a good way of controlling the spread of Pleioblastus species, which are short but can run rapidly. Cream-striped *P. variegatus*, gold variegated *P. auricomus* and little *P. pygmaeus* are all very effective in wide, shallow pots and can be pruned back to compost level every spring. This helps to curtail their vigour, but more importantly produces a flush of fresh, colourful new leaves. Large-leaved Indocalamus

they have reached their final height, as pruning too early can make culms abort. Newly-emerged culms that are cut back or snapped off to ground level – they are quite brittle at this stage – generally abort completely. This is the best way of controlling the spread of a bamboo: simply snap or mow off emerging culms where they are not wanted, and the plant will automatically divert its growth elsewhere.

All bamboos benefit from the regular removal to ground level of their oldest, weakest or obviously dead culms; this allows more light into the clump and makes space for new ones to arise and keeps the plant looking fresh. Low-growing species such as *Pleioblastus auricomus* and Sasa are usually cut hard back to ground level in Japan, so that the fresh new growth of spring can be enjoyed undiluted. The bamboo in the raised bed in the sequence above [A] looks tired and heavy. Firstly, cut out all the thin, weak and dead culms down to ground level [B]. Then prune off the lower branches of the remaining culms so their colour can be better appreciated [C]. The rejuvenated plant can be 'dressed' with a few carefully chosen stones to give an Oriental feel [D].

Container grown bamboos Although many bamboos adapt well to pot cultivation, it is vital not to allow them to go too short of water – droughted container-grown

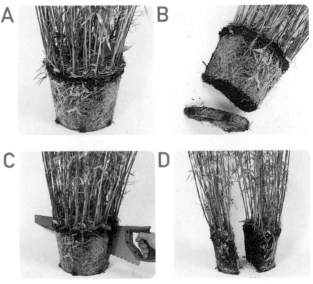

A B

C D

depth of pot, it is important to saw a slice a few centimetres (1–2in) thick off the base of the rootball [B], as bamboos in pots invariably heave their rootballs up above the original soil level. If you want to replant into the same-sized pot, it will be necessary to divide it. Alternatively, pot it on into a larger container.

Bamboo rhizomes are extremely tough because, like the culms, they are full of silica, so dividing a plant is often best carried out with a sharp saw [C] or even an axe, though for less congested and smaller plants, sharp secateurs should be adequate. Look for a natural line between culms, and saw the rootball in half (or more sections, if desired) [D].

Because the most vigorous part of the rootball is invariably found around its edges, replant with the 'outside' of the rootball turned around so that it faces the centre of the pot. Place a layer of soil-based compost into the bottom of the pot, and sit the plant on top before filling around with compost and firming gently. Leave 2.5–5cm (1–2in) of space between the compost surface and the rim of the pot to allow for watering. A surface mulch of gravel will help retain moisture and sets the plant off nicely. The remaining divisions can either be planted out into the garden, potted-up themselves or given away.

species can also spread rapidly, but in a large pot are much better behaved and their broad blades look effortlessly tropical.

It is also perfectly possible to prune back the culms of taller pot grown species quite hard if they are growing too tall. Allow the new culms to grow to their full height and begin to leaf out before shortening by cutting just above a well-branched node, because cutting new culms that are still shooting up can cause them to abort and die back completely.

Regular splitting and repotting of such plants is therefore vital. In the case of running species such as Indocalamus and Sasa, unless the container is very large, annual repotting may be advisable. Remember to feed container grown plants with a balanced liquid fertilizer, or mix a pelleted slow-release fertilizer into the compost, according to the manufacturer's instructions.

Repotting a container grown bamboo

Begin by removing the bamboo from its pot [A]. If this proves difficult, slide a blade down the inside of the pot and carefully work it around the rootball. If the plant is extremely potbound, it may be necessary to break the pot to free it. If the plant is to be repotted into the same

Many bamboos will outgrow their pots despite repeated divisions. Time to plant outdoors…

Mulching

Whether they are grown in the open ground or in pots, most plants will benefit from the application of a mulch over the soil or compost surface. Grasses and bamboos in particular seem to thrive on this, both in terms of encouraging their growth and making them look their best. A mulch is simply a layer of loose material, and can be organic or inorganic. Inorganic mulches include gravel, pebbles or more obviously decorative material such as glass chippings. These can look extremely effective, and will both reduce moisture loss from the underlying substrate and make it more difficult for weeds to establish, providing they are used a few centimetres (an inch) or more deep. To prevent such mulches from working their way into the underlying soil, in the open garden they are often used on top of a 'landscape fabric', a tough, woven sheeting that allows water through but keeps soil and mulch apart. Organic mulches include bark chippings, compost, well-rotted manure (NOT fresh manure, which often releases nutrients too quickly in damaging concentrations), and even grass clippings. These retain moisture and suppress weed growth like inorganic mulches, but have the additional benefit of slowly

Old dried leaves are an excellent mulch for bamboos

Inorganic mulches can be extremely decorative

Manure makes a highly effective organic mulch, but ensure it is well-rotted

breaking down under microbial activity, releasing nutrients gradually for the plants they surround. Except on very poor soils, bamboos and grasses need little if any feeding, and indeed overfeeding them with chemical fertilizers can be detrimental – it encourages lush growth, which can be 'top-heavy' and flop over, and which is also more prone to damage from winter cold and winds. Organic mulches should be spread thickly, at least 5cm (2in) deep, and while bamboos relish mulch among their culms, keep organic materials away from the crown or clump of grasses and grass-like plants. Direct proximity can keep the growing points too moist, encouraging rots, or release nutrients in concentrations that are too high, 'burning' the plants by drawing moisture out of them. As organic mulches break down slowly, they will need topping up occasionally, depending on the speed of breakdown.

Propagation

Another factor that makes grasses and bamboos such rewarding plants to grow is their ease of propagation. It is usually simply a matter of cutting the plant into pieces, as most spread by underground stems (rhizomes), which root as they go. Dividing these plants is actually of positive benefit, as inevitably the oldest, central parts of a clump tend to lose vigour, as growth is concentrated around the fresh soil on the edges. Nevertheless, it is important to carry out division in the right way and at the right time of year, and to give newly-divided plants the right aftercare.

Raising from seed

Most grasses, sedges and grass-like plants can also be raised from seed, but the characteristics of specific cultivars will probably not be passed on to their progeny, as the seeds have been produced sexually by pollen from another plant. Some species of grass are annual, dying after they set seed, and these must be raised from seed on an annual basis.

Bamboos can also be raised from seed, but most flower so rarely – 60–70 years or longer between flowerings is not unusual – that seed is rarely available. It is a myth that when a bamboo flowers, it invariably dies. Seed production is so copious that the plant is severely weakened and will die back, but if cut back to ground level it will often recover.

Most grasses are so easy to raise from seed that their self-seeding around the garden can actually be an irritation. In order to prevent this, deadhead before the seed begins to be shed from the seedheads. Either sow three to six seeds into individual 9–12cm (3–4in) pots [A], or sprinkle thinly over the surface of a seed tray full of multi-purpose compost. Cover thinly with another layer of compost [B], water well with a fine-rosed watering can [C] and place in a light place such as a windowsill or greenhouse, or outside in a sheltered area.

Depending on the species, germination is usually rapid, but it can be erratic. Keep the young plants well-watered, and plant out when they have formed nice chunky little clumps. Sowing several seeds in small pots has the advantage of producing clumps more quickly, but keeping a section of seed tray compost together produces the same effect. Bamboo seed, if you can get it, is best sown singly, but the method is the same.

Division of grasses & sedges

Dividing established grasses is a simple matter of digging up the clump and lifting it [A] and physically cutting the plant into sections [B] before potting up each section [C]. Alternatively, clumps can be prised apart with back-to-back garden forks (see top left, page 24). Division has the major advantage that as it is a vegetative form of propagation, the resulting plants are

TIP

It is best to divide grasses just as they come into growth, usually in early spring. Plants divided in autumn or winter do not heal as quickly and their damaged root systems are much more prone to root rots and frost damage.

23

A

B

C

D

tearing them, then ease the rest of their root systems apart gently [C], and either pot up each division [D] or plant them out.

Division of bamboos

Because they flower so rarely, this is the main method of propagating bamboos. Early autumn is the best time to carry out the operation, giving the plant time to recover before the worst of the winter weather while not interfering with new culm production in spring.

identical to their parents, keeping all the characteristics of named cultivars. Early spring is probably the best time of year, as the plants are coming back into growth. Autumn is also possible, but the damaged root systems can then be vulnerable to cold and wet winter conditions.

It is also often possible to divide newly purchased container grown plants at planting out time. Most of the species covered in this book have fine, fibrous root systems that are easy to divide. Simply remove from the pot and either gently tease obvious clumps apart with the fingers (with many species, little 'sub-clumps' are obvious around the edges of the main clump) or cut the plant into sections with a sharp blade. Do not be afraid of damaging the plants, as they recover rapidly, and usually with vigour. Plant the divisions out into the garden, or pot-up to grow on.

Some of the non-grass species like Ophiopogon, Luzula and Acorus have fleshier root systems, but again it is usually obvious where to divide them. Choose a flourishing pot-grown specimen, such as this Acorus [A]. Try and cut the rhizomes linking the mini-clumps together cleanly with a sharp blade [B] rather than

Look for a vigorous section of new culms, ideally forming a discrete clump, and carefully dig around its edges. A trowel is often the best bet for this operation. You are looking for the rhizomes connecting it to the main body of the plant. These are often tangled, particularly with clump-forming species, and may go down deeper than is immediately obvious. Cut through each with secateurs or a saw, trying to make the cuts as clean as possible.

If the division is going to be planted elsewhere in the garden, dig all around it with a spade and try to lift with as much soil attached to the rootball as possible, to minimize root disturbance, replant immediately and water in well. If destined for a pot or for transport elsewhere, carefully lift the rootball and work as much of the soil from the roots as possible. Wrap the root system in wet cloth and/or plastic for transport. Don't be afraid to shorten the division's culms by up to two thirds, cutting each cleanly above a node.

If you want to raise a larger number of plants from an established clump, the division itself can be divided using a technique known as rhizome cuttings. This seems drastic, and works best on the more vigorous bamboos, but has a high success rate. Cut away all the mature culms from the division close to their base, leaving only short stumps and clean away as much soil as possible from the rhizomes, teasing them apart where necessary. Cut the rhizomes into short sections of around 15–20cm (6–8in) using sharp secateurs or a knife, trying to ensure each piece has at least three buds (usually obvious as swellings on the upper surface), and ideally plenty of roots [A]. Pot up each cutting singly in a good multipurpose compost, so the rhizome sits just below the surface [B] and water in [C]. Place the potted up rhizome cuttings in a sheltered part of the garden, cold frame or cold glasshouse and ensure they are kept well watered. It may take them several months to establish themselves, but they should then start throwing up new culms and growing away strongly [D].

Planting styles

Although most of the species profiled in this book are versatile and amenable plants that can be used in gardens of any type, there are species and cultivars that are best suited to particular styles of gardening. A specimen bamboo would look rather odd in a traditional herb or cottage-style garden, and large grasses would look out of place in a rock garden dominated by alpine plants. There is such a range of sizes, forms, leaf colour and textures within the grasses and bamboos that there is a plant that will sit comfortably within the existing planting of virtually any garden. A word of warning, however – bamboos and grasses often prove addictive to many gardeners and there is always room for 'just one more', changing their gardening style on a gradual basis. Of course, there is nothing wrong with this; gardens by their very nature are ever-changing, evolving and altering, but if you find yourself lifting sections of your lawn to fit in more grasses and bamboos, or adding a bog garden to the side of your pond to make room for more sedges and rushes, don't say I didn't warn you!

Containers

Many of the plants in this book make excellent, relatively low-maintenance pot plants. A large bamboo in a substantial glazed oriental-style pot needs no companions and will provide a beautiful focal point for any garden. In a pot it will even work in a garden with a totally different style, its exotic appearance merely emphasized by its contrast with everything else. Statuesque grasses such as Stipa or Miscanthus can be equally arresting in containers.

Suitable species: many bamboos including *Phyllostachys nigra*, *P. violascens*, *P. bambusoides* and *Pleioblastus auricomus*; large grasses, including *Stipa gigantea*, *S. arundinacea*, *Miscanthus sinensis*, *M. floridula* and *M. sacchariflorus*, *Cortaderia selloana* 'Pumila', *Molinia caerulea* subsp. *arundinacea*.

Flamboyant grasses in pots – such as this *Hakonechloa macra* 'Aurea' – make dramatic statements

Many bamboos can be used singly in containers as focal points

Groups of bamboos in contrasting sizes, colours and shapes are even more effective

Contemporary 'minimalist' style

Low maintenance gardening has probably never been more popular, particularly in small modern gardens, where the whole 'look' is defined as much by the clean lines of decking, galvanized containers and liberal use of strong colours like blue and terracotta as by the plants themselves. Bamboos and grasses have clean, 'architectural' lines themselves, so are natural choices for this style of gardening. Whether in the ground or in pots, automated watering systems, particularly controlled by timing switches, mean busy gardeners can virtually leave their plot to look after itself.

Suitable species: most bamboos including all Phyllostachys, particularly *P. nigra* (black bamboo), *Fargesia nitida* and *F. muriele*, *Pleioblastus auricomus*; virtually all grasses particularly Stipa, Miscanthus and *Festuca glauca*; most sedges including *C. elata* 'Aurea', *C. comans*, *C.* 'Frosted Curls'; all Juncus, Cyperus, Luzula and horsetails (Equisetum) if kept moist.

In a contemporary garden, blue-leaved *Festuca glauca* provide an effective background, echoing the Agapanthus

Smaller species and cultivars, particularly with contrasting leaf colours and forms, can be planted together in a pot or a series of containers (ideally of similar design and colour), each with a single plant, and grouped together. Grasses mixed with plants of contrasting, broad-leaved form such as hostas and heucheras and even slow-growing shrubs can also produce exquisite tableaux, providing focal points and helping break up large expanses of patios or paving.

Suitable species: bamboos, including Sasa, Thamnocalamus, *Pleioblastus variegatus* and *P. pygmaeus*, *Shibataea kumasaca*; most smaller grasses, including *Pennisetum alopecuroides*, *P. orientale*, *P. villosum*, *Festuca glauca*, *F. amythestina*, *Deschampsia caespitosa*, *D. flexuosa*, *Stipa tenuissima* and Imperata; most sedges; Acorus, Luzula, Ophiopogon and all horsetails (Equisetum).

Japanese gardens are characterized by understated, unchanging calm

Japanese style Japanese gardens usually use bamboos relatively sparingly, and plain green leaves are preferred to brighter variegated ones. Rocks and gravel are a common presence, and ponds, even very small ones, are a feature of most. The look is evergreen and essentially unchanging, with the exception of spring flowering cherries, camelias or magnolias and the vivid colours of Japanese maples (*Acer palmatum* cultivars) marking autumn. Less is usually more in Japanese gardens, with every plant carefully chosen and the use of empty space and rocks as important as the plants.

Suitable species: most clumping bamboos (used sparingly), particularly Semiarundinaria, Phyllostachys, Pseudosasa, especially *P. japonica*, and Shibataea species – Sasa, Indocalamus and smaller Pleioblastus can also be used but are best confined; many plain-leaved grasses including Hakonechloa, Imperata, *Deschampsia cespitosa* and cultivars; most sedges, especially *Carex oshimensis* and *C. comans* and their cultivars, *C. glauca* and *C. pendula* 'Moonraker'; all Acorus, Luzula, Juncus, Ophiopogon, Phalaris and smaller Cyperus, providing the site is not too dry.

Gravel gardens Gravel gardening is another style growing in popularity as it is so low-maintenance. It particularly suits those species that like well-drained conditions and full sunlight. Separate the gravel layer from the soil below by tough, woven-plastic 'landscape fabric', as this both avoids gravel working its way into the underlying soil and physically prevents weeds from rooting. X-shaped cuts in the fabric allow plants to be planted into the soil, and the fabric to be folded back around their crowns. Most species of grass and bamboos look great planted into gravel, but as with the Japanese style, less is often more, with empty space surrounding discreet groups of plants, with or without rocks, the most successful approach. Grasses can be allowed to seed into the top layer of gravel – simply retain the seedlings you want and remove the others.

In gravel gardens, space out plants so that the stones remain visible

Suitable species: clump forming bamboos of all sizes including Phyllostachys, Fargesia, Pseudosasa and Shibataea – on drier sites, *Bashania fargesii*, *Chusquea culeou*, *Pseudosasa japonica* and *Sasaella ramosa*; most grasses, including Eragrostis, Festuca, Holcus, *Melica altissima*, *Panicum virgatum* and cultivars *Pennisetum alopecuroides*, Stipa and Miscanthus species and cultivars; sedges such as *Carex comans*, *C. morrowii* and *C. buchaenii*, provided soil is not too dry.

On heavier soils, or if you are prepared to water regularly, most of the non-aquatics in this book will grow happily in gravel.

Prairie or 'New European' style

One of the most interesting and exciting styles of gardening to emerge in recent years is the mixing of larger grasses such as Miscanthus and *Stipa gigantea* with equally tall and stately herbaceous perennials such as cone flowers (Echinacea), Achillea, fennels (Foeniculum) and Actaea. It is a naturalistic style of planting that takes its inspiration from natural communities such as the North American Prairies and Russian Steppes. Either intermingled in a deliberately random way or planted in irregular drifts, such combinations usually peak towards the end of summer and autumn, but look attractive at all times of the year. The dead, bleached grasses and herbaceous stems and seedheads retain the structure of the planting over winter, and are not usually cut back until early spring. Most of the species used are drought-tolerant, making the style extremely low-maintenance and self-sustaining once established.

Suitable species: bamboos are not native to the Prairies and Steppes, and would look out of place, as would moisture-lovers like sedges and rushes – most lack the size and vigour to compete with big grasses and perennials anyway; Miscanthus, particularly the many cultivars of *M. sinensis* reign supreme here, but *Stipa gigantea*, *S. tenuissima*, most Cortaderia, Calamagrostis species, particularly *C.* x a*cutifolia* and its cultivars, *Deschampsia cespitosa* and cultivars, *Molinia caerulea* subsp. *arundinacea* and cultivars, are all good choices.

Alternative lawns

For those gardeners seeking the ultimate in formal, contemporary looks, massed plantings of small, tussock-forming grass species in regular shapes bounded by paths or even box hedging and mulched with bark chippings, gravel or even glass chippings hark back to the magnificent formal parterres of the past such as those at Versailles and Hampton Court, but the repetitive, blocky appearance of such areas also provide a modern, cutting edge feel to a garden. This is not a style for the faint-hearted, but the fact that grasses lend themselves to such formal use as well as the studied naturalism of the Prairie style, in both cases creating arresting, low-maintenance plantings, serves to emphasize their versatility as garden plants. This is one

style where the invasive tendencies of the smaller running bamboos is a positive advantage, and they can be relied on to produce equally good ground cover but with a more open, airy look.

Suitable species: smaller running bamboos such as *Pleioblastus viridistratus*, *P. variegatus*, *P. pygmaeus*, and Sasa and Indocalamus species and cultivars; tussock-forming grasses, particularly variegated or coloured leaved cultivars; most Festuca species and cultivars, particularly bright steel-blue *F. glauca* 'Elijah Blue', 'Blaufuchs' and 'Blauglut', *F. amythestina*, smaller Cortaderia, including *C. fulvida* and *C. richardii*, *Milium effusum* 'Aureum' and Pennisetum cultivars, especially purple-bronze *P. setaceum* 'Rubrum'; sedges, including *Carex buchananii*, *C. comans* and *C. glauca* and their selections are good choices for sites that do not dry out too much.

Water and bog gardens

With so many herbaceous bog plants such as hostas, ornamental rhubarb (Rheum), Ligularia and huge *Gunnera maculata* producing large, verdant leaves, the fine, upright foliage of many sedges and grass-like plants form a beautiful contrast. Whether a pool is formal, or informal and wild-looking, species of sedge, rush, reeds and reed-mace are excellent choices as emergents for planting around the edges, with their roots in the water and their leaves standing proud of it.

Emergent plants blur pond boundaries, linking them to the rest of the garden

Rushes and sedges make an invaluable contribution to water gardens

Even if there is no standing water, low-lying, heavy ground is perfect for many of the moisture-loving plants profiled in this book, particularly teamed with perennials and ferns that enjoy similar conditions.

If your garden is on the dry side, ponds and bog gardens can be excavated and lined with water-retaining sheeting such as butyl rubber (make a few slits in the lowest-lying part of the liner in a bog garden to avoid excessive waterlogging) to form the conditions they enjoy. Providing they remain moist enough, most of these species will cope with more exposure to sun and wind than they would in drier areas.

Suitable species: no bamboos tolerate constant waterlogging, but Chimonobambusa, *Chusquea montana* and *C. uliginosa*, *Pseudosasa japonica* and *Shibataea kumasaca* thrive in permanently moist soils; relatively few grasses are suited to wet conditions, but *Calamagrostis* x *acutifolia* and its cultivars, *Dactylis glomerata*, *Deschampsia caespitosa*, *Milium effusum* and *Molinia caerulea* subsp. *arundinaceae* and their cultivars will put up with such conditions, provided they are not combined with deep shade; permanently moist or waterlogged sites, and the edges of standing water, are the preserve of almost all sedges, as well as all Acorus, Cyperus, Luzula, Juncus, Phalaris, Phragmites, Typha and Equisetum – those that grow as emergent plants are highlighted in the A–Z species profile section of this book.

Bamboos & Grasses

This section considers the wide range of grasses, bamboos, sedges, rushes, horsetails and other grass-like plants available to the gardener.

These pages are organised in alphabetical order by genera (a genus is a group of closely related species that are classified together). The most useful or ornamental species in each genus are described, together with their best cultivars (selections of a species). The conditions they prefer are outlined – the type of soil they like, amount of drought they will tolerate, and whether they prefer sun or shade. Suggestions for how and where to use them, and which styles of garden they are best suited to, are also included.

Each entry includes a care chart, summarizing the plants' needs, and where more than a single species is covered, a variety chart comparing the characteristics of the different species and cultivars. Bear in mind few of these 'rules' are set in stone – bamboos and grasses in particular are fairly accommodating plants and it is often worth trying them out in a less-than-ideal position to see how they react, as if a plant is obviously not thriving it can be lifted and replanted elsewhere.

Likewise, the sizes of most plants covered can vary considerably according to conditions. In particular, it is difficult to be specific about the ultimate size of bamboo plants in cultivation as it depends so much on where they are planted. Theoretically, bamboo clumps can go on spreading indefinitely. In this A–Z section three sizes are given for bamboos, 200cm+, 400cm+ and 600cm+ to give an idea of their relative vigour in average conditions, but a better guide to their rate of spread or capacity to 'run' can be found in the plant description.

The list is by no means exhaustive – the grass family alone is one of the largest in the plant kingdom, though many have little horticultural merit – and is biased towards plants that are relatively freely available to buy.

Acorus

Sweet rush *or*
Sweet flag

Neither a grass nor a bamboo, the Acorus genus actually belongs to the aroid family, so has more in common with peace lilies and arum lilies than true grasses. Its members are perennial evergreens.

Acorus flowers, although not large or showy, have the family's distinctive, arum-like central spike of many tiny flowers (spadix) cupped in what looks like a single petal (spathe). Most species are relatively small, slow-growing and evergreen plants that prefer moist conditions and semi-shade, although they will adapt to more open positions given plenty of water.

Perhaps the most apt common name is 'sweet rush', for Acorus are usually found close to water in the wild and their roots and leaves contain calamus, a sweet smelling essential oil reminiscent of liquorice used in perfumes, beers and gins. The narrow, flat, grasslike leaves are produced from a fleshy rootstock and form distinct 'fan' shapes, unlike any grass.

Two main species in cultivation are, *Acorus calamus*, whose leaves reach 45cm (18in) and form fairly stiffly arching clumps, and *A. gramineus*, a smaller plant native to Japan which has narrower, more grass-like, arching leaves 15–25cm (6–10in) long, forming a carpet of greenery around 10–15cm (4–6in) high.

I must admit to having a soft spot for Acorus, particularly for the ornamental variegated selections (which are much

site	Shaded, sheltered spots and watersides. Good container subjects
soil	Moisture retentive neutral to acid soils; dislike alkaline soils such as chalk
watering	Keep these plants evenly moist, as they dislike being droughted. Will cope well with permanently damp sites
general care	Slow growing – keep away from anything too vigorous. Comb out damaged leaves in early spring
pests & diseases	Do not plant too deep; the top of the rootstock should be at ground level to avoid fungal rots

Acorus gramineus 'Ogon'

Acorus gramineus var. pusillus

easier to find than plain green), as they are so undemanding and low maintenance, quietly getting on with life in their refined, evergreen way. Variegated selections also retain their striping well even in quite dense shade.

A. calamus 'Argenteostriatus' (often sold as 'Variegatus') has leaves half green and half creamy-white, the white often

Acorus gramineus 'Hakuro-nishiki'

Acorus gramineus 'Variegatus'

beautifully tinged pink in cooler conditions. *A. gramineus* 'Variegatus' is white striped, while *A. g.* 'Ogon' is green and yellow.

Acorus leaves look wonderful rimed with frost, and they are one of the few plants associated with boggy areas that never become invasive, making them ideal for the edges of the smallest ponds or water features. *A. calamus* can also be grown as an emergent.

They make excellent container plants, but should not be teamed with anything too vigorous, and prefer a moisture retentive loam based compost such as John Innes to a peat based one. Prolonged drought is the one thing they will not tolerate.

Propagation is primarily by division, ideally in early spring; use an extremely sharp knife to slice carefully through the fleshy rootstock as cleanly as possible to either remove obvious offsets or split the main clump in half. Plants can take some time to recover vigour.

	SPRING	SUMMER	AUTUMN	WINTER	height (cm)	spread (cm)	leaf colour	
Acorus calamus	🍃🍃🍃	🍃🍃🍃	🍃🍃🍃	🍃🍃🍃	45	45		Plain green form of sweet flag; can be difficult to find
A. calamus 'Argenteostriatus'	🍃🍃🍃	🍃🍃🍃	🍃🍃🍃	🍃🍃🍃	45	45		Variegation often flushed with pink
A. gramineus	🍃🍃🍃	🍃🍃🍃	🍃🍃🍃	🍃🍃🍃	15-20	15-20		Japanese species; variegated selections easier to find
A. gramineus 'Golden Edge'	🍃🍃🍃	🍃🍃🍃	🍃🍃🍃	🍃🍃🍃	15-20	15-20		Centre of leaves green, yellow-gold edges
A. gramineus 'Hakuro-nishiki'	🍃🍃🍃	🍃🍃🍃	🍃🍃🍃	🍃🍃🍃	10	10		Dwarf golden selection
A. gramineus 'Licorice'	🍃🍃🍃	🍃🍃🍃	🍃🍃🍃	🍃🍃🍃	15-20	15-20		Selection with particularly strong scent
A. gramineus 'Masamune'	🍃🍃🍃	🍃🍃🍃	🍃🍃🍃	🍃🍃🍃	10	10		Gold selection of var. *pusillus* (see below)
A. gramineus 'Oborozuki'	🍃🍃🍃	🍃🍃🍃	🍃🍃🍃	🍃🍃🍃	15-20	15-20		Yellow gold leaves with slight green striping
A. gramineus 'Ogon'	🍃🍃🍃	🍃🍃🍃	🍃🍃🍃	🍃🍃🍃	25	25		Popular and easy to find cultivar
A. gramineus var. *pusillus*	🍃🍃🍃	🍃🍃🍃	🍃🍃🍃	🍃🍃🍃	10	10		Miniature, naturally occuring variety
A. gramineus 'Variegatus'	🍃🍃🍃	🍃🍃🍃	🍃🍃🍃	🍃🍃🍃	25	25		Popular and easy to find

🍃 *in leaf*

Agrostis
Bent grass

If you have a lawn, the chances are you already have Agrostis in the garden; there are several native species of bent grass and some, such as *Agrostis tenuis* (browntop) and *A. canina* (velvet bent grass) are widely used in turf and lawn seed mixes.

There are annual and perennial species, most of which spread by underground stems (rhizomes), forming low mats close to the ground rather than upright clumps, and most of which have fairly narrow leaves and relatively open flowerheads (panicles).

Few Agrostis are grown as ornamentals, probably because they are relatively small and inconspicuous, without particularly showy flowers. They are important constituents of many British meadows, as their small size and relative lack of vigour means they do not swamp companion wildflowers. They are equally well-behaved in the garden, and happy in most soils, except really dry ones, coping with full sun or partial shade.

Probably the most ornamental selection is *A. canina* 'Silver Needles' (also known as striped brown bent) – found as a chance seedling in a London garden. A small plant with even more narrow leaves than the species, its leaves are cleanly margined in white and grow to only 8cm

site	Unfussy grasses; do well in sun or partial shade; make good container grasses
soil	All, except free draining, permanently waterlogged or extemes of acid or alkalinity
watering	Dislikes sodden conditions or bone-dryness. Requires more frequent watering in sun and exposed conditions
general care	Divide regularly in spring to avoid loss of vigour in centre of clumps, and dead-head to avoid self-seeding
pests & diseases	This plant is relatively trouble free, as there are not usually any problems with pests and diseases

(3in), spreading as a low mat up to 30cm (12in) across. It produces showy flowers for an Agrostis, up to 20cm (8in) tall forming a purple haze that can obscure its foliage. Its low growth habit and small stature make 'Silver Needles' an excellent edging plant, for the front of borders or mixed-planting containers where it contrasts beautifully with more upright grasses or slow-growing perennials.

The other widely grown bent grass, *A. nebulosa*, would probably be more popular if it was perennial rather than annual, needing to be raised from seed every year (see page 23), although it can be sown in-situ in spring or autumn. As the species name implies, its flowers are airy and cloud-like, held well above the foliage, and also dry well.

Agrostis canina

Agrostis canina

	SPRING	SUMMER	AUTUMN	WINTER	height (cm)	spread (cm)	leaf colour	
Agrostis canina	🍃🍃	🍃 ✹ ✹	🍃 🍃		20	30		Open, reddish brown flowers
Agrostis canina 'Silver Needles'	🍃🍃	🍃 ✹ ✹	🍃 🍃		8	30		Small grass for pots and borders, red-purple flowers
Agrostis nebulosa	🍃🍃	🍃🍃🍃🍃	🍃 🍃		20	30		Annual species, airy light brown flowerheads

🍃 *in leaf*　✹ *flowering*

Aira
elegantissima
Hair grass

A small genus of grass, Aira have extremely narrow leaves, giving the common name 'hair grass'. Only one species is widely cultivated, *Aira elegantissima*. Like *Agrostis nebulosa*, it is annual and a fairly small, dainty grass, its leaves reaching only 15cm (6in), forming tight clumps reaching a maximum of only 20cm (8in) across.

Aira elegantissima is definitely happiest in full sun, but it will cope with semi-shade, and will tolerate most soils. Like most annual grasses, Aira will grow well even on fairly dry, poor soils, although its foliage will often begin to brown off once the seedheads begin to mature.

This plant's flowers are its most attractive feature, and like many annual grass species, the sheer volume of flowers produced is impressive. The panicles are open with purple-tinged stems, pyramidal in structure and tipped with spikelets of tiny, distinctly silvery seeds on flowering stems up to 30cm (12in), held well above the foliage. It can be sown in situ where it is to flower equally successfully in either autumn or spring, and flowers from mid- to late summer. Alternatively, raise seedlings of this grass in small pots or modules, thinning them out to the three strongest seedlings as they germinate, and plant out in late spring. The flower spikes dry well, but pick them before they are fully open to avoid them shedding too many of their seeds.

A versatile annual, Aira is equally at home in borders and pots. Its fine structure means it contrasts well with wider leaved species such as sedges and woodrushes, while complementing other fine-leaved species such as Festuca. However, it is important not to overwhelm this delicate plant with much larger neighbours.

Aira elegantissima

site	Full sun but will stand semi-shade, although flowering may not be so effusive
soil	Unfussy as to soil type, and will cope with dryness if not prolonged
watering	Keep this plant well watered in spring when in full growth, drier once flowering begins
general care	Needs to be raised from seed every year. Leaves can begin to bleach as flowering progresses
pests & diseases	This plant is relatively trouble free as there are not any problems in terms of pests and diseases

Aira elegantissima

Alopecurus
Foxtail grass

A genus of mostly diminutive but really attractive grasses whose stature makes them ideal for containers and even alpine troughs, Alopecurus are also known as foxtail grasses, from the dense tufts of their flowerheads.

Several species are from high altitude, and although fully hardy in cold climates, like other alpine plants they dislike too much winter wet, having evolved to sit snug under a carpet of snow during the coldest months. They spread by underground rhizomes, so theoretically there is no limit to their spread, but cannot be described as invasive, expanding only slowly.

The easiest to grow and largest in cultivation are selections of *Alopecurus pratensis*. The species itself is seldom seen, but *A. pratensis* 'Aureovariegatus', golden foxtail grass, is a definite improvement on the species with yellow leaves with narrow green stripes. In spring, its colour outshines virtually all other yellow grasses, though others overtake it in summer. It forms a slowly spreading, upright clump with leaves to 40cm (16in) up to 30cm (12in) across and produces dense, fawn coloured flower spikes resembling mini bullrushes on tall stems held well above the foliage. 'Aureus' is a similar, all yellow selection of slightly less vigour.

site	*A. pratensis*, is easy to grow. *A. alpinus* and *A. lanatus* need full sun
soil	Are happy in most soils; alpine species need sharp drainage
watering	Moderately when in growth; protect *A. alpinus* and *A. lanatus* from excessive winter wet
general care	Will succeed in most situations. *A. alpinus* and *A. lanatus* are more difficult, but worth the effort
pests & diseases	This plant is relatively trouble free, as there are not usually any problems with pests and diseases

A. alpinus, blue foxtail grass, and its even bluer subspecies *glaucus*, are little gems, both reaching no more than 20cm (8in) and spreading into discontinuous clumps. Leaf colour varies from grey-blue with purple overtones to real steel-blue, and stubby, purplish flowers are produced in spring. It prefers well-draining soil and companions that are similarly slow and not invasive mat formers, such as *Ajuga reptans*. *Alopecurus lanatus*, silver foxtail grass, is similar to *A. alpinus*, but even dwarfer, and downright tricky to grow, being particularly intolerant of winter wet. It repays the effort, however, with exquisite thick, woolly leaves that look distinctly silver over a grey base.

Alopecurus pratensis 'Aureus'

	SPRING	SUMMER	AUTUMN	WINTER	height (cm)	spread (cm)	leaf colour	
Alopecurus alpinus	🌿🌿🌿	✸✸✸🌿 🌿			25	45	▨	Beautiful alpine species
A. alpinus subsp. *glaucus*	🌿🌿🌿	🌿🌿🌿🌿	🌿🌿	🌿🌿🌿	20	30	▨	Usually evergreen, rarely flowers
A. lanatus	🌿✸	✸🌿✸🌿	🌿🌿		10	15	▨	Leaves densely covered in silver hairs. True alpine
A. pratensis 'Aureovariegatus'	🌿🌿	✸✸✸🌿 🌿			30	30+	▨	Ornamental, bright and easy to grow
A. pratensis 'Aureus'	🌿🌿🌿	✸✸✸🌿🌿			30	30+	☐	Slightly less vigorous than 'Aureovariegatus'
A. pratensis 'No Overtaking'	🌿🌿🌿✸	✸✸✸🌿🌿			30-40	30+	▨	A new introduction with white variegation

🌿 in leaf ✸ flowering

Andropogon
Bluestem

A North American genus of grasses commonly known as bluestems, Andropogon are handsome, colourful, perennial deciduous plants grown for their silvery blue, often purple-tinted stems and silky, white haired flowers.

Only two species, *Andropogon gerardii* and *A. virginicus*, are widely grown at present, but given their popularity for the Prairie and New European planting styles, wide natural distribution and inherent variability in form and colouring, it seems only a matter of time before named selections begin hitting the market. As Prairie grasses, bluestems do best on well drained soils in full sun and tend not to colour or flower well in shade.

A. gerardii, the big bluestem, is a striking grass both in stature and colouring. Its size varies widely in the wild, its flower stems reaching 3m (10ft) in optimum conditions but only 1m (3ft) on the southern fringes of its range. The forms in cultivation in Europe are towards the lower end, flower stems reaching 1.2m (4ft) with the foliage shorter. Big bluestem forms tight clumps of upright, silvery blue stems and arching, blue-grey leaves usually tipped with purple. The purple

staining often intensifies after midsummer. The flowers are reddish-purple with white hairs on long, slender stems, borne from late summer to autumn, before the whole plant turns an attractive dark brown in autumn. It makes a good specimen grass, or is ideal in Prairie type plantings mixed with other grasses and statuesque, late-flowering perennials such as asters. Gravel gardens are also much to its liking.

A. virginicus, or silver beardgrass, is smaller, its dense green leaves reaching only 30cm (12in), and is grown primarily for its flowers. These are spiky, held on long waving stems to 90cm (3ft) and appear from midsummer, opening to show the relatively long, silky white hairs that give the grass its common name. It has good autumn colour, the whole plant usually turning shades of purple and orange before bleaching to buff as the leaves and stems die off.

Andropogon gerardii

Andropogon virginicus

site	This plant is best in full sun, and it copes well with exposure
soil	Unfussy as to pH. Prefer light, well drained, not too rich soils. Dislike heavy clay
watering	Adapted to relatively dry environments, particularly in summer. Give more water in spring
general care	Generally easy to maintain and cultivate. Dead leaves and stems can be left for winter structure
pests & diseases	Largely trouble free, any problems usually associated with excessive winter wet

	SPRING	SUMMER	AUTUMN	WINTER	height (cm)	spread (cm)	leaf colour	
Andropogon gerardii		in leaf	flowering		120	60		Late flowering grass, good autumn and winter presence
Andropogon virginicus		in leaf	flowering		90	60		Smaller species grown for flowers, good autumn colour

 in leaf   flowering

Arrhenatherum elatius subsp. bulbosum 'Variegatum'

Variegated bulbous oat grass

Only a single cultivar of a subspecies of Arrhenatherum is common in cultivation, _A. elatius_ subsp. _bulbosum_ 'Variegatum'. The name of this plant is a bit of a mouthful, as is the common name of variegated bulbous oatgrass, but both are worth learning, as it is perhaps the best of the white variegated small grasses.

Although technically an annual, this plant's unique self-propagation method makes it particularly easy to raise. Its leaves reach only 30cm (12in), growing in a tight, upright clump up to 30cm (12in) across, with clean looking, relatively broad leaves striped and margined with pure white on a grey-green base. The flowers are produced from mid-summer, in narrow, upright panicles on stems up to 60cm (2ft). This is definitely a grass for

site	Best in light shade, especially in warmer areas, where it holds its variegation well
soil	Moisture retentive, slightly acidic soils. Dislikes heavy, wet soils and dry ones
watering	Thi plant is best kept evenly moist. Irrigate it freely if it is growing in the full sun. Little else is required
general care	Generally easy to maintain and cultivate. Little is needed with regard to general care
pests & diseases	Problems tend to be cultural, through unsuitable soil or hot weather. Tired foliage can be cut hard back

Arrhenatherum elatius subsp. bulbosum 'Variegatum'

cooler climes; in full sun and warm conditions the foliage can start to look tired and begin to bleach during the summer. Either grow in a shadier spot, or be ruthless and cut hard back, as given plenty of water a second flush of fresh leaves will be produced.

The name bulbous oat grass comes from the odd way this subspecies self-propagates. Late in the season, the nodes (joints) on the stem and the stem bases themselves swell into strange, bulb-like structures which, when the leaves die back in autumn, are shed onto the soil and can grow into new plants. As this is a form of vegetative propagation, they also inherit the variegated nature of their parent and are easy to collect and plant up, or can be left where they fall to grow in situ. If too many are emerging in one spot, thin out, retaining the strongest seedlings.

Variegated bulbous oatgrass is best used either in small groups of individual plants or as a foreground contrast plant with darker leaved grasses or perennials, either in borders or in pots. However, given its short stature do not plant it close to anything that is too vigorous.

Arrhenatherum elatius subsp. _bulbosum_ 'Variegatum'

Arundo
Giant reed

Arundo is one of the giants of the grass world, the stature of its species rivals that of the temperate bamboos, quite an achievement for a non-woody, herbaceous species. Given their size and rhizomatous growth habit, they can be invasive however, and all are deciduous plants.

Arundo donax var. *versicolor*

Arundo donax, the giant or Provencal reed, is a common sight in moist areas around the Mediterranean. It can reach 4.5m (15ft), with stems more than 2.5cm (1in) across, sheathed by grey-green leaves as much as 10cm (4in) wide and 60cm (2ft) long.

Not the hardiest of grasses, *A. donax* does best in full sun in a wet, sheltered spot, or can be grown as an emergent in large ponds, where it makes a spectacular specimen plant. It also lends an instant touch of the tropics combined with other large sub-tropical looking species such as tree ferns, bananas, *Fatsia japonica* and cannas, and can even be used as a hedge.

The foliage can begin to look tired by late summer, and the usual practice is to cut the plant back to ground level in late autumn. Stems only flower in their second year however (and only in warm areas), so if you want to enjoy the spectacular fluffy white panicles, up to 60cm (2ft) long and 25cm

(10in) across, try nursing at least a few stems through the winter.

Occasional variegated individuals occur in the wild, and are available as *A. donax* var. *versicolor*, their broad leaves variably margined and striped with creamy white. Much less vigorous than the plain form, these usually reach no more than 2.1m (7ft), and are also much more tender, succeeding outside only in virtually frost-free areas without winter protection.

A. formosana is an even more bamboo-like species reaching 2.1m (7ft) with an upright, arching shape. *A. pliniana* is a distinctly spiky customer with blue-green culms (stems) punctuated by short, stiff leaves only 10cm (4in) long, but coming to a point strong enough to pierce the skin.

site	Full sun and sheltered spots. All require winter protection in colder areas
soil	Rich, heavy and moist soils, or grow as emergents in large water bodies
watering	Water these plants freely when in growth – Arundo are all plants of wetlands and watersides
general care	Easy to grow given full sun and moisture. Cut back to ground level for over-wintering in containers
pests & diseases	Generally trouble free. Cultural problems usually related to drought or cold damage

Arundo formosana

	SPRING	SUMMER	AUTUMN	WINTER	height (cm)	spread (cm)	leaf colour	
Arundo donax		in leaf	flowering		450	200+		Largest hardy grass
A. donax var. versicolor		in leaf	flowering		210	200+		Smaller and more tender than species
A. formosana		in leaf	flowering		210	200+		Particularly bamboo-like
A. pliniana		in leaf	flowering		180	200+		Short, spiky foliage

in leaf   flowering

Arundinaria gigantea
Switchcane, canebrake

Formerly one of the largest bamboo genera, following several revisions of their taxonomy (botanical classification), most arundinaria species have now been assigned to other genera. Of the remainder, only *Arundinaria gigantea* is widely cultivated in temperate climes.

It has the distinction of being the only bamboo species native to North America, where it used to form large groves around watercourses in the deep south. It lacks the hardiness of many Phyllostachys species (but will withstand temperatures as low as –20°C/-4°F) and is less exposure tolerant, but nevertheless a well grown clump can make an impressive specimen plant. It is a true clump-former (pachymorphic), expanding only slowly, and does best in damp, open glades with some shelter.

A. *gigantea* reaches 9m (30ft) in the wild, and produces culms up to 4cm (1.5in) across, with leaves up to 20cm (8in) long, but is usually much smaller in European gardens. As with many bamboo species, it is a variable plant in the wild, so some clones in cultivation are much more attractive plants than others.

The culms are thin walled, emerging light green with persistent, purplish culm sheaths, but quickly age to dull yellow. Young shoots are an attractive deep purple colour on emergence, and clusters of relatively short branches emerge around the nodes, quickly producing soft, pale yellow-green leaves.

A. *gigantea* subsp. *tecta* is said to be better adapted to boggy soils, as its rhizomes have internal air spaces. Otherwise, its main distinguishing characteristic is the fact that it produces red flowers, rather than the straw coloured ones typical of the species, is slightly smaller and has longer branches. Given the rarity of bamboo flowering and natural variability within the species, whether it deserves subspecies status is questionable. In cultivation, the two are fairly indistinguishable.

Arundinaria gigantea

site	Prefers some shelter, but will cope with full sun or light shade
soil	Ideally moisture-retentive and rich, but will grow in all but very dry soils
watering	Evenly moist soils, dislikes both dry and wet sites. Subspecies *tecta* is said to do better in wet soils
general care	Cut out thin, old and dead culms annually to keep tidy. The leaves are naturally yellowish in hue
pests & diseases	There are no real pest and disease problems. Growth can be poor on exposed or dry sites

	SPRING	SUMMER	AUTUMN	WINTER	height (cm)	spread (cm)	culm colour	
Arundinaria gigantea	𝄢𝄢𝄢	𝄢𝄢𝄢	𝄢𝄢𝄢	𝄢𝄢𝄢	180	600+		Rarely tops 1.8m (6ft) in the UK; much larger in warmer areas
A. gigantea subsp. *tecta*	𝄢𝄢𝄢	𝄢𝄢𝄢	𝄢𝄢𝄢	𝄢𝄢𝄢	180	600+		Very similar to species form

𝄢 in leaf

Avena
Oats

Avena is a genus of annual grasses that are nevertheless widely grown – *Avena sativa* and its selections are better known as oats, widely grown for animal (and human) fodder.

Wild oats are minor constituents of many grassland communities and meadows (hence their reputation for being widely sown), flower abundantly even compared to other annual grasses, and with their relatively broad leaves are actually rather attractive. A case of familiarity breeding contempt in the eyes of the gardener, perhaps. Like many annual grasses, the stems and leaves often begin to die off and bleach of colour just as the flowers are reaching their peak.

The openess of the panicles and relatively large size of the individual spikelets of this plant are characteristic of the genus, and oat flowerheads seem almost to 'dance' when blown by even the slightest breeze. Far more common in cultivation, however, is *A. sterilis*, the animated oat. It is so called as the long hairs (awns) attached to each spikelet are extremely sensitive to changes in atmospheric humidity, twisting and writhing when it changes even when they have been dried. *A. sterilis* forms a loose clump of arching leaves up to 60cm (2ft) in height and spread, rarely larger.

One of the few annual species that grows well on heavy soils, Avena prefers an open position in full sun. Cut flower stems for drying while still with some green in them to avoid seeds being shed, and dead-head garden plants in order to prevent them from self-seeding.

Grow a small clump of wild or animated oats in a shady spot or a pot and invite your gardening friends to admire them – then watch the consternation on their faces when you inform them that something very similar produced the porridge in their larder!

Avena sativa

site	Full sun preferred. Probably best sown in situ where they are to flower in spring
soil	Any soil, including heavy and moisture retentive, and unfussy as to pH.
watering	Water freely if necessary when in full growth in spring. Prefers drier feet in summer
general care	Among the easiest grasses to grow, and flower stems dry well. Relatively short season of interest
pests & diseases	Generally trouble free as there are no problems regarding pests and diseases for this plant

Avena sativa

	SPRING	SUMMER	AUTUMN	WINTER	height (cm)	spread (cm)	leaf colour	
Avena sativa					90	30		Wild oat
Avena sterilis					90	25		Animated oat

 in leaf   flowering

Bambusa ventricosa

Bambusa

Bambusa is a mostly tropical bamboo genus, but several species and their cultivars will withstand some frost. They do prefer warm summers however, so in northern climes or at altitude, hardier species such as Phyllostachys or Fargesia may be a safer bet, or grow in a pot in a sheltered spot and give winter protection.

Bambusa multiplex is an elegant bamboo, reaching 'only' 5m (16ft), that adapts well to container culture. The leaves are relatively large, up to 10cm (4in) long and 3cm (1in) across and paddle shaped. Its cultivars are more commonly grown and include: 'Alphonso-Karrii', which has bright yellow culms irregularly striped with green; 'Rivieriorum', an elegant dwarf form growing to only 1.8m (6ft), ideal for pot culture and said to be hardier than the species, with much smaller leaves; 'Silver Stripe', which is similar to the species but with irregular white variegation on the leaves and faint white striping on the culms.

Something of an oddity, *B. ventricosa* is known as 'Buddha's belly' because of its characteristically swollen nodes on vivid green culms. It is most commonly sold as a rather forlorn looking indoor bonsai only a few inches high, but is hardy down to -7°C (20°F).

B. vulgaris is possibly the most widely grown bamboo in the world, with green culms and capable of topping 15m (40ft) in the subtropics but will not tolerate frost. It is relatively drought tolerant for a bamboo, and so adapts well to pot culture. It is sometimes sold as a large houseplant. *B. vulgaris* 'Vittata' is a selection with bright yellow and green striped culms, while in 'Wamin', the gaps between the nodes are compressed, making it shorter and bushier than the type.

site	Prefers sheltered spot away from cold winds; adapts well to pot culture
soil	Moisture retentive preferred but relatively drought tolerant for a bamboo
watering	Once established, in garden should only require watering in dry periods. Keep potted specimens evenly moist
general care	*B. vulgaris* needs to be kept frost-free. Loam based John Innes compost for potted specimens
pests & diseases	No real problems in terms of pests and diseases. Will shed leaves if droughted but relatively quick to recover

Bambusa ventricosa

	SPRING	SUMMER	AUTUMN	WINTER	height (cm)	spread (cm)	culm colour	
Bambusa multiplex	🗲🗲🗲	🗲🗲🗲	🗲🗲🗲	🗲🗲🗲	500	600+		Elegant and variable species. Usually much less than 5m (16ft)
B. multiplex 'Alphonso-Karrii'	🗲🗲🗲	🗲🗲🗲	🗲🗲🗲	🗲🗲🗲	500	600+		Boldly-striped culms
B. multiplex 'Rivieriorum'	🗲🗲🗲	🗲🗲🗲	🗲🗲🗲	🗲🗲🗲	200	600+		Dwarf form good in pots
B. multiplex 'Silver Stripe'	🗲🗲🗲	🗲🗲🗲	🗲🗲🗲	🗲🗲🗲	500	600+		White variegation on leaves and culms
B. ventricosa	🗲🗲🗲	🗲🗲🗲	🗲🗲🗲	🗲🗲🗲	250	400+		'Buddha's Belly' is its common name
B. vulgaris	🗲🗲🗲	🗲🗲🗲	🗲🗲🗲	🗲🗲🗲	1500	600+		Tender species but adapts well to pots
B. vulgaris 'Vittata'	🗲🗲🗲	🗲🗲🗲	🗲🗲🗲	🗲🗲🗲	1500	600+		Form selected for vivid yellow/green striped culms
B. vulgaris 'Wamin'	🗲🗲🗲	🗲🗲🗲	🗲🗲🗲	🗲🗲🗲	1500	600+		Internodes not usually as short in temperate areas

🗲 *in leaf*

Bashania

A relatively little-known genus of bamboos related to Arundinaria, Bashania has much in common culturally with the better known Pleioblastus species.

Tough, exposure tolerant and extremely hardy, only two species are as yet available in the West, although this situation may change as interest in bamboos generally continues to grow.

Perhaps the most important characteristic of Bashania is that they are not clump-forming, but 'running' species, with leptomorphic rhizomes. As such, they are best used where their invasive tendencies are either not important, planted as shelter-belts or hedges where use can be made of their hardiness and relative drought tolerance, or confined using paving slabs set edge-on into the earth or a rhizome barrier. Their vigour makes them unsuited to all but the largest containers.

Bashania fargesii is an extremely tough customer; hardy down to -25°C (-13°F), exposure tolerant, vigorous and capable of thriving on all but the driest of sites. The culms can top 10m (30ft), although they are usually considerably smaller, and in common with most running species of bamboo, relatively widely spaced – Bashania forms fairly open groves rather than tight clumps. Culms are an attractive grey-green colour, as are the leaves, which are up to 15cm (6in) long by 2.5cm (1in) across, which is fairly substantial for a bamboo leaf. Each culm node (joint) initially puts out three branches, with a number more developing later.

The wonderfully named *Bashania qingchengshanensis* (by a Chinese botanist, clearly), is relatively new to cultivation, but seems to be proving just as hardy as its better known cousin. It is considerably smaller in size, reaching only 4m (13ft), but with even larger leaves up to 25cm (10in) long. Culms are marked grey-

Bashania fargesii

yellow below the nodes, with persistent culm sheaths. Its leaves seem to overwinter with less damage than those of *B. fargesii*, and with an overall smaller stature it may be better suited to use this plant as a hedge. *Bashania qingchengshanensis* is slightly less vigorous, but ultimately just as invasive.

site	Extremely tough and hardy, will cope with real exposure and very low temperatures
soil	All types except permanently wet. Tolerates drier soils than most bamboos
watering	Prefers even moisture but will cope well with all but the most prolonged droughts once established
general care	Not so ornamental but among the best for hedges and windbreaks. Invasive if not physically constrained
pests & diseases	Relatively trouble free as there are not usually any problems regarding pests and diseases

	SPRING	SUMMER	AUTUMN	WINTER	height (cm)	spread (cm)	culm colour	
Bashania fargesii	🍃🍃🍃	🍃🍃🍃	🍃🍃🍃	🍃🍃🍃	1000	600+		Hardy, exposure tolerant but invasive
B. qingchengshanensis	🍃🍃🍃	🍃🍃🍃	🍃🍃🍃	🍃🍃🍃	400	400+		Smaller than *B. fargesii* but just as invasive

🍃 *in leaf*

Bothriochloa
Beard grass

Bothriochloa has become a genus with a cosmopolitan distribution across much of the northern hemisphere thanks to taxonomic revisions, and deserves to be much better known than it currently is in most countries.

Beard grasses are perennial, deciduous species with handsome flowerheads produced over a long period, and often spectacular red and purple autumn colour. In this they resemble smaller versions of the much more widely known Miscanthus species and cultivars, and like them prefer drier soils and full sun. They mix equally well with other grasses and late-flowering perennials, or can be used at the front of Prairie style plantings and in gravel gardens.

B. bladhii is actually native to Malaysia and Indochina, but seems reliably hardy in a temperate climate. It forms pale green fountains of leaves, up to 60cm (2ft) high. From mid-summer until the first severe frosts, a succession of thin stems rise above the foliage, tipped with thin, branched panicles looking like a coarse bottle brush. These are a vivid maroon, against which the relatively large cream pollen sacs they produce are particularly striking. In autumn, the whole plant turns an arresting maroon-purple, ultimately bleaching to straw. It does best in sun and on soils that are not too wet, or makes an excellent specimen for a container with a contrasting glaze colour, sitting particularly well in Japanese style gardens.

B. barbinoides, cane bluestem (like *B. ischaemum*, it was formerly classified in Andropogon and the common name has stuck), is a New Mexico native forming tall, upright, relatively narrow clumps to 30cm (12in) across. Flower stems reach up to 90cm (3ft) and are similar to those of *B. bladhii*. *B. ischaemum*, yellow bluestem, is a tussock-forming species native to a wide swathe of the Old World from Southern Europe to Japan. Its blue-green leaves are narrower than those of *B. bladhii*, but its autumn colour can be just as good. It is semi-evergreen, so it can retain this colouring through milder winters, in which case cut clumps back to ground level in early spring. Flower stems can reach 1.2m (4ft), and are dark purple in full sun.

Bothriochloa ischaemum

Bothriochloa ischaemum

site	All species of this plant prefer full sun, and will stand exposure
soil	Prefer freer-draining soils and relatively drought tolerant. Unfussy about pH
watering	Keep this plant on the dry side, irrigation necessary only in prolonged dry periods
general care	Easy to grow grasses with good autumn colour, attractive flowerheads and winter structure
pests & diseases	Largely pest and disease free. Cultural problems only likely on soils that are too wet, particularly in winter

	SPRING	SUMMER	AUTUMN	WINTER	height (cm)	spread (cm)	leaf colour	
Bothriochloa barbinoides					90	30		Slightly short season of interest
B. bladhii					60	90		Purple flowers and good autumn colour
B. ischaemum					90	60		Semi-evergreen in mild winters

🌿 in leaf   ✹ flowering

Bouteloua

Two species of Bouteloua, which are both native to the drier, southern US shortgrass prairies are in cultivation, though neither are particularly widely grown. However, the plant is gradually becoming more popular.

These plants are creatures of habitats that are dry and baked through the summer, and rarely wet in the winter, so they need free-draining conditions and as much sun as possible in wetter, cloudier climates. Both are clump-forming, and best suited to Prairie-style plantings, gravel gardens or dry meadows with sharp drainage. Once established they are extremely drought and exposure tolerant.

Bouteloua gracilis, the mosquito or signal-arm grass, is reputedly so called because the crowded, brownish purple spikelets hang down from the flower stems, which are held almost horizontally, like a row of mosquito larvae at the water surface. Flower stems emerge silver but gradually darken to purple as they mature, and are produced throughout the summer. The light grey-green, narrow leaves form dense mounds only around 15cm (6in) tall, and the whole plant flushes purplish in autumn before bleaching straw in the winter. Relatively small and delicate, *B. gracilis* also makes a good front of border or container plant, where its intriguing flowers can be best appreciated, provided drainage is good, and is sometimes recommended for rock gardens.

B. curtipendula, sometimes called side-oats, is larger than mosquito grass and altogether more imposing, with upright panicles up to 75cm (30in) high, bearing large, spikelets down one side – hence the name 'sideoats' – only. These are an attractive reddish purple when young, aging to fawn. The leaves are grey-green, reaching around 45cm (18in).

Bouteloua curtipendula

Bouteloua curtipendula

site	Full sun, do not grow well in shade. Tolerant of wind and exposure
soil	Do well on poor and dry soils once established. Intolerant of winter wet
watering	Watering usually not required unless plants are establishing or in prolonged drought
general care	Good, non-invasive, clump-forming grasses. Particularly effective planted in drifts
pests & diseases	Suffers from few pests or diseases. Culturally, only winter wet on heavy soils can be problematical

	SPRING	SUMMER	AUTUMN	WINTER	height (cm)	spread (cm)	leaf colour	
Bouteloua curtipendula					80	60		Hardy, exposure and drought tolerant
B. gracilis					30	60		Unusual flowers

🍃 in leaf ✿ flowering

Briza
Quaking grass

Briza maxima is probably the most popular of annual grasses, but there are several other species also worth growing, some of them perennial. Their common name comes from the fact their large spikelets hang from almost impossibly delicate-looking, hair like branches, and sway in the slightest of breezes.

Briza maxima

Briza flower early, and are unusual in that on many sites, even the annuals may stay green throughout the winter, but die off in mid-summer following flowering (this summer dormancy characteristic betrays the Mediterranean origins of several species, and means Briza can be useful contributors to the winter garden). Perennial species begin to reappear in autumn. Medium-sized grasses, quaking grasses are suited to a range of gardening styles, including mixed borders and the front of Prairie plantings. Their flowerheads complement those of species with either dense or more filamentous natures. Flowerheads dry well.

Briza maxima has the largest flowerheads, which hang like scaly little lockets from late spring to mid-summer. Clumps reach 40cm (16in) tall by 30cm (12in) across. Flower stems can top 60cm (2ft). *B. minor* is the smaller of the well-known annuals, reaching 23cm (9in) with much smaller spiklets, but these are produced in even larger numbers.

Briza media can reach a similar size to *B. maxima*, but is perennial. It prefers richer soils than the annuals, and will also grow

Briza media

well in semi-shade. Its leaves are more blue-green. Although the spikelets are smaller than those of *B. maxima*, they are arguably more striking, distinctly heart-shaped and tinged purple. Its cultivar 'Limouzi' grows slightly larger, with more intense colouring in both leaves and flowers.

Two other perennial quaking grasses are becoming more freely available. Of a similar size to *B. media* and enjoying similar conditions, *B. subaristata* is a clumping grass with dull green foliage and small, curled, purple green spikelets held on relatively small, open panicles. *B. triloba* produces more dense, arching flowerheads from which hang, green, pearl-like flowers.

site	Annual species full sun, perennials full sun or partial shade
soil	Annuals tolerate poor and dry soils, perennials prefer richer and more moist
watering	Annuals of this plant are more drought tolerant, perennials prefer more even moisture
general care	All Briza are accommodating, easy to grow grasses. Annuals must be sown every year
pests & diseases	Relatively trouble free, as there are not usually any problems in terms of pests and diseases

	SPRING	SUMMER	AUTUMN	WINTER	height (cm)	spread (cm)	leaf colour	
Briza maxima	🌿 🌿	● ●	🌿 🌿	🌿 🌿	30	23		Popular annual, unusual flowers
B. media	🌿 🌿 ●	● ●	🌿 🌿	🌿 🌿	60	60		Perennial
B. media 'Limouzi'	🌿 🌿	●	🌿 🌿	🌿 🌿	70	70		Slightly larger selection, better leaf and flower colour
B. minor	🌿 🌿	● ●	🌿 🌿	🌿	23	15		Annual with its own subtle charms
B. subaristata	🌿 🌿 ●	● ●	🌿 🌿	🌿 🌿	60	60		Perennial, unusual curled spikelets
B. triloba	🌿 🌿 ●	● ●	🌿 🌿	🌿 🌿	60	60		Perennial, pearl-like spiklets

🌿 *in leaf*   ● *flowering*

Bromus
Brome grass

Bromus is one of the lesser known grass genera, with largely annual members, although a few species are perennial. Several are natives of meadowland communities, found particularly in meadows that were annually cleared, a traditional farming practice that has declined markedly with the intensification of farming in recent years.

Most of the species in cultivation are medium-sized clump formers that associate well with other grasses and herbaceous perennials alike, suited to a wide range of informal garden styles.

Bromus brizaeformis is an annual species which resembles *Briza maxima*, as its name implies. It is larger than Briza, the soft, relatively wide leaves reaching 50cm (20in) and forming tight clumps. Flowerheads are large, up to 75cm (30in) with drooping spikelets like those of quaking grasses, but these are longer and more pointed. They also appear throughout the summer.

Bromus do not take the mid-summer break that characterizes the quaking grasses, the foliage dies back over winter. It dries well, and can be sown in situ where it is to flower. Unlike most annual grasses, it will tolerate some shade.

B. intermis 'Skinner's Gold' is a beautiful, intensely yellow variegated improvement of a less than striking perennial species. It reaches 75cm (30in), forming tight, arching clumps and holds its colour well in semi-shade. *B. ramosus* is a perennial British native. Known as the wood or hairy brome, it is a woodland grass, so adapted to lower light levels than most, although it will stand full sun on good soils with moisture. It reaches 45cm (18in), producing open, branched heads of drooping spikelets in mid and late summer with a bristled, rather wispy effect.

B. macrostachys var. *lanuginosus* is a compact annual grass reaching only 25cm (10in), grown for its unusual flowers. Flowerheads are compact, near white and so hairy they appear almost woolly. Sow in situ in sun or shade. *B. madritensis* is a compact annual grass whose flowerheads are strongly flushed purple, a colour which suffuses the whole plant before it bleaches in autumn.

site	Full sun or part shade, annuals tolerate exposure, perennials more shade
soil	Unfussy as to pH, all soils except dry and extremes of acidity or alkalinity
watering	Annuals more drought tolerant than perennials, which need moist soils grown in full sun
general care	Easy to grow and reliable. Annuals may need to be resown in situ each year, but usually self-seed
pests & diseases	No real pest, disease or cultural problems, although perennials in full sun dislike droughting

Bromus intermis 'Skinner's Gold'

Bromus brizaeformis

	SPRING	SUMMER	AUTUMN	WINTER	height (cm)	spread (cm)	leaf colour	
Bromus brizaeformis					50	50		Tall flower spikes; annual
B. intermis 'Skinner's Gold'					75	75		Perennial, holds colour well in shade
B. macrostachys var. lanuginosus					25	25		Unusual white flowerheads
B. madritensis					30	30		Purple-flushed flowerheads and autumn colour
B. ramosus					45	45		Long flower stems

🖋 in leaf ● flowering

Calamagrostis
Feather reed grasses

Calamagrostis is a grass genus that has found much favour with designers in recent years for use in the Prairie and New European style of informal drift planting mixing large grasses with tall herbaceous perennials. The best known is a hybrid, *Calamagrostis* x *acutiflora*.

Most species form tight clumps of foliage 60–90cm (2–3ft) tall, with large, striking, narrow flowerheads up to 1.6m (5ft) high, produced in quantity that seem to float well above their foliage. As a genus, although deciduous, they have good brownish autumn colour, and both leaves and flowers hold their structure extremely well over the winter, usually only needing to be cut back in spring just before the new growth appears.

C. x *acutiflora* is usually encountered in two widely available cultivars, 'Stricta' and 'Karl Foerster'. 'Stricta' is the more upright of the two, introducing a strong vertical element into any planting scheme that contrasts well with both broader leaved perennials and more arching grasses. The flowers can top 1.6m (5ft). 'Karl Foerster' is slightly less upright and around 25cm (10in) taller, with broader, fluffier panicles, which unlike 'Stricta' it continues to produce as the summer progresses.

C. x *acutiflora* 'Overdam' is a variegated cultivar, making densely-arching clumps of strongly white striped foliage, which often emerge tinged an attractive

Calamagrostis x *acutiflora* 'Karl Foerster'

Calamagrostis x *acutiflora* 'Overdam'

site	Tolerant of exposure and full sun. Grows in semi-shade, upright habit lost
soil	Dislike only constantly wet soils, do best on free-draining ones. Any pH
watering	Relatively drought tolerant, though appreciate occasional watering in dry springs
general care	Most popular grasses for mixing with perennials. Versatile genus that looks good with most other plants
pests & diseases	No pest and disease problems. Cultural problems only really in heavy soils during wet winters

pink. It reaches 60–90cm (2–3ft) producing narrow, purple-tinged, feathery flowerheads. The colour of the foliage tends to fade as it ages, but clumps can be cut hard back to initiate a flush of bright new growth in summer.

	SPRING	SUMMER	AUTUMN	WINTER	height (cm)	spread (cm)	leaf colour	
C. x *acutiflora* 'Karl Foerster'	in leaf	flowering	flowering	flowering	150	100		One of the most popular Prairie- and European-style grasses
C. x *acutiflora* 'Stricta'	in leaf	in leaf / flowering	flowering	flowering	125	100		Slightly later flowering and more upright than 'Karl Foerster'
C. x *acutiflora* 'Overdam'	in leaf	in leaf / flowering	flowering		100	100		Showy white variegated grass
C. brachytricha	in leaf	in leaf / flowering	flowering		90	100		Leaves emerge bronze tinted
C. emodensis	in leaf	in leaf / flowering	flowering		45	90		Pretty new grass from Nepal
C. epigejos	in leaf	in leaf / flowering	flowering		60	90		Very drought tolerant

in leaf   *flowering*

Carex
Sedges

The Carex genus is very large, most of its members well adapted to life in or near water, many also evergreen and adapted to grow in shade. Variegated selections abound, and there is a veritable rainbow of different leaf colours. Often lumped together with grasses because they look similar, sedges are only distantly related to true grasses; they evolved much earlier.

Most Carex are fairly low-growing; few top 90cm (3ft), forming arching mounds, adapting well to pot culture given enough moisture. Choosing sedges for the damper and more shady areas of a garden in colours that echo those of grasses used in open areas in full sun helps a garden design hang together, and grouping by colour is also a good way of introducing some of the myriad Carex available.

site		Most prefer partial or full shade; New Zealand species full sun
soil		Moist to heavy soils, some grow in water, New Zealand species free-draining to dry
watering		Keep most carex moist to wet. Some species grow as emergents. New Zealand sedges dislike winter wet
general care		Low maintenance species. Remove dead flowerheads and comb out dead leaves from evergreens in spring
pests & diseases		Relatively trouble free regarding pests and disease free. New Zealand sedges can rot if too wet in winter

White and cream variegated sedges

Variegated sedges fall into two main groups: those with a broad central stripe and green edges, and those with green centres and coloured margins. Unlike many variegated plants, they hold their colouring well in shade.

Carex oshimensis 'Variegata' forms a low spreading mound to 25cm (10in) tall and 45cm (18in) across with a broad white stripe down the middle of each leaf and small brown flowers in spring. Similar is *C. ornithopoda* 'Variegata'. *Carex morrowii* also has a 'Variegata', altogether more spiky and upright, with thick, tapering leaves up to 60cm (2ft) long margined white. There is also a dwarf form, 'Nana Variegata'. The beige and cream flowers of 'Variegata' in early spring are quite showy

Carex brunnea

Carex siderosticta 'Kisokaido'

for a sedge, but it is deciduous. *C. morrowii* 'Fisher's Form' is similar but slightly larger with cream variegation rather than white.

Carex 'Silver Sceptre' is if anything more heavily variegated, the leaves also slightly twisted. *C.* 'Ice Dance' has darker green, similarly twisted leaves with intensely white striping. *C. comans*, New Zealand hair sedge, has leaves barely a millimetre wide, evenly whitish-green in the species, but even whiter in more compact forms. All of these variegated sedges are great for

Carex phyllocephala
'Sparkler'

lighting up shade plantings with ferns and broad leaved perennials like hostas, ligularia and astilbes.

White variegated dwarf sedges are ideal for pots and planting around small pools. One of the best is *C. saxatilis* 'Variegata', to only 7.5cm (3in) with unusual twisted leaves that can form a low growing carpet. It is evergreen, but loses the central white stripe in winter. Deciduous *C. siderosticta* 'Kisokaido' is a new Japanese cultivar with leaves emerging white tipped, developing irregular white stripes.

Carex comans
'Frosted Curls'

	SPRING	SUMMER	AUTUMN	WINTER	height (cm)	spread (cm)	leaf colour	
C. brunnea 'Variegata'	in leaf	flowering / in leaf	in leaf	in leaf	25	30		Tender sedge best grown indoors
C. comans 'Frosted Curls'	in leaf	in leaf	in leaf	in leaf	45	100		Smaller than species, whiter and shy-flowering
C. 'Ice Dance'	flowering / in leaf	in leaf	in leaf	in leaf	60	100		Unusual twisted leaves
C. morrowii 'Fisher's Form'	flowering / in leaf	in leaf	in leaf	in leaf	75	100		Popular and widely available. Stands some dryness
C. morrowii 'Nana Variegata'	flowering / in leaf	in leaf	in leaf	in leaf	30	30		Smaller form of Variegata
C. morrowii 'Variegata'	flowering / in leaf	in leaf	in leaf	in leaf	60	75		One of the best variegated evergreen sedges
C. ornithopoda 'Variegata'	flowering / in leaf	in leaf	in leaf		15	30		Small, deciduous
C. oshimensis 'Variegata'	in leaf / flowering	in leaf	in leaf	in leaf	25	45		Like morrowii 'Variegata', but smaller
C. phyllocephala 'Sparkler'	in leaf / flowering	flowering / in leaf	in leaf	in leaf	30	60		Tender, spiky cultivar best grown indoors
C. saxatilis 'Variegata'	flowering	in leaf			10	100		Low growing, deciduous, twisted leaves
C. siderosticta 'Kisokaido'	flowering / in leaf	in leaf	in leaf		30	60		Leaves emerge white-tipped
C. 'Silver Sceptre'	in leaf / flowering	in leaf	in leaf	in leaf	45	100		Twisted leaves, heavily variegated

Yellow variegated and yellow leaved sedges

Carex oshimensis 'Evergold' is perhaps the most popular garden sedge, with a bright yellow band running between dark green edges to 25cm (10in) tall. Larger and more imposing is *C. pendula* 'Moonraker', whose young leaves emerge almost white,

Carex oshimensis 'Evergold'

becoming striped with rich creamy yellow, and more green as the summer goes on. It forms wide arching clumps up to 75cm (30in) tall, and in summer bears tall wands with pendulous, catkin-like flowers.

C. muskingumensis 'Oehme', gold palm-leaved sedge, is a beautiful deciduous yellow striped selection to 75cm (30in), as is *C. dolichostachya* 'Kaga-nishiki', a Japanese fountain sedge forming dense, arching mounds to 25cm (10in). *C. nigra* 'On Line', often sold as 'Variegata', is a narrow leaved, yellow margined plant to about 30cm (12in) with black flowers.

Carex flava, strictly speaking, is not variegated, but has soft greenish-yellow leaves particularly effective in shade, as has *C. aurea*, the golden fruit sedge. There

in leaf   flowering

is also an all-yellow palm sedge, *C. muskingumensis* 'Wachtposten', which is so pale some find it insipid. Perhaps the best gold sedge is, however, *C. elata* 'Aurea', Bowles' golden sedge, which forms dense tussocks of arching yellow leaves thinly edged in green. 'Knighthayes' is similar but all yellow. Both reach 75cm (30in) in height.

Carex elata 'Aurea'

	SPRING	SUMMER	AUTUMN	WINTER	height (cm)	spread (cm)	leaf colour	
Carex aurea					35	35		Stands full shade
C. dolichostachya 'Kaga-nishiki'					25	40		Forms arching clumps
C. elata 'Aurea'					75	90		Popular and widely available
C. elata 'Knighthayes'					75	90		Similar to 'Aurea' but lacks green leaf margins
C. flava					35	60		Soft pale yellow, good in shade
C. muskingumensis 'Wachtposten'					60	100		Pale almost sickly yellow
C. muskingumensis 'Oehme'					60	100		Golden palm leaved sedge. Spreads slowly
C. nigra 'On Line'					30	200+		Greyish leaves edged yellow, arching habit
C. oshimensis 'Evergold'					25	45		Popular and widely available
C. pendula 'Moonraker'					75	100		Leaf colour develops from cream over summer

Blue sedges

There are several blue leaved sedges for shady areas where blue leaved grasses would not be happy. *Carex glauca* and *C. flacca* subsp. *flacca* look very similar, both steely grey-blue forming low clumps to 30cm (12in) in height. *C. flacca* 'Bias' has a white margin down one side of each leaf, while *C. panicea* is a similar soft blue colour but much shorter, to only 23cm (9in). Both species and their forms have chocolate-brown flowers in summer and stand sun or shade.

New Zealand also has a bluish sedge, the best selection of which is *C. trifida* 'Chatham Blue', an imposing broad leaved sedge to 90cm (3ft). Its hardiness in a temperate climate is as yet relatively untested.

Carex trifida 'Chatham Blue'

	SPRING	SUMMER	AUTUMN	WINTER	height (cm)	spread (cm)	leaf colour	
Carex flacca					45	200+		Low steel-blue clumps, can be invasive
C. flacca 'Bias'					30	200+		Variegated, leaves striped white down one side
C. flacca subsp. *flacca*					30	200+		Better behaved than the species
C. glauca					25	60		Broad leaved, good strong blue-grey
C. panicea					25	200+		Similar to *C. f. s. flacca*, but smaller and less spreading
C. trifida 'Chatham Blue'					90	100		Even bluer selection. Resembles N. Zealand flax

 in leaf · flowering

Bronze and Brown sedges

Most brown and bronze leaved sedges are from higher altitudes in New Zealand, and are much more attractive in the flesh than they sound. Their unusual colouring goes surprisingly well with foliage colours including blues, silvers, reds and black, as well as green, but not all are of proven hardiness. *Carex buchananii* is quite upright, growing to around 60cm (2ft), needing good drainage and is pretty drought tolerant like many New Zealand sedges. *C. flagellifera* is much more lax and darker brown, its long

Carex buchananii

leaves trailing along the ground in all directions, excellent in a tall pot or on steep slopes. There are several named cultivars, including 'Auburn Cascade', 'Coca-Cola' and 'Rapunzel', which are all fairly similar.

Carex testacea

Carex comans' bronzy-red selections of varying shades are grouped as *C. comans* bronze. 'Dancing Flame' is particularly reddish, as is the more compact 'Taranaki', still often sold as 'Small Red'. *C. tenuiculmis* is a paler brown, and more fountain-shaped, its leaves arching up to around 45cm (18in) tall. *C. berggrenii* is equally pale, but short and broad-leaved, around 10cm (4in), forming stubby, spreading clumps. *C. uncifolia* is reddish leaved, forming low clumps around 23cm (9in) high and 30cm (12in) across. Two evergreen New Zealand species are more changeable in colouring: *C. dipsacea* is dark olive green in summer, developing shades of red, yellow and brown in streaks and patches during the winter. *C. testacea* is an unusual olive-yellow with bronzy tints, turning almost orange in sun.

	SPRING	SUMMER	AUTUMN	WINTER	height (cm)	spread (cm)	leaf colour	
Carex berggrenii					10	200+		Short, broad leaved and spreading. Good drainage
C. buchananii					60	60		Upright growth, curled leaf tips
C. comans bronze					30	75		Narrow, thread-like leaves. Good drainage
C. comans 'Dancing Flame'					30	75		More red than Bronze form. Good drainage
C. comans 'Taranaki'					20	75		Sometimes sold as C. comans small red
C. dipsacea					30	75		Olive green leaves, orange and red patches in winter
C. flagellifera					45	100		Leaves arch out of clump then trail, bleaching at tips
C. flagellifera 'Auburn Cascade'					45	100		Similar to species. Good in pots
C. flagellifera 'Coca-Cola'					45	100		Similar to species. Good in pots
C. flagellifera 'Rapunzel'					45	100		Similar to species. Good in pots
C. kaloides					50	20		Prefers full sun
C. tenuiculmis					45	45		Upright, fountain-shaped growth. Good drainage
C. testacea					45	45		Orange leaves in sun, near-green in shade. Likes moisture
C. testacea 'Old Gold'					45	45		More yellow-orange than species Likes some moisture
C. uncifolia					23	30		Likes more moisture than most brown sedges

⌀ in leaf   ✷ flowering

Green sedges

Green leaved does not necessarily mean dull in the Carex genus. *Carex trifida* makes bold clumps up to 90cm (3ft) tall with pleated leaves. *C. hispida* reaches a similar size but has narrower leaves of a brighter green. *C. caryophyllea* 'The Beatles' forms tight 'mopheads' of foliage.

C. muskingumiensis 'Little Midge' is an excellent choice for smaller gardens and does well in a pot, as does *C. secta*, a moisture loving oddity from New Zealand

Carex plantaginea

with pretensions of being a tree fern, since it forms a distinct 'trunk' of dead roots and leaf bases up to 90cm (3ft).

Although sedges are not usually grown for their flowers, *C. grayi*, the mace sedge, an evergreen North American species, produces spiky green flowers like mini medieval maces, while *C. pseudocyperus*, hop sedge, is festooned with large, dangling hop-like flowers.

	SPRING	SUMMER	AUTUMN	WINTER	height (cm)	spread (cm)	leaf colour	
Carex atrata					15	30		Black alpine sedge. Native to the UK
C. baccans					90	90		Crimson seed sedge. Needs shelter or winter protection
C. brunnea					30	30		Forms upright, spiky clumps
Carex caryophyllea 'The Beatles'					30	90		Narrow-leaved mophead clump former
C. grayi					60	45		Mace sedge, spiky flowerheads. Moist soil or in water
C. hispida					90	90		Narrow leaved clumps
C. lurida					35	35		Sallow sedge. Prefers shade and moisture
C. muskingumensis					60	100		Palm sedge. Leaves like mini parasols. Shade tolerant
C. muskingumensis 'Little Midge'					10	30		Dwarf form. Good in pots
Carex pendula					90	100		UK native with large, hanging, catkin-like flowers
C. plantaginea					20	60		Broad leaved, showy dark flowers, shade tolerant
C. pseudocyperus					120	90		Big upright sedge, hop-like dangling flowers. In water
C. secta					100	100		Unusual in forming a 'trunk'. Moist or in water
C. sylvatica					60	60		Wood or forest sedge. Moisture and shade
C. trifida					90	100		Imposing, broad leaved sedge, hardy

in leaf   *flowering*

Chasmanthium latifolium

Northern sea oats

This North American grass species is the only member of its genus commonly grown in Europe, and is one of the best perennial grasses for shady area, being native to woodlands and woodland edges.

It produces an arching mound of relatively wide, fresh green leaves 60–90cm (2–3ft) tall, and handsome flowerheads that resemble those of Briza, the quaking grasses.

Held on flower stems up to 1.2m (4ft) tall, the panicles hold pendulous, large scaly-looking, flattened spikelets with an intricate, overlapping structure much larger than those of Briza which emerge olive green from mid-summer and age to an attractive bronze, contrasting beautifully with the apple-green leaves, and holding their colour well into winter. The foliage often develops a beautiful pink tinge as autumn progresses before bleaching to brown, and both leaves and flowerheads

Chasmanthium latifolium

hold their structure well through winter. Cut the clumps back in late spring if you have enjoyed the plant's winter effect.

Northern sea oats will grow in most soils, but prefers evenly moist, relatively rich soils, particularly in only semi shade, but resents both drought for any extended period and permanently waterlogged soils.

site		Prefers at least partial shade; very shade-tolerant for a true grass
soil		Rich, evenly moist. Dislikes excesses of dryness and waterlogging. Most pH suit
watering		Evenly moist is the ideal for this plant. Irrigate regularly in dry periods or if growing in full sun
general care		Easy to grow and tolerant species with good autumn colour and keeps winter structure well
pests & diseases		No pest and disease problems; cultural problems usually related to excesses of dryness or winter wet

It will stand full sun providing it is kept moist, but seems to enjoy life best in at least partial shade, whether this be from other plants or garden structures and houses. If planting under mature trees, make sure it does not have to compete with the trees too hard for moisture or keep it well watered, and avoid shallow-rooted trees such as birches.

A handsome, medium sized grass with much to recommend it, Chasmanthium mixes well with other shade-lovers such as Briza, the contrastingly finer leaves of *Deschampsia flexuosa*, and *Hystrix patula*, the so-called bottlebrush grass, whose compact, furry flowerheads could not be more different. Non-grassy partners in differing leaf shades such as Luzula (woodrushes) or black Ophiopogon also enjoy similar conditions, as do many species of fern.

Chasmanthium latifolium

Chimonobambusa

A particularly leafy bamboo genus whose members are relatively small forest under-storey plants, enjoying sheltered conditions, some shade and moist soils.

Chimonobambusa have leptomorphic (running) rhizomes, and can be invasive in conditions to their liking, however the smaller species are easier to control than some – simply snap or mow off culms emerging in the wrong places. For groundcover in wooded areas, few bamboos are more attractive. Smaller selections can also make good container plants. New culms (stems) are produced in late summer and autumn, only leafing out the following spring.

Chimonobambusa tumidissinoda

leaves 10cm (4in) long. Undeniably lush and impressive, with a 'herringbone' of fresh green leaves on arching culms, it can prove a rampant spreader. A variegated form, 'Variegata' has green stripes on its yellow culms and a few rather unimpressive white stripes on the foliage. *C. quadrangularis* is an oddity, since its larger culms, which can top 7m (22ft), are four-sided and matt grey-green in colour.

Chimonobambusa were once thought relatively tender, but most seem hardy down to -20C (-4F). *Chimonobambusa macrophylla* forma *intermedia* is a beautiful dwarf bamboo, said to reach 1.8m (6ft) but usually only half that, with delicate leaves 5cm (2in) long and prominent nodes. It needs a relatively high humidity, so does best in a sheltered, shady spot or in a well-watered container. A vigorous Japanese native, *C. marmorea* reaches 3m (10ft) with

Chimonobambusa marmorea

site	Prefer semi or full shade, shelter and high humidity. Stands some sun if moist
soil	Evenly moist, dislike dry soils. Nutrient-poor soils curb invasive tendencies
watering	Even moisture; established plants need irrigating during dry periods. Foliage appreciates moisture
general care	Beautiful bamboos, but running, not for exposed or small gardens. Good ground cover for large areas
pests & diseases	No real pest or disease problems; cultural problems occur only on dry or waterlogged sites

	SPRING	SUMMER	AUTUMN	WINTER	height (cm)	spread (cm)	culm colour	
C. macrophylla f. intermedia	🌿🌿🌿	🌿🌿🌿	🌿🌿🌿	🌿🌿🌿	200	200+		Usually nearer 90cm (3ft) in cultivation
C. marmorea	🌿🌿🌿	🌿🌿🌿	🌿🌿🌿	🌿🌿🌿	300	600+		Very leafy, but can be rampant spreader
C. marmorea 'Variegata'	🌿🌿🌿	🌿🌿🌿	🌿🌿🌿	🌿🌿🌿	300	600+		Culms can turn red in sun, but just as invasive as its parent
C. quadrangularis	🌿🌿🌿	🌿🌿🌿	🌿🌿🌿	🌿🌿🌿	700	600+		Square culms, but not hardiest. Copes with full shade
C. quadrangularis 'Suow'	🌿🌿🌿	🌿🌿🌿	🌿🌿🌿	🌿🌿🌿	700	600+		Soft yellow stems with green stripes, some leaf variegation
C. quadrangularis 'Nagaminea'	🌿🌿🌿	🌿🌿🌿	🌿🌿🌿	🌿🌿🌿	700	600+		Very similar to 'Suow', with extra green stripe above branches
C. tumidissinoda	🌿🌿🌿	🌿🌿🌿	🌿🌿🌿	🌿🌿🌿	600	600+		Gorgeous but rampant runner

🌿 *in leaf*

Chionochloa
Snow grasses

A genus of tussock-forming (rounded clumps), evergreen grasses largely from New Zealand, coming increasingly into vogue with gravel and Prairie-style gardeners. Although most are plants of high altitude, alpine origins, relatively few are reliably hardy in colder climates.

Mixed with other New Zealand natives such as phormiums (spiky, upright New Zealand flax), and the many species of Carex found

	site	Prefer full sun, however will cope with exposure and wind
	soil	Free draining. Happy on moist soils, but dislike alkaline conditions
	watering	Even moisture is required for these plants, and they dislike winter wet in particular. Little else needed
	general care	Low-maintenance evergreen grasses. Benefit from combing out dead and damaged leaves in spring
	pests & diseases	There are no real pest, disease or cultural problems provided winter sogginess avoided

there, a whole planting style essentially mimicking nature known as 'tussock gardening' has evolved which is equally striking, naturalistic and low maintenance employed elsewhere.

Chionochloa rubra

Chionochloa resemble the pampass grasses, Cortaderia, though they are smaller and altogether more elegant-looking. The best known is *Chionochloa conspicua*, plumed tussock grass, which forms mounds of pale green leaves with an orange midrib to 1.2m (4ft) tall, and from late spring, green flower spikes up to 1.8m (6ft) from one side of which hang the creamy seedheads that last through summer.

C. flavescens, broad leaved tussock, has wider leaves than *C. conspicua*, is slightly lower-growing and its flowerheads are more yellowish in colour, held on more arching stems. It is reputed to be the hardiest species in the genus so is probably the best choice for the coldest areas. *C. flavicans* looks broadly similar, but is nowhere near as hardy, requiring a sheltered position in well-drained soil and ideally full sun.

Perhaps the most attractive snow grass is *C. rubra*, red tussock grass, which forms more upright clumps of foxy, red-brown leaves that are usually held rolled up in themselves like seaside marram grass.

Chionochloa flavescens

	SPRING	SUMMER	AUTUMN	WINTER	height (cm)	spread (cm)	flower colour	
Chionochloa conspicua					180	120		Clump forming evergreen grass, long flowering period
C. conspicua subsp. *cunninghamii*					180	120		As for species
C. conspicua subsp. *conspicua*					180	120		Reputedly freer flowering
C. flavescens					90	90		Broader leaves and hardiest in genus
C. flavicans					90	90		Quite tender- sheltered, well-drained spot
C. rubra					100	100		Red-brown colouring, shorter flowering season

🍃 *in leaf*   ✺ *flowering*

Chusquea

Bamboos are invariably associated with the Orient, but several genera are native to the Americas, the most useful of which is Chusquea; several of its species are from the southern tip of South America, Argentina and Chile, or from high altitudes in the Andes almost up to the permanent snowline.

Little known as yet, this is a group of bamboos that seem set to increase in popularity. Many of the species in cultivation have yet to be widely grown, so their performance in different areas is uncertain.

Chusquea's branching pattern produces many more branches than other bamboos around each node, distributed halfway around its circumference not from a single point like most bamboos, giving a leafy, 'bottlebrush' effect. All cultivated species are clump-forming (pachymporphic), although some are large and vigorous.

Some Chusquea are not reliably hardy, but are paradoxically also intolerant of high temperatures, as the temperate species are largely from humid, mountain cloud forests where they rarely experience temperatures above 25°C (77°F). The continental European climate of cold winters and hot summers seem not to suit chusquea, however they thrive better in milder, maritime climates.

The best known is *Chusquea culeou*, a variable species first introduced in 1890. It can reach 6m (20ft) and is short-branched,

Chusquea macrostachya

Chusquea gigantea

Chusquea culeou

site	Full sun to part shade. Tolerant of exposure in humid areas
soil	Hardy species unfussy if moist. Mediterranean species dry, free draining
watering	These plants do best kept evenly moist. Mediterranean-type species more drought tolerant
general care	More tender species need winter protection. Thin out old, weak and dead culms in spring
pests & diseases	No real pest and disease problems. Hardiness and exposure tolerance of some species uncertain

givng it a particularly 'fox brush' or 'shuttlecock' look. It forms dense clumps of yellow-green culms, is shade-tolerant and is reliably hardy down to -18°C (0°F). A beautiful dwarf form, *C. culeou* 'Tenuis', that reaches only 1.8m (6ft), is sometimes available and is excellent for smaller gardens. *C. macrostachya* is a relatively recent introduction and similar to *C. culeou*, but slightly taller, more arching and with rich purple new culms.

C. cumingii reaches only 1.5m (, and as it is from near Mediterranean conditions, is relatively drought tolerant, preferring drier alkaline soils. It has bunched, stiff branches and narrow, blue-green leaves only 5cm (2in) long. *C. montana* is similarly compact but from high altitude making it hardy to -15C (5F) with distinctive swollen nodes and short branches bearing leaves to 7cm (3in) long. It prefers moist, acid soils and some shade.

At the other extreme, the culms of both *C. gigantea* and *C. valdiviensis* can reach 15m (50ft). *C. gigantea* has attractive yellow culms, well-branched with leaves up to 12cm (5in) long, preferring damp climates.

C. valdiviensis is a climber in the wild, scrambling its way through evergreen forests. Its culms are arching, and root where they touch the ground. The branches are backward pointing, acting like 'grappling hooks'. More an oddity than an ornamental, it is (perhaps fortunately) not the hardiest. *C. quila* has a similarly climbing habit but reaches only 4m (13ft), and is more attractive, if just as untidy. From a Mediterranean climate, it is quite drought tolerant. *C. uliginosa* is a slightly larger scrambler that prefers it warm and wet. Both seem hardy to around -10°C (14°F).

Chusquea culeou 'Tenuis'

Chusquea culeou

C. coronalis is one of the more tender species, but adapts well to life in a container where winter protection can be given, standing a couple of degrees of frost, but only suitable for planting out in the mildest areas. It can reach 7m (22ft), but is much smaller in a pot, looking better with its large main branches removed. *C. sulcata* is smaller, to 4m, with golden culms and long, thin leaves, preferring part sun but of similar borderline hardiness. Marginally more hardy is *C. pittieri*, with culms that are widely arching and a beautiful shiny purple.

	SPRING	SUMMER	AUTUMN	WINTER	height (cm)	spread (cm)	culm colour	
Chusquea coronalis	🌿🌿🌿	🌿🌿🌿	🌿🌿🌿	🌿🌿🌿	700	200+		Barely frost hardy, winter protection in all but mildest areas
C. culeou	🌿🌿🌿	🌿🌿🌿	🌿🌿🌿	🌿🌿🌿	600	200+		Recently flowered, good seed-raised plants available
C. culeou 'Tenuis'	🌿🌿🌿	🌿🌿🌿	🌿🌿🌿	🌿🌿🌿	180	200+		Lovely dwarf form
C. cumingii	🌿🌿🌿	🌿🌿🌿	🌿🌿🌿	🌿🌿🌿	150	200+		Small and very attractive
C. gigantea	🌿🌿🌿	🌿🌿🌿	🌿🌿🌿	🌿🌿🌿	150	200+		Large but slow spreading
C. macrostachya	🌿🌿🌿	🌿🌿🌿	🌿🌿🌿	🌿🌿🌿	700	200+		More elegant and arching than *C. culeou*
C. montana	🌿🌿🌿	🌿🌿🌿	🌿🌿🌿	🌿🌿🌿	150	200+		Small, swollen nodes, likes shade and moisture
C. pittieri	🌿🌿🌿	🌿🌿🌿	🌿🌿🌿	🌿🌿🌿	800	200+		Gorgeous but distinctly tender
C. quila	🌿🌿🌿	🌿🌿🌿	🌿🌿🌿	🌿🌿🌿	400	200+		Scrambling climber, drought resistant
C. sulcata	🌿🌿🌿	🌿🌿🌿	🌿🌿🌿	🌿🌿🌿	400	200+		Tropical looking but only stands a few degrees of frost
C. uliginosa	🌿🌿🌿	🌿🌿🌿	🌿🌿🌿	🌿🌿🌿	500	200+		Scrambling climber, likes moisture
C. valdiviensis	🌿🌿🌿	🌿🌿🌿	🌿🌿🌿	🌿🌿🌿	150	200+		Scrambling giant, rampant, hardy only to -7°C (20°F)

🌿 in leaf

Coix lacryma-jobi

Job's tears

The only species of this grass genus in general cultivation is an annual grown not for its flowers or foliage, but for its unusual seeds. These dry to become hard, oval, grey and pearl-like, and were used in times gone by as cheap and readily available beads.

It was the widespread use of the seeds for necklaces and particularly for rosaries which most probably explains where the unusual biblical common name came from.

Coix lacryma-jobi

Job's tears is a not unattractive grass, reaching 75cm (30in) and forming an upright, relatively narrow clump spreading to 45cm (18in). The leaves are broad and fresh green, with a prominent, paler central midrib. It really prefers warmer climes, and needs a long, hot summer to produce its 'tears' in any profusion. Treat it like a tender bedding plant, sowing in a glasshouse or sunny windowsill in mid-spring. Rather than using a seed tray, sow three seeds to a 9cm (3in) pot, and pot on regularly, as Coix resents both root disturbance and any check to growth. Do not plant out into the final flowering position until all risk of frost has passed, and harden off carefully before this.

Give Coix the hottest, driest spot in the garden – the base of a south-facing wall is ideal, or where it will get as much full sun as possible. Water moderately when in full growth and hope for long spells of unbroken sunshine in mid- to late summer.

Even when happy in its position, Coix forms a fairly sprawling, untidy looking clump and does not produce its flowers in either particularly large or numerous panicles. If harvesting the 'tears' for drying, leave them until the whole plant has bleached and they begin to turn grey.

site	Give this plant as open an aspect and as much full sun as possible
soil	Not fussy, and will grow in all but the heaviest and most waterlogged
watering	Keep evenly moist as seedlings, but they will cope with drought when planted out
general care	Avoid low temperatures and checks to growth as seedlings. Little else is required
pests & diseases	No real pest and disease problems. Cultural problems if potbound or during cold, wet summers

Coix lacryma-jobi

Cortaderia
Pampass grasses

Cortaderia is a genus of large, handsome, evergreen grasses whose reputation has unfortunately suffered because the popularity and overuse of *Cortaderia selloana*, 'the' pampass grass, during the 1970s made it as unfashionable as bell bottoms, afros, and dwarf-conifer-plus-heathers plantings. This is a shame, as it is hardly the fault of the plant that it was marooned in the middle of too many suburban front gardens.

Cortaderias are some of the toughest, hardiest and most exposure-tolerant grasses around, and are not confined to the Argentinian pampass – the horticultural merits of an increasing number of New Zealand species are becoming better appreciated. The smaller forms at least are surprisingly versatile and can look attractive next to a range of other grasses or broad-leaved perennials, or dotted alone in gravel gardens. They form large, arching clumps of evergreen foliage armed with sharp, toothed edges (always handle pampass grasses wearing gloves), with large flowers that open as silky threads, becoming fluffy and looking glorious placed so the sun can shine through them.

C. fulvida, the New Zealand toe-toe, forms a mound of arching leaves to 1.5m (5ft) tall and more across. The flowerheads arch high above this, producing one sided, drooping, shaggy plumes in white or pink. Dieback of the foliage can be a problem with this species in summer.

C. richardii is similar in habit but larger, with more slender plumes in white or cream. Both are hardy in most temperate areas, making good specimen

site	Will withstand most conditions, including dry and exposed
soil	This plant is unfussy as to soil, disliking only permanently wet soils
watering	Prefer dryish feet, very drought tolerant when established, with exception of *C. fulvida*
general care	Cut out bleached leaf tips, collapsed flower stems and dead leaves in spring. Be sure to wear thick gloves
pests & diseases	No real pest or disease problems. Severe water-logging in winter can cause dieback

plants or additions to expansive grass and perennial plantings.

The hardiness, sheer size and impact, flowering potential and low-maintenance qualities that made *C. selloana*, the pampass grass, so popular are all still there, and have resulted in many selections. It is undeniably big – in flower, 3m (10ft) high and wide – and a rapid spreader, but its perceived 'naffness' is perhaps due more to the unimaginative way it was often used. At the back of a border, it can fade into the background for the summer before throwing up its huge plumes in autumn, and contribute evergreen structure for the winter. However, placed at the centre of a group of other Cortaderia, Miscanthus and other big grasses, it reveals it also has harmonizing qualities.

The dwarf cultivar 'Pumila' is an excellent choice for smaller gardens, even its flower plumes rarely topping 1.8m (6ft), and its size makes it easier to associate. *C. selloana* 'Albolineata' is even more compact at 1.2m (4ft), as is 'Silver Stripe', both of

Cortaderia selloana 'Sunningdale Silver'

Cortaderia selloana 'Pumila'

them with attractive white margins and stripes to the leaves. 'Aureolineata' has leaves with broad gold edging that gets richer as the summer progresses, reaching around 1.5m (4ft).

Of the larger cultivars, *C. selloana* 'Monstrosa' is probably the tallest, with pure white plumes. 'Sunningdale Silver' forms a taller leaf mound and has fuller, stouter

Cortaderia selloana 'Albolineata'

plumes. 'White Feather' and recently inroduced 'Silver Feather' ('Notcort') are both white flowered and slightly smaller at around 2.4m (8ft).

Pink plumes on plants the size of pampass grasses look frankly odd. 'Rendatleri' is at least dark pink suffused with purple, but the flower stems are weak and often break. 'Rosea' is white with a faint blush of pink and almost attractive, unlike shockingly flamingo-pink 'Pink Feather'.

Cortaderia selloana 'Pumila'

Cortaderia richardii

	SPRING	SUMMER	AUTUMN	WINTER	height (cm)	spread (cm)	flower/leaf colour	
Cortaderia fulvida	in leaf	flowering	flowering	flowering	240	180		Prefers more moisture than other species, fairly hardy
C. richardii	in leaf	flowering	flowering/in leaf	in leaf	300	300		New Zealand species, fairly hardy
C. selloana	in leaf	in leaf	in leaf/flowering	flowering	300	240		Flower size and showiness varies
C. selloana 'Aureolineata'	in leaf	in leaf	in leaf/flowering	flowering/in leaf	150	150		Dwarf gold variegated form
C. selloana 'Albolineata'	in leaf	in leaf	in leaf/flowering	flowering/in leaf	120	120		Dwarf form with white margins and stripes to leaves
C. selloana 'Monstrosa'	in leaf	in leaf	in leaf/flowering	flowering	300	180		One of largest cultivars, narrow clumps
C. selloana 'Pumila'	in leaf	in leaf	in leaf/flowering	flowering	180	180		Best plain leaved dwarf form, free flowering
C. selloana 'Pink Feather'	in leaf	in leaf	in leaf/flowering	flowering/in leaf	240	240		Too loud to even be planted as ironic
C. selloana 'Rendatleri'	in leaf	in leaf	in leaf/flowering	flowering/in leaf	240	240		Pink-purple flowers, not as long lasting as some
C. selloana 'Rosea'	in leaf	in leaf	in leaf/flowering	flowering	240	240		Blush pink flowers
C. selloana 'Silver Feather' ('Notcort')	in leaf	in leaf	in leaf/flowering	flowering	240	240		New cultivar, white flowers
C. selloana 'Sunningdale Silver'	in leaf	in leaf	in leaf/flowering	flowering	300	150		Large but narrow clumps, free flowering
C. selloana 'White Feather'	in leaf	in leaf	in leaf/flowering	flowering	240	240		White flowers

in leaf   flowering

Corynephorus canescens
Grey hair grasses

Only a single species of the genus, *Corynephorus canescens*, is in cultivation, and it would be fair to say that grey hair grass is better known by ecologists and botanists than gardeners. This is a shame, as not only is it an increasingly rare British native, it is also a small perennial with real ornamental qualities.

The overall colour is more grey than blue, and the plant forms low growing, tight tussocks up to 30cm (12in) tall when in flower and about the same across. The basal stems and lower parts of the leaves are often shaded an attractive rusty red. The flower spikes are initially compact, forming loose panicles on opening and are blue-grey initially, becoming more reddish.

The leaves appear very thin and fine, as they are rolled in on themselves, a water-conserving adaptation that suits grey hair grass to its favoured habitat, coastal sand dunes where it often appears as a pioneer species, spreading slowly by runners and helping to consolidate sand dunes. In cultivation, this makes it extremely drought tolerant and useful for dry, poor soils. It associates well with other low-growing, dry area specialists like sedum, thymes and Armeria (thrift), and many alpines, as well as smaller coloured leaved grasses enjoying similar acidic soils, such as festucas.

Grey hair grass is more common in mainland Europe, in a swathe from the south

site	This plant requires full sun, and it copes well with exposure
soil	Prefers poor, free draining soils but grows in any non-alkaline soils
watering	Extremely drought tolerant once established. Very little extra watering should be required
general care	Very low maintenance: give clumps a spring haircut, and dead head to avoid self-seeding
pests & diseases	Relatively trouble free. No pest or disease problems. Dislikes only permanent wetness

of Norway to Portugal. Britain is actually right at the northern limit of its range, which experimental work has shown coincides with the line of average temperatures in mid-summer of 15°C (59°F). This is the main flowering season, and temperatures below this interfere with flowering and seed germination, making Corynephorus a classic example of an ecological limiting factor. Paradoxically, while British conservationists are attempting to halt its decline in the UK, in the Eastern USA it is showing signs of becoming a problem, invasive introduced species.

Corynephorus canescens

Corynephorus canescens

Cymophyllus fraserianus

Fraser's sedge

The plant formerly known as *Carex fraseri*, Fraser's sedge is still commonly sold as such, but in the interests of botanical correctness has been separated from the Carex entries.

Although still in the sedge family, the Cyperaceae, *Cymophyllus fraserianus* never bore much resemblance to the other Carex species, having broad, leathery, strap-like leaves up to 2.5cm (1in) across, looking more like those of a tulip than a sedge. As is usual in taxonomy, the reclassification of Fraser's sedge was based on its flowers, their detailed structure considered sufficiently different from those of Carex to warrant a different genus.

Fraser's sedge is an evergreen denizen of the moist woods of the US Appalachian states, several of which list it as threatened or endangered across much of its former range. Its leaves are dark green, arching then trailing on the ground at their tips, and up to 45cm (18in) long, forming lax clumps up to 35cm (15in) high and up to 60cm (24in) across. The flowers appear in late spring as the new leaves unfurl, and look like odd, tiny white drumsticks. Against the dark leaves they are striking if not beautiful. In cultivation, it prefers a deep, moisture-retentive and lime free soil, and ideally full shade, although partial shade will be tolerated if the ground stays moist enough.

Despite its rather lax habit, *Cymophyllus fraserianus* mixes very effectively with other

Cymophyllus fraserianus

site	Sheltered and shady sites preferred, good woodland groundcover
soil	Moist, deep, acidic and rich soil is preferred, and it dis-likes lime
watering	Keep evenly moist but be careful not to waterlog this plant. Little else is required reagrding watering
general care	Removing old and damaged leaves as new ones unfurl in spring keeps plants tidy. Little else is needed
pests & diseases	Relatively trouble free from pest or disease problems. Easy to grow if kept shaded and moist

woodland dwellers. The broad leaves contrast nicely with the more finely divided fronds of ferns such as the lady fern (*Athyrium filix-femina*), or echo the undivided leaves of Hart's tongue fern (Asplenium), and the heart shaped paddles of woodland arum lily relatives, the Asarums. Trilliums are also good partners, especially as they originate from the same areas of North America and flower at around the same time. The thinner leaves of other sedges, particularly Bowles' golden sedge, *Carex aurea*, or the many gold and silver variegated shade tolerant cultivars, also contrast beautifully with this plant.

Cymophyllus fraserianus

Cyperus
Umbrella plants

The umbrella plants are the sedge genus that gave the family its name, the Cyperaceae, although they look like few other sedges.

Predominantly deciduous aquatics that grow best with their feet in the water, their unusual growth pattern of leaves held like spokes atop thick stems, often with whorls of small brown flowers make these plants look unfailingly exotic.

Most species are tender, but four are reliably hardy outdoors in temperate areas, two of them being rare natives to Britain. *Cyperus longus*, the sweet galingale, grows to 90cm (3ft), producing whorls of foliage, each stem terminating in flat, branched flower stems holding small brown flowers. More showy but slightly less hardy is American galingale, *C. eragrostis*, which forms a loose, leafier clump topped by more ball-like, pale brown flowerheads.

The largest hardy umbrella is *C. ustulatus*, which can reach 1.8m (6ft). It has broad leaves of a pale lime green suffused with light coffee-brown, with red midribs.

The other British native, *C. fuscus*, or brown cyperus, is smaller, rarely topping 15cm (6in), and is annual. All four can be grown as emergents with their rootballs in containers or seem equally happy in permanently moist soil, and will stand sun or shade.

Of the tender species, the most handsome is undoubtedly *C. papyrus*, which has furnished Egypt with paper for millennia. All tender species need high humidity levels.

Cyperus papyrus

Cyperus fuscus

Cyperus papyrus

site	Tender species indoors; standing in water, as light as possible
soil	Unfussy, provided permanently moist or waterlogged
watering	Water these plants profusely as they react badly to drought. Do not let them dry out or they will fail
general care	Cut hardy species back to ground level after stems collapse. Remove fading stems from tender species
pests & diseases	No pest and disease problems. Cultural problems usually related to lack of water or low humidity

	SPRING	SUMMER	AUTUMN	WINTER	height (cm)	spread (cm)	leaf colour	
Cyperus albostriatus					60	100		Tender, needs humidity indoors
C. eragrostis					90	75		Hardy South American species
C. fuscus					30	30		Rare native, annual
C. involucratus					100	100		Tender, humid indoors
C. involucratus 'Nanus'					30	30		Miniature form
C. involucratus 'Variegatus'					90	90		Variegated cultivar, tends to revert to plain green
C. longus					90	90		Hardy British native
C. papyrus					360	360		Tender but magnificent. High humidity indoors
C. papyrus 'Nanus'					60	60		Dinky dwarf form, sold as houseplant, needs humidity
C. ustulatus					180	120		Largest hardy species, red midribs

🗡 in leaf   ✺ flowering

Dactylis glomerata 'Variegata'

Striped cock's foot grass

The only form of this grass commonly grown is variegated a brilliant white on green, forming eye-catching, dense tussocks up to 30cm (12in) high. The flowers are not particularly prominent, forming relatively short, one sided, drooping panicles.

This grass is not a fast grower – clumps expanding only slowly – but it is relatively well-behaved, not a rampant self-seeder, reliably hardy and perennial. It is also unfussy as to soil type and mixes well with other grasses, particularly those with plain coloured leaves which are either broader or more narrow than Dactylis' own rather middling blades. Given that it has so many virtues, it is a mystery, then, as to why it is not more popular and more widely grown.

The short answer to this question is that, like many grasses, striped cock's foot seems particularly loathe to shed its dead leaves, and clumps become so clogged with brown, papery cast-offs that they seem to physically prevent the production of fresh new growth, so that what was once a shining, white-striped mound becomes an increasingly dull lump, declining to the point of complete disappearance.

The good news is that this problem can be avoided by a regular combing through of the clump with the fingers; be quite firm and the dead leaves should come away relatively easily while the live ones remain more strongly attached. Growing in a pot makes this easier, but whether the gardener thinks it is worth such a chore at least twice a season, in spring and autumn, when there are many other variegated grasses available around the same size, is a matter of personal choice. This is also one of the grasses that benefits from regular division, best carried out in spring just as the new leaves begin to emerge. Replant immediately and keep well-watered during re-establishment.

site	Prefers full sun to keep variegation strong, prone to revert to green in shade
soil	Unfussy, disliking only very dry or permanently wet conditions
watering	Keep evenly moist, but will stand short periods of drought as long as it does not become too dry
general care	This plant needs a regular combing out to remove dead leaves in order to remain fresh and vigorous
pests & diseases	No real pest or disease problems. Culturally, suffers in extremes of drought or winter waterlogging

Dactylis glomerata 'Variegata'

Deschampsia
Hair grass

A beautiful genus of grasses grown primarily for their finely divided, airy flowers which smother the plants from late spring, long before most other grasses, and often last well into autumn or winter. Deschampsia has the additional advantage of being shade tolerant, mixing well with broad leaved herbaceous plants like hostas and ferns.

Deschampsia cespitosa 'Goldtau'

Deschampsia looks particularly at home in informal planting styles such as Prairie and gravel gardens, coping with sun if the ground is moist enough. A word of warning: they self-seed, and seedlings of named cultivars do not come true.

The best known species, *Deschampsia cespitosa*, or tufted hair grass, forms arching clumps of dark green leaves 30–60cm (12–24in) tall, producing arching flower stems 75–90cm (30–36in) tall. The panicles open into clouds of airy spikelets coloured from golden yellow to bronze, lasting well and often obscuring the leaves. In much of Britain it is semi-evergreen. Good cultivars include 'Bronzeschleier' or 'Bronze Veil', with bronzy-red spikelets; 'Goldehange' ('Gold Shower') and 'Goldschleier' ('Gold Veil'), both slightly taller growing at 1.2m (4ft) with rich yellow spikelets; and slightly smaller 'Goldtau' ('Golden Dew'). *D.*

cespitosa var. *vivipara* (sometimes sold as 'Fairy's Joke') produces small plantlets that can drop off and root instead of seeds.

D. flexuosa (wavy hair grass) is smaller than *D. cespitosa*, with extremely fine, dark green and usually evergreen leaves only 15–25cm (6–9in) long, but produces airy flowers on stems up to 75cm (30in) tall. Native to woodland clearings, it copes with shade and wet soils better than most other grasses. 'Tatra Gold' is a lovely bright yellow cultivar with reddish brown flowers.

Deschampsia cespitosa

site	Unfussy; if kept moist will withstand sun or shade and a degree of exposure
soil	Moisture retentive, copes with acidic soils, dislikes free-draining, alkaline soils
watering	Best kept evenly moist, may need irrigation in dry periods, however little else is required
general care	Unfussy and easy to grow grasses. Benefit from a spring haircut to remove dead leaves and flowers
pests & diseases	Relatively trouble free from pests and diseases, however dryness can cause problems to the plants

	SPRING	SUMMER	AUTUMN	WINTER	height (cm)	spread (cm)	leaf colour	
Deschampsia cespitosa					90	75		Tufted hair grass, hardy and attractive
D. cespitosa 'Bronzeschleier'					90	75		Often sold as 'Bronze Veil'
D. cespitosa 'Goldehange'					120	100		Often sold as 'Gold Shower' or 'Gold Pendent'
D. cespitosa 'Goldschleier'					120	100		Often sold as 'Golden Veil'
D. cespitosa 'Goldstaub'					90	75		Often sold as 'Gold Dust'
D. cespitosa 'Goldtau'					90	75		Often sold as 'Gold Dew'
D. cespitosa 'Northern Lights'					90	90		Multicolour variegation, best as specimen or in a pot
D. cespitosa var. *vivipara*					100	100		Produces small plantlets instead of seeds
D. flexuosa					75	60		Wavy hairgrass, shade and moisture tolerant
D. flexuosa 'Tatra Gold'					15	15		Yellow leaved form, dwarfer than species

🌿 in leaf ⚫ flowering

Elymus

Blue wheat grass

Few other garden plants can compete with the intense, almost icy, silvery-blueness of some of the species in this small grass genus, which puts even *Festuca glauca* and its blue cultivars to shame.

Elymus magellanicus

Elymus have broader leaves and a more lax, arching habit than the fescues. Elymus need full sun. The silver-blue colour often indicates exposure tolerance. They are unfussy as to soil type, disliking only really heavy clays.

Elymus hispidus (blue wheatgrass) forms loose clumps up to 60cm (2ft) high, and has narrow, deeply ridged, evergreen leaves that emerge upright, becoming more arching through the season. The flowerheads are dense and narrow, with a herringbone structure similar to an ear of wheat, hence the common name.

They emerge silver blue but fade through yellow to beige. *E. magellanicus*, from the tip of South America, is similarly coloured but smaller, to 45cm (18in), and more lax and sprawling in habit. It is not reliably hardy in colder, temperate regions.

Reliably hardy is *E. canadensis* from Canada, which is grey-green leaved and larger than *E. hispidus*, forming more substantial clumps to 1.5m (60in), without becoming invasive; f. *glaucifolius* is a particularly intense blue. *E. villosus* also grows to 1.5m (60in), with bristly green flowerheads and is deciduous, the foliage turning butter yellow in autumn. *E. villosus* var. *arkansanus* is of a similar size, with bright green leaves on mahogany-brown stems. It has red flower stems, green flowerheads tinged red and more open, rye-like seedheads from early summer.

Elymus hispidus

site	Full sun. Cope well with exposure but do not do well in shade
soil	Unfussy, disliking only heavy clays; relatively drought-tolerant
watering	Keep evenly moist, but not permanently wet; the plants will take some dryness if necessary
general care	Evergreens benefit from spring comb-out of dead leaves; deciduous species best cut back hard in spring
pests & diseases	No real pest or disease problems. Shade and excessive winter wet can lead to cultural problems

	SPRING	SUMMER	AUTUMN	WINTER	height (cm)	spread (cm)	leaf colour	
Elymus canadensis	🌿🌿	●●●●●	●●●●●	🌿🌿	150	100		Large but slow spreading
E. canadensis f. *glaucifolius*	🌿🌿	●●●●●	●●●●●	🌿🌿	150	100		Much bluer leaves than species
E. hispidus	🌿🌿🌿	●●●●●	●●●●●	🌿🌿🌿	60	60		Intensely blue evergreen grass
E. magellanicus	🌿🌿🌿	●●●●●	●●●●●	🌿🌿🌿	45	45		Smaller and less hardy than *E. hispidus*
E. villosus	🌿🌿	●●●●●	●●●●●	🌿🌿	150	100		Hardy, good butter yellow autumn colour
E. villosus var. *arkansanus*	🌿🌿	●●●●●	●●●●●	🌿🌿	150	100		Similar to species with bronzy overtones

 🌿 in leaf ● flowering

Equisetum
Horse tails

At the risk of alienating those who have grappled with *Equisetum arvense*, an invasive weed common in allotments, I would like to introduce some more ornamental cousins. Horsetails, also known as scouring rushes, are an ancient and unusual plant lineage that produce spores, having evolved long before seed bearing plants, with more in common with mosses and liverworts than the comparative newcomers, grasses and bamboos, that form the bulk of plants in this book.

Some 345 million years ago, horsetails were tree sized, and formed much of the coal mined today as fuel. Only a few small species survive today, reproducing largely vegetatively, but are widely distributed. The temperate species are bone-hardy, down to -30°C (-22°F).

Horsetails are moisture lovers, several species growing as emergents, and spread by underground rhizomes (stems). There are deciduous and evergreen species, some of which are invasive in conditions they like, and are perhaps best confined in a pot (ensure they never dry out), or in shady, humid areas. There are two main types, those that branch at the nodes, forming spiky, 'bottlebrushes' and unbranched, ramrod-straight species that are often attractively striped at the nodes. Curious, light, cone-like reproductive structures appear at the tips of some that are interesting rather than truly ornamental.

Of the unbranched species, *Equisetum hyemale*, the rough horsetail or scouring rush is fairly typical, its stems reaching 1.5m (5ft) and attractively striped black at the nodes. Var. *affine* is up to 60cm (2ft) taller and more robust. Both adapt to life as emergents. *E. ramosissimum* var. *japonicum* is similar, reaching 1m (39in). *E. variegatum* rarely reaches 30cm (12in) but has black bands highlighted with white 'teeth', and *E. scirpoides* is even smaller, to 15cm (6in), fresh green with darker green nodes. All prefer permanently damp soil.

The 'leaves' of branched horsetails are actually stems, the true leaves are fused into the banded sheaths that mark the nodes.

Equisetum hyemale var. affine

site	Full sun to partial shade, exposure tolerant if kept moist
soil	Unfussy; they will adapt to virtually any soil, including waterlogged
watering	Several species happy growing in water, to evenly moist soil. Dislike really dry areas
general care	Extremely easy to grow. Some species prove invasive, and are best grown in pots
pests & diseases	Not usually any pest or disease problems. Culturally, only dry conditions detrimental

	SPRING	SUMMER	AUTUMN	WINTER	height (cm)	spread (cm)	stem colour	
E. hyemale var. *affine*	𝄄 𝄄 𝄄	𝄄 𝄄 𝄄	𝄄 𝄄 𝄄	𝄄 𝄄 𝄄	210	200+		Unbranched, brown-black nodes
E. ramosissimum var. *japonicum*	𝄄 𝄄 𝄄	𝄄 𝄄 𝄄	𝄄 𝄄 𝄄	𝄄 𝄄 𝄄	100	200+		Unbranched, prominent black nodes
E. scirpoides	𝄄 𝄄 𝄄	𝄄 𝄄 𝄄	𝄄 𝄄 𝄄	𝄄 𝄄 𝄄	15	200+		Usually unbranched, darker green nodes
E. sylvaticum		𝄄 𝄄 𝄄	𝄄 𝄄 𝄄		60	200+		Highly branched, deciduous 'bottlebrush'
E. telmateia	𝄄 𝄄	𝄄 𝄄 𝄄	𝄄		180	200+		Great horsetail; large, deciduous, branched species
E. variegatum	𝄄 𝄄 𝄄	𝄄 𝄄 𝄄	𝄄 𝄄 𝄄	𝄄 𝄄 𝄄	30	200+		Unbranched, black and white banded nodes

𝄄 in leaf

Eragrostis
Love grasses

Love grasses are dainty plants with narrow leaves and diffuse, long lasting feathery flowers from summer to autumn, forming substantial, arching clumps wider than they are high and as happy in a pot as they are planted en masse.

Not dissimilar to Deschampsia but less shade-tolerant, these plants associate equally well with broader leaved and more upright grasses and herbaceous plants, are unfussy about soil type and look lovely trailing over the sides of pots. Planted en masse, they are excellent as ornamental weed suppressors. About their only disadvantage is that they are not the hardiest of grasses, since several are native to southern Africa, although most species will survive an average winter in colder regions providing they do not stay too wet.

Eragrostis curvula, African love grass, has dark green, hair-like leaves up to 90cm (3ft) long. From the centre of its clumps in mid-summer arise arching flower stems bearing diffuse, grey-green panicles on delicate, feathery stems that shift in the slightest breeze. The leaves bleach to pale fawn in autumn but the flowerheads remain green-grey. 'Totnes Burgundy' is a lovely selection, with dark red, plum-coloured flowers. *E. chloromelas*, Boer love grass, is similar but larger at 1.2m (4ft), with grey-blue leaves, an intense blue in some individuals.

Eragrostis trichodes

Eragrostis trichodes

Eragrostis curvula 'Totnes Burgundy'

Bamboos & Grasses

site	Prefer full sun, but they are relatively tolerant of exposure
soil	Free-draining soils, but will grow in all but heavy clay and permanently wet sites
watering	Keep these plants evenly moist or on the dry side. They dislike winter wet. Little else required
general care	Not the hardiest – leaving dead leaves until spring gives some winter protection
pests & diseases	No real pest or disease problems. Cuturally, winter wet and low temperatures can cause dieback

	SPRING	SUMMER	AUTUMN	WINTER	height (cm)	spread (cm)	flower colour	
Eragrostis airoides					30	30		Lovely new introduction
E. chloromelas					120	120		Handsome glaucous grass
E. curvula					90	120		Grey-green, feathery flowers bleach bluff
E. curvula 'Totnes Burgundy'					90	120		Red flowered cultivar
E. spectabilis					60	60		Purple flowered
E. trichodes					90	90		Light purple flowers

in leaf   flowering

Fargesia

Fargesia is one of the largest and most useful of the temperate bamboo genera. Largely from Himalayan regions, several species are extremely hardy, standing up well to exposure and dryness, making them useful as windbreaks or even hedging.

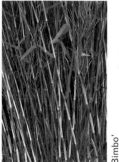

Fargesia murielae 'Jumbo'

Fargesia murielae 'Bimbo'

haves for Oriental style gardens. Several species are new to cultivation in the West, with more to come, but the whole genus is under taxonomic review so names may change and species be split or amalgamated; like many bamboos, they are extremely variable plants.

Fargesia murielae may well be the most widely grown of all temperate bamboos, and it is deservedly popular for its hardiness, down to -29°C (-20°F), tolerance of exposure and dry conditions, and graceful habit. The culms are

In very cold or exposed positions, they can become deciduous, their leaves browning and falling, but being replaced by fresh new growth in the spring. Others are more delicate, with relatively small, narrow leaves leaves and often attractively coloured culms (stems). Most are well-behaved clump-formers with an attractive, slightly arching habit that spread only slowly. Fargesias usually produce 4–5 branches per node, with a 45-degree upward slope that characterizes the genus, and have small leaves produced in large quantities. They make elegant specimen plants and also integrate beautifully into plantings with other grasses, and are must-

site	Sun or partial shade. More exposure tolerant than most bamboos
soil	These plants grow well in any soils but permanently wet or very dry
watering	Even moisture is the ideal, but they will thrive in drier conditions than most bamboos
general care	Graceful, easy to grow bamboos suited to a range of garden styles. Most adapt well to pots
pests & diseases	Relatively trouble free as there are not usually any problems in terms of pests and diseases

	SPRING	SUMMER	AUTUMN	WINTER	height (cm)	spread (cm)	culm colour	
Fargesia angustissima					700	600+		Young culms white bloomed, purple sheaths
F. denudata					500	400+		Similar to *F. murielae*
F. dracocephala					500	400+		Long leaves, full sun, new
F. fungosa					450	400+		Purple-red new shoots, culms red in sun
F. murielae					400	400+		Popular and hardy
F. murielae 'Bimbo'					200	200+		Semi-dwarf, good in pots
F. murielae 'Harewood'					100	200+		Dwarf, good in pots
F. murielae 'Jumbo'					450	400+		Larger than species
F. murielae 'Simba'					200	200+		Semi-dwarf, good in pots
F. murielae 'Willow'					400	400+		Longer, narrower leaves than species
F. nitida					400	400+		Exposure tolerant, good windbreak or hedge

in leaf

Fargesia robusta

but the same elegant habit. *F. dracocephala* is of a similar size and habit, and even newer in cultivation, with narrow leaves double the length of those of *F. denudata*. It prefers full sun, as does *F. fungosa*, a promising, slightly smaller new import with culms that emerge purple-red, colour to mid green and can be a strong rust-red in full sun.

Fargesia nitida was one of the first bamboos to reach the West and is widely grown across Europe. It is as bone-hardy as *F. murielae*, but even more exposure tolerant, making an excellent windbreak or hedge. Its greenish culms, purple-flushed in some individuals, reach 4m (13ft) and do not branch out until their second year. There are several named selections. 'Anceps' is an elegant plant with longer leaves than the species and a lax, almost weeping habit. 'Eisenach' has smaller leaves than the species, is slower growing and its culms curve from their base. *F. robusta* is a recent introduction that is similar to *F. nitida* but more upright, with relatively large leaves to 13cm (5in) long. It has dark green culms, that emerge with prominently white sheaths that give an attractive variegated apppearance as the stems lengthen. Its cultivar 'Pingwu' is larger leaved and more robust, while 'Red Sheath' has red sheaths and branch bases. *F. utilis* is a relatively coarse, rapid spreading species not recommended for smaller gardens that seems less hardy than most, while undeniably handsome *F. angustissima*, a small leaved species reaching 7m (23ft) with purple sheaths seems reliable only to -9°C (15°F).

The best of the new introductions may well prove to be *F. yulongshanensis*, a Chinese species from high altitudes with rich green culms to 7m (23ft) that emerge with a blue bloom and small leaves.

light green, up to 4m (13ft) tall, and form tight, arching clumps spreading only slowly. The leaves are around 8cm (3in) long and fairly narrow. After a major flowering period in the 1970s and 1980s, a variety of named cultivars have become available. The best of these include 'Bimbo' and 'Simba', dwarf selections to 2.1m (7ft), and 'Harewood', which barely reaches a metre (39in). All three are excellent in pots. 'Jumbo' is wider leaved than the species and slightly taller, while 'Willow' has narrower leaves and is more arching.

F. denudata is a fairly new introduction broadly similar to *F. murielae*, with mid-green culms to 5m (16ft) that colour rich yellow in sun and slightly smaller leaves, to 5cm (2in)

Fargesia nitida

F

Bamboos & Grasses

	SPRING	SUMMER	AUTUMN	WINTER	height (cm)	spread (cm)	culm colour	
F. nitida 'Anceps'	𝄢 𝄢 𝄢	𝄢 𝄢 𝄢	𝄢 𝄢 𝄢	𝄢 𝄢 𝄢	400	400+	▨	Longer, narrower leaves. Heat tolerant
F. nitida 'Eisenach'	𝄢 𝄢 𝄢	𝄢 𝄢 𝄢	𝄢 𝄢 𝄢	𝄢 𝄢 𝄢	400	400+	▨	Smaller leaved and more arching than species
F. robusta	𝄢 𝄢 𝄢	𝄢 𝄢 𝄢	𝄢 𝄢 𝄢	𝄢 𝄢 𝄢	400	400+	▨	Upright growth for a Fargesia, larger leaved than most
F. robusta 'Pingwu'	𝄢 𝄢 𝄢	𝄢 𝄢 𝄢	𝄢 𝄢 𝄢	𝄢 𝄢 𝄢	450	400+	▨	Larger and more robust than species
F. robusta 'Red Sheath'	𝄢 𝄢 𝄢	𝄢 𝄢 𝄢	𝄢 𝄢 𝄢	𝄢 𝄢 𝄢	400	400+	▨	Red sheaths and nodes
F. utilis	𝄢 𝄢 𝄢	𝄢 𝄢 𝄢	𝄢 𝄢 𝄢	𝄢 𝄢 𝄢	700	600+	▨	Fast-growing and vigorous
F. yulongshanensis	𝄢 𝄢 𝄢	𝄢 𝄢 𝄢	𝄢 𝄢 𝄢	𝄢 𝄢 𝄢	700	600+	▨	Promising new introduction, culms emerge blue

𝄢 *in leaf*

Bamboos & Grasses

Festuca
Fescues

The fescues are small, narrow leaved grasses primarily found on poor, acidic soils. Important constituents of meadows and lawns, it is however the blue and grey leaved species that are most often grown as ornamentals.

Festuca glauca 'Seeigel'

In cultivation, these tend to form small tussocks rarely higher or wider than 90cm (3ft), usually much smaller, and are both easy to grow and attractive. There are many named forms, primarily selected for their unusual leaf colours, and most species are evergreen, although some of the foliage can brown off after flowering (deadheading can help prevent this). Most do best divided every 2–3 years, which prevents dieback in the middle of clumps, and all benefit from a spring haircut just as the new leaves begin to emerge. Avoid planting fescues in alkaline limestone or chalk areas, but otherwise they will adapt to most soil types, doing best in full sun and good drainage. Soggy winters can cause dieback problems, particularly in the centres of clumps.

site	Full sun is preferred and necessary to achieve the best possible colour
soil	Average to free-draining, dislike heavy clay and alkalinity
watering	Like to be kept on the drier side, particularly in winter, and react badly to waterlogging
general care	Mostly evergreen grasses. Benefit from a spring haircut and deadheading as flowers bleach
pests & diseases	Relatively trouble free in terms of pest and disease problems, but can be prone to rots if wet in winter

Festuca glauca 'Elijah Blue'

Fescues look particularly at home teamed with sedges or grasses of around the same size in contrasting colours, but will not stand real shade, in gravel gardens or with other grasses and perennials of similar vigour that will not swamp them. The blue and silver selections marry well with other grey leaved plants such as Eryngium and lavenders, and the smaller forms make good edging plants for the front of borders. They also make wonderful container plants, particularly in pots glazed a harmonizing or contrasting colour to their leaves, or used en masse, as an easy-care lawn alternative. The steely

	SPRING	SUMMER	AUTUMN	WINTER	height (cm)	spread (cm)	leaf colour	
F. amythystina					45	45		Like a large *F. glauca*
F. erecta					45	45		Upright grower from Falklands
F. eskia					8	15		Carpet forming dwarf grass
F. glauca					30	60		Variable colour from silver to blue
F. glauca 'Azurit'					40	60		Slightly larger than species
F. glauca 'Blaufuchs'					15	30		Often sold as 'Blue Fox'
F. glauca 'Blauglut'					15	30		Often sold as 'Blue Glow'
F. glauca 'Elijah Blue'					30	60		Probably the most intensely coloured

in leaf · *flowering*

for their exceptional colour. 'Elijah Blue' is perhaps the brightest blue, and a gorgeous garden plant forming tight blue mounds to 30cm (1ft). 'Azurit' is slightly taller, and lighter and more silvery in colour. 'Harz' is several shades darker, forming an interesting contrast. 'Seeigel' ('Sea Urchin') is more upright and green leaved, and there is even a good yellow, 'Golden Toupee', which emerges bright yellow in spring fading to more green-yellow as the summer goes on, making clumps to 30cm (12in).

Of the other species, the largest is probably *F. mairei*, Maire's fescue, forming clumps of relatively broad, shiny, grey-green leaves up to 60cm (2ft) in height and spread, appearing silvery from a distance. *F. paniculata* is similar, slightly smaller with greener leaves that are the broadest in the genus, and larger than average flowerheads.

F. amythystina can make 45cm (18in) but is pale grey-blue, not the purple its name suggests. *F. valesiaca* looks similar, often a little smaller, and its bluer variant var. *glaucantha* looks very similar to *F. glauca*.

More spiky, upright fescues that contrast well with more arching grasses include *F. erecta*, a Falklands Islands grass forming clumps to 45cm (18in) of a grey, leaden pale blue, and smaller *F. punctoria*, porcupine grass with sharply pointed, silver blue leaves forming short clumps to 15cm (6in) tall and 30cm (12in) across. Even smaller is *F. eskia*, a beautiful little carpeting grass growing no more than 6cm (3in) tall in clumps 15cm (6in) across.

Festuca glauca 'Golden Toupee'

Festuca amethystina

blueness of *Festuca glauca* and its selections are particularly loved by designers of modern, clean-lined 'outdoor room' gardens as they look especially at home among galvanised containers and in raised beds.

By far the most popular fescue is *F. glauca*, which occurs in a range of colours from pale and silvery to intense blue-grey, the colour usually most intense in spring and fading to a greener blue in winter. It is evergreen, up to 30cm (12in) high in clumps to 60cm (2ft) across, flowering from late spring to midsummer. The flower spikes are not particularly eye-catching but emerge the same colour as the leaves, opening to fairly small, loose panicles and ageing to biscuit brown. There are many named selections, most of which are fairly similar and chosen

	SPRING	SUMMER	AUTUMN	WINTER	height (cm)	spread (cm)	leaf colour	
F. glauca 'Golden Toupee'					25	30		Turns more lime green in summer
F. glauca 'Harz'					30	60		Good contrast to lighter cultivars
F. glauca minima					10	20		Gorgeous little miniature, good with alpines
F. glauca 'Seeigel'					30	30		Often sold as 'Sea Urchin', spiky and upright
F. mairei					60	60		Silvery looking, broad leaved and large for a fescue
F. paniculata					50	50		Broad leaved and large flowered
F. punctoria					15	30		Porcupine grass, narrow leaved and upright
F. valesiaca					30	30		Similar to F. glauca
F. valesiaca var. glaucantha					30	30		Very similar to F. glauca
F. valesiaca 'Silbersee'					12	12		Semi dwarf form, often sold as 'Silver Sea'
F. vivipara					15	30		Produces small plantlets instead of seeds, unusual

🌿 in leaf   ✹ flowering

Glyceria maxima var. variegata

Striped mana grass

Glyceria maxima, the only species commonly cultivated, is most commonly seen in its variegated form, G. maxima var. variegata, although the plain green leaved species is not without its merits.

Striped mana grass is however one of the best of the white variegated grasses. It is deciduous, the leaves emerging in spring strongly flushed pink, fading down the leaf as it emerges to near purple where the blades join the stem.

The leaves are up to 60cm (2ft) long, 5cm (2in) across and arching, with prominent white or cream stripes on a deep green base, retaining their colouring well through the season.

The plant forms broad clumps to 60cm (2ft) tall, with an open, arching shape.

Flowers are produced on slightly taller stems in mid- and late summer, and form highly branched, open panicles of creamy white. The species form of this grass is of similar size and stature, if faster growing and even more invasive, but much more rarely offered for sale.

Mana grass is a native of wet, boggy habitats and loves to grow close to water, where its vigorously spreading, rhizomatous root system (of indefinite spread like those of bamboos) can make it highly invasive.

In such conditions it goes well with other

Glyceria maxima var. variegata

site	Full sun for the best variegation, and ideally moist and sheltered
soil	Grows best in moist to waterlogged soils, and of any pH
watering	Happy with its feet in the water permanently, or kept moist, dislikes drought, so water regularly
general care	Easy to grow, but can be invasive in wet conditions. Much less of a problem kept drier
pests & diseases	No real pest and disease problems, only cultural problems tend to be drought-induced

moisture lovers like ferns, Astilbe and Ligularia, and looks good when contrasted with the ramrod-straight, plain green leaves of rushes and horsetails.

It will grow quite happily in less moist conditions however, where its wandering tendencies are somewhat curtailed, making a particularly good companion for blue-leaved plants like some junipers and hostas, but dislikes real dryness and free draining conditions, and needs a relatively sunny spot to retain the freshness of its variegation.

Hakonechloa macra

Hakone grass

I am biased when it comes to this beautiful, hardy Japanese grass and its cultivars, but I am not the only one – it is a favourite of many for its quiet charm and the fact that it associates so well with such a wide range of plants.

It forms a low, rounded hemisphere of densely overlapping leaves and is deciduous, but has wonderful autumn colours of pink and purple before turning a shrivelled brown for the winter. About its only 'fault' is the flowers are relatively inconspicuous, forming small, loose panicles that often rest on the leaves in autumn. It is also a fairly slow-grower, and young plants are invariably 'one sided', only forming the domed shape with age and size.

The plain green species is little seen, sadly, as it is considerably larger than its variegated selections at 45cm (18in) by up to a metre (39in) across. It is magnificent in an oriental-style garden, however its cream and

Hakonechloa macra 'Aureola'

yellow striped selections are also some of the few variegated plants that do not look out of place in the green foliage dominated world of the Japanese garden.

The variegated selections are unfortunately often misnamed and confused in the nursery trade, so examine the colour and pattern of the stripings carefully. *H. macra* 'Alboaurea', golden Hakone grass, has rich golden yellow leaves with only thin stripes of green, and occasional splashes of white, held on thin red stems. In autumn, it flushes pink, then red-purple. It is 15–23cm (6–9in) tall, but up to 90cm (3ft) across, although slow growing. The other common gold-leaved cultivar is 'Aureola', broadly similar, if anything even brighter, but lacks the white splashes completely. The two are much confused.

H. macra 'Albolineata' is cream rather than white striped and more vigorous than the gold forms, reaching 30–38cm (12–15in), largely because the green stripes are much broader. Even more vigorous is 'Mediovariegata', which can reach 45cm (18in), approaching the size of the plain green species.

site	Prefer sheltered spot in part shade, but will stand full sun if moist enough	
soil	Garden loams preferred, dislike free-draining, heavy, and alkaline soils	
watering	Keep these plants evenly moist, and do not allow potted plants in particular to dry out	
general care	Easy in the right conditions, but slow growing for a grass, particularly the gold leaved forms	
pests & diseases	No real pest or disease problems. Cultural problems generally drought related	

Hakonechloa macra 'Aureola'

	SPRING	SUMMER	AUTUMN	WINTER	height (cm)	spread (cm)	leaf colour	
Hakonechloa macra	🌿🌿🌿❋	❋❋❋❋	❋❋❋	45	100		Difficult to find but worth the effort
H. macra 'Alboaurea'	🌿🌿🌿🌿	❋❋		25	90		True cultivar also has white splashes
H. macra 'Albolineata'	🌿🌿🌿🌿	❋❋		40	90		More vigorous than gold selections
H. macra 'Aureola'	🌿🌿🌿	❋❋		25	90		Similar to 'Alboaurea' but lacks white splashes
H. macra 'Mediovariegata'	🌿🌿🌿🌿	❋❋❋❋		45	100		Understated variegation, almost as vigorous as species

🌿 *in leaf*   ❋ *flowering*

Helictotrichon
Blue oat grass

Helictotrichon are attractive, clump-forming grasses, the most popular of which are grown for their steely blue leaves. These prefer full sun, becoming much duller in shade. They are undemanding grasses in cultivation, disliking only permanently wet soils, and are reasonably drought tolerant.

Helictotrichon sempervirens

They associate well with other relatively small grasses like festuca, particularly the blue *Festuca glauca* cultivars such as 'Elijah Blue', and with yellow-leaved species and cultivars. Although evergreen, blue oat grasses can be cut back hard in early spring as the fresh new foliage has the best colouring.

Helictotrichon sempervirens, the blue oat grass, cannot compete with Elymus in colouring, being a slightly duller, greyer blue, but it makes a more shapely plant, having more upright, narrower and less lax leaves. It is evergreen and grows to around 60cm (24in), with tall flower stems up to 1m (39in) in early and mid-summer, initially grey-blue but opening into one sided oat-like panicles that quickly bleach to straw and end up near white. Its variety *pendulum* has much more arching flowerstems that contrast nicely with the relatively upright leaves. There are several named forms chosen for their blueness, the best of which is probably 'Saphirsprudel', named in Germany.

H. pratense has two-tone leaves, blue on the upper surface and green beneath, which give an interesting effect if the wind is strong enough to rustle them. It produces more open flowers than *H. sempervirens* on shorter stems with large spikelets bearing long hairs (awns). *H. filifolius* is larger than *H. pratense* with the same leaf colouring, but is more upright and broad leaved, forming an upright tussock to 30cm (12in). A word of warning: its leaves are tough and taper to points strong enough to pierce the skin.

site	Full sun to part shade is preferred, and they are relatively exposure tolerant
soil	Free-draining preferred, but adapt to all but permanently wet substrates
watering	These plants prefer to be kept on the dry side, during winter especially; summer watering should be minimal
general care	Easy to grow. Benefit from either combing out dead leaves or cutting hard back in spring
pests & diseases	For some reason attractive to ants, which may establish nests in clumps. Treat with a proprietary ant pesticide

	SPRING	SUMMER	AUTUMN	WINTER	height (cm)	spread (cm)	leaf colour	
Helictotrichon filifolius	in leaf	flowering	in leaf	in leaf	70	60		Sharp leaves, more upright than others
H. pratense	in leaf	flowering	flowering	in leaf	30	60		Smallest in general cultivation
H. sempervirens	in leaf	flowering	in leaf	in leaf	100	100		Leaf clumps to 60cm (24in), flowers taller
H. sempervirens var. *pendulum*	in leaf	flowering	in leaf	in leaf	75	100		Smaller form with arching flowers
H. sempervirens 'Saphirsprudel'	in leaf	flowering	in leaf	in leaf	100	100		Vivid blue selection

🍃 in leaf   ✹ flowering

H

Bamboos & Grasses

Hibanobambusa

Hibanobambusa tranquillans is thought to be a hybrid between two species from different bamboo genera (an inter-generic hybrid) that was found in the wild after the simultaneous flowering of *Sasa veitchii* and *Phyllostachys nigra* 'Henonensis'.

Hibanobambusa tranquillans 'Shiroshima'

Given the infrequency most bamboos flower, if it is a hybrid it may well be unique, combining the characteristics of what are two dissimilar bamboos – the large leaves of Sasa with the taller, stouter culms of Phyllostachys. It has also inherited the running tendencies of Sasa, but fortunately is nowhere near as invasive. It makes a fine specimen bamboo, is happy in most soils and contrasts excellently to smaller-leaved bamboos and other grasses. It looks particularly good near water and in Oriental style gardens or mixed with other sub-tropical looking plants like cannas, bananas and tree ferns.

H. tranquillans can reach 5m (16ft) but is usually smaller, its culms having prominent nodes and ridges common in Phyllostachys species, with usually two branches emerging from each node. The culms are green, taking on lighter yellow-green highlights in sun. The leaves, however, are much larger than any Phyllostachys – up to 23cm (9in) long and 5cm (2in) across they are like those of *Sasa palmata*. Unlike Sasa, they

site	Full sun to part shade is preferred, it stands some exposure
soil	Unfussy, disliking only permanent wetness or very dry conditions
watering	Keep this plant evenly moist, particularly as culms are emerging and new leaves appearing
general care	Does run, so snap off culms emerging too far away from main clump, and thin out old and dead culms annually
pests & diseases	Relatively trouble free regarding pest or disease problems. Dislikes prolonged drought

do not bleach around the edges to pale straw in the winter, remaining a bright, rich green. It is hardy down to -20°C (-4°F)

H. tranquillans 'Shiroshima' is a deservedly popular variegated form, with some of the largest, brightest variegated leaves of any garden plant. This can make it more difficult to associate with other plants, but as a stand-alone specimen plant it is hard to beat. The leaves are conspicuously striped with creamy-white, and often take on delightful pink and purple overtones when young or in full sun. The striping seems to have little effect on the vigour of the plant as it is just as strongly growing as the plain leaved form. *H.* 'Kimmei' is another named selection that seems smaller but otherwise differs little from the species, but both it and 'Shiroshima' have conspicuously hairy sheaths.

Hibanobambusa tranquillans

	SPRING	SUMMER	AUTUMN	WINTER	height (cm)	spread (cm)	culm colour	
Hibanobambusa 'Kimmei'	🌿🌿🌿	🌿🌿🌿	🌿🌿🌿	🌿🌿🌿	400	600+		Similar to species
H. tranquillans	🌿🌿🌿	🌿🌿🌿	🌿🌿🌿	🌿🌿🌿	500	600+		Large leaved and exotic looking
H. tranquillans 'Shiroshima'	🌿🌿🌿	🌿🌿🌿	🌿🌿🌿	🌿🌿🌿	500	600+		Leaves variegated creamy white

🌿 *in leaf*

Himalayacalamus

Himalayacalamus is a bamboo genus largely from the Himalayas. Its species form part of the understory of broad leaved deciduous forests, so have evolved to enjoy shady, sheltered and humid conditions. As a genus they do not cope well with drought or exposure, but given a degree of shelter are not difficult to grow and can adapt well to life in pots.

H. f. 'Damarapa'

The species currently in cultivation in the West are unfortunately not particularly hardy, and it is to be hoped more cold-tolerant species or forms from higher altitudes will be imported.

The best known species is *Himalayacalamus falconeri*, an upright, elegant, tightly clumping bamboo from Nepal and Bhutan, which can reach 7m (23ft) in the wild but barely half that in cultivation, and is only reliably hardy down to -8°C (18°F). It grows well in pots, however, allowing it to be moved under protection in cold snaps. Its leaves are up to 9cm (3.5in) long. Its culms have the odd characteristic of emerging covered in a jelly-like substance, thought to be an insect repellant.

H. falconeri 'Damarapa' was long thought a separate species, and was sold as *H. hookeriana* (*H. hookerianus* is in fact a completely different plant, see below), but has now been placed as a cultivar of *H. falconeri*. Its culms are beautifully marked with cream

site	Partial shade is preferred by this plant, as well as sheltered conditions
soil	It is not fussy if not too dry and free draining. Likes moist soil
watering	This plant likes humid conditions, keep moist. Leaves enjoy a splash of water in dry spells
general care	Not reliably hardy in temperate regions, particularly drier areas. Winter protection advisable
pests & diseases	Relatively trouble free as there are not usually any problems regarding pests and diseases

and green stripes, with reddish tinges developing. Unfortunately cold and wind tend to cause loss of colouration, particularly on new culms produced late in the season. Like its parent, it is not the hardiest of bamboos.

The true *H. hookerianus* is known as the blue bamboo as its culms emerge a waxy blue, ageing to yellow or purple green. A beautiful plant, it is as yet rare in cultivation. The leaves are slightly larger than those of *H. falconeri*, and the culm sheaths are longer and narrower. It seems to be slightly hardier than falconeri too, down to -10°C (14°F). Relatively new to cultivation is *H. asper*, a small-leaved species reaching 6m (20ft).

Himalayacalamus falconeri 'Damarapa'

	SPRING	SUMMER	AUTUMN	WINTER	height (cm)	spread (cm)	culm colour	
Himalayacalamus asper					600	600+		Lovely arching bamboo but quite tender
H. falconeri					700	600+		More upright and slightly hardier
H. falconeri 'Damarapa'					700	600+		Handsomely striped culms
H. hookerianus					900	600+		Blue bamboo, rare, slightly hardier than others

🗡 *in leaf*

Holcus mollis

Yorkshire fog

Yorkshire fog, or creeping soft grass, is a relatively common British native grass, widely distributed in moist grasslands and water meadows. It spreads by rhizomes at or just under the soil surface, and can form extensive mats where conditions suit it, up to 75cm (30in) tall.

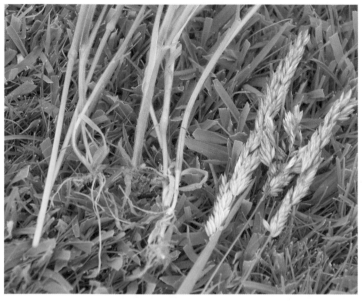

Holcus mollis 'White Fog'

rockeries, between cracks in paving, and is even resilient enough to mowing to be used as a variegated lawn. It also mixes well with the smaller sedges, liking similarly shady conditions: it keeps its variegation well and does not enjoy full sun, particularly in summer, looking its freshest early and late in the season.

Considerably larger is *H. mollis* 'White Fog', which has a similarly spreading habit but grows to 30cm (12in), flowering in mid-summer. If anything, its white stripes are broader than those of 'Albovariegatus', and the leaves have an attractive pink blush to them on emergence. It copes better with sun than 'Albovariegatus', and tends to retain the pink colouring in good light. It will also succeed on drier soils.

The stems are quite stout with prominent nodes at which the broad, soft, fresh green leaves attach. It is a useful meadow component on heavy soils but has little ornamental merit grown alone. It remains green through most winters.

The same cannot be said of its most commonly available cultivar, *Holcus mollis* 'Albovariegatus', striped creeping grass, which grows no taller than 15cm (6in) forming sprawling tufts 30cm (12in) or more across and is one of the best and brightest white variegated grasses. Leaves can be up to 20cm (8in) long and are fresh green in the centre, thickly margined with white. The flowers are greenish white but small and not particularly decorative, appearing from mid-summer. Striped creeping grass is small enough to mix with alpines and grow in

site	Semi- to full-shaded areas are preferred; 'White Fog' requires more sun
soil	This plant prefers heavier, moist soils; 'White Fog' drier ones
watering	Keep evenly moist, particularly as new leaves emerge in spring. Little else is required
general care	Simply pull up unwanted parts spreading too far; rhizomes are fragile and easily broken
pests & diseases	No real pest or disease problems. 'White Fog' less tolerant of winter wet than others

	SPRING	SUMMER	AUTUMN	WINTER	height (cm)	spread (cm)	leaf colour	
Holcus mollis	🍃🍃🍃	✺ ✺ ✺	🍃🍃🍃	🍃🍃🍃	75	200+		Little ornamental merit
H. mollis 'Albovariegatus'	🍃🍃🍃	✺ ✺ ✺	🍃🍃🍃	🍃🍃🍃	15	200+		One of the best white variegated grasses
H. mollis 'White Fog'	🍃🍃🍃	✺ ✺ ✺	🍃🍃🍃	🍃🍃🍃	30	200+		Larger than 'Albovariegatus'; pink tinged variegation

🍃 *in leaf*   ✺ *flowering*

Hordeum
Barleys

Hordeum is a grass genus of huge commercial importance for it contains barley, _Hordeum vulgare_, one of the first domesticated (in the Neolithic Near East) and most widely grown temperate crop plants, different cultivars of which are used to make everything from animal feeds to Scotch whisky.

Cultivated barley remains broadly similar to _H. spontaneum_, a wild species still found in Turkey and Syria. The barleys are unfussy as to soil type and relatively drought-tolerant, particularly as their flowerheads develop into seeds in late summer to early autumn, at which point the leaves usually bleach to a pale straw as well.

Although barley itself is quite a handsome grass, it has more refined near-relatives. Two of these are commonly cultivated, usually as annuals as they are not the hardiest – although they are in fact short-lived perennials. _H. jubatum_, squirrel tailed barley, forms similarly compact flowerheads to cultivated barley, which are arranged in tightly packed rows down either side of the flowerstem, each tapering into a long silky hair (awn). However, unlike ordinary barley these are tinted an attractive and strking shimmering pink or red. As they swell into seeds, they turn brown and the

site	Full sun is preferred but will take a little shade if necessary
soil	These plants are unfussy as long as kept in free-draining to quite heavy soil
watering	Prefer even moisture in spring, will take quite dry conditions around flowering and seeding time
general care	Easy to grow and tolerant of most conditions. Usually grown as annuals but short-lived perennials
pests & diseases	There are no particular pest or disease problems and these plants are tolerant of most conditions

whole flowerhead develops a twist along the main axis, making it look even larger. They dry well at the pink stage, but shatter and shed the seeds once they mature (this is the characteristic Neolithic man seems to have bred out of common barley at an early stage, allowing him to harvest the seedheads whole). The leaves are mid-green, appearing as early as late winter in mild areas and upright to arching, forming a loose clump around 23cm (9in) high and about the same across.

H. hystrix is the other species commonly grown as an ornamental; it is similar to _H. jubatum_, but with slightly smaller flowerheads and a shorter flowering season. Both are usually grown as annuals, but if left to overwinter and cut back to ground level in spring, may re-shoot.

Hordeum jubatum

	SPRING	SUMMER	AUTUMN	WINTER	height (cm)	spread (cm)	leaf colour	
Hordeum hystrix					23	23		Pink-red flowerheads ageing brown
H. jubatum					30	30		Similar to _H. hystrix_, slightly larger and longer flowering

🌿 in leaf   ✹ flowering

Hystrix patula
Bottle brush grass

A semi-evergreen grass that copes well with shady conditions rather better than most grasses, including quite dry shade, bottle brush grass is the only species of its genus in cultivation. It is aptly named, hystrix being Latin for porcupine.

This plant's flower stems can reach a metre (39in), the leaf mound around 90cm (3ft) and the plant forms upright, arching clumps of broad, mid-green leaves up to 60cm (2ft) across. The flowerheads are most attractive, each up to 10cm (4in) long, and made up of relatively widely spaced flowers (spikelets), each held horizontally and tipped with two long hairs (awns), giving the characteristic hairy bottlebrush appearance. The spikelets emerge a lovely jade green, tinted pink at the base from mid- to late summer, shattering once the seeds have matured from early autumn but sometimes persisting later. The flowers dry well if picked, with some colour still in them.

Hystrix patula is quite versatile, and will happily grow in full sun if kept moist enough, but it comes into its own in shady areas where it associates well with other shade lovers like *Chasmanthium latifolium* (northern sea oats), and both variegated and plain yellow leaved sedges like *Carex aureum* and *C. elata* 'Aurea' (Bowles' golden sedge). Given that its plain green, rather lax leaves are not its most attractive feature, smaller plants can be placed in front of it as disguise, still allowing the flowers to be appreciated. The new leaves emerge relatively late, so clumps can be interplanted with the star-shaped, blue and white flowers of wood anemones (*Anemone blanda*) for an earlier show that is dying back when the grass begins to emerge, with hardy ferns and broad-leaved woodland perennials such as hostas and Trillium.

Hystrix patula

Hystrix patula

	site	Any site from full sun to shade, and will stand some exposure
	soil	Stands dryness in shade, prefers even moisture in sunnier spots. Most soils
	watering	Keep dry in shade, and moist in sun, but should only need watering in dry spells
	general care	Easy to grow and tolerant, but not the longest-lived perennial grass. Benefits from a spring tidy up
	pests & diseases	Relatively trouble free as there are not usually any problems in terms of pests and diseases

Imperata

Imperata is a small genus of Japanese grasses most famous for producing the only genuinely red (rather than bronze) grass in cultivation, *Imperata cylindrica* 'Rubra', Japanese blood grass. Unfortunately slow growing and not the hardiest, it is nevertheless unique and quite startlingly beautiful.

It is deciduous, the leaves emerging in late spring pale green with a substantial red tip. As the season progresses, the red staining moves slowly down each ramrod-straight leaf, becoming more and more intense until by early autumn, the entire leaf can be a vivid, blood red. With low late season sun behind them, the relatively thin leaves glow like a glass of red wine held to the light. Blood grass may reach 45cm (15in) but is usually considerably smaller, and needs full sun and moisture to colour well. In most temperate regions, it is best grown in a pot where it can be moved under cover during cold snaps. It seems to need warm summers in order to flower well. The plain green species is nowhere near as striking and seldom available, but is of similarly upright habit, and larger, reaching 70cm (27in).

The only other Imperata species in cultivation is *I. brevifolia*, known as the satintail, which is grown more for its flowers than its leaves and is hardier than *I. cylindrica*. Also deciduous, the leaves emerge in late spring a translucent light green and are similarly upright, gradually developing a bronzy-red flush, colouring a beautiful purplish-red in autumn. The flowers are in cylindrical panicles, developing long, silky, cotton-like hairs as they open, giving a fluffy effect from mid-summer.

Both Imperata species spread slowly by underground stems (stolons) in conditions they like, ideally moisture-retentive soils in humid areas such as streambanks, but in full sun, not shade. They mix well with sedges that will stand full sun and complement plain green, yellow or blue coloured plants particularly well.

Imperata cylindrica 'Rubra'

Imperata cylindrica 'Rubra'

site	Full sun to colour well, but dislike exposure. Adapt well to pot culture
soil	Constantly moist, rich soils preferred. Dislike limy conditions
watering	Keep this plant moist, as drying out can cause the leaves to turn brown, but avoid waterlogging
general care	Gorgeous, slow growing grasses, not the hardiest – blood grass in particular may need winter protection
pests & diseases	No real pest or disease problems. Dislike combined winter cold and wet, and summer drought

	SPRING	SUMMER	AUTUMN	WINTER	height (cm)	spread (cm)	leaf colour	
Imperata brevifolia		🌿 ✹ ✹ ✹ 🌿	✹ ✹ 🌿	🌿 🌿	60	200+		Attractive flowers and bronze flushed leaves
I. cylindrica		🌿 🌿 🌿 🌿	🌿 🌿		70	200+		Not easy to find, understated
I. cylindrica 'Rubra'		🌿 🌿 🌿 🌿	🌿 🌿		45	200+		Red flush develops as season progresses

🌿 in leaf   ✹ flowering

Indocalamus

The temperate bamboo genus which has the largest leaves, many Indocalamus species are rampantly invasive running (leptomorphic) species, and of little horticultural merit. Five are worth growing however, and spread more slowly, making good ground cover in shade or sun.

Indocalamus look effortlessly tropical, but are in fact surprisingly hardy. In smaller gardens, they are all better grown in large pots, where they will thrive given enough moisture and regular repotting.

The pick of the genus, *Indocalamus tessellatus*, has huge, dark green, spear-shaped leaves 40cm (16in) long and occasionally larger. The culms can reach 1.8m (6ft), but are usually bent over by the weight of the leaves to form a broad green dome barely a metre (39in) high. It first reached the West from China as long ago as 1845, and is reliably hardy down to -25°C (-13°F). It spreads slowly enough to be safely planted out in the average garden, or makes a good pot plant, and will grow in sun or shade.

Larger and more upright growing are *I. latifolius*, with culms to 3m (10ft) and leaves to 30cm (12in), an architectural plant that does not spread too quickly (but quicker than *I. tessellatus*), and *I.*

Indocalamus tessellatus

site	Unfussy with reference to site, sun or shade and relatively exposure tolerant
soil	Moisture retentive preferred, but will succeed on most soils
watering	Like to be kept evenly moist, but will withstand short periods of drought once established
general care	The species in cultivation are some of the better behaved running species; not as invasive as some
pests & diseases	No real pest or disease problems. Cultural problems only on dry, exposed sites

tessellatus f. *hamadae*, a statuesque beauty with culms up to 5m (16ft) bearing huge, paddle-like leaves up to 60cm (2ft) long. The latter is spectacular but does run, so give it space or surround it with some sort of rhizome barrier such as paving stones sunk into the ground edge-on, or stout landscape fabric. Both species are hardy to -20°C (-4°F).

I. longiauritus is more akin to *I. tessellatus*, with culms to 2.5m (9ft). Its leaves are up to 30cm (12in) in length and the culms are conspicuously noded. They age to a colour that is near black. This plant spreads energetically, and barring culm colour, is inferior to *I. tessellatus*.

Grasses

	SPRING	SUMMER	AUTUMN	WINTER	height (cm)	spread (cm)	culm colour	
Indocalamus latifolius	🌿🌿🌿	🌿🌿🌿	🌿🌿🌿	🌿🌿	300	600+		Similar to *I. tessellatus* f. *hamadae*, but does run
I. longiauritus	🌿🌿🌿	🌿🌿🌿	🌿🌿🌿	🌿🌿	250	600+		Small but vigorous spreader
I. solidus	🌿🌿🌿	🌿🌿🌿	🌿🌿🌿	🌿🌿	300	600+		Similar to *I. longiauritus* and vigorous
I. tessellatus	🌿🌿🌿	🌿🌿🌿	🌿🌿🌿	🌿🌿	180	600+		Slowest spreading and most attractive species
I. tessellatus f. *hamadae*	🌿🌿🌿	🌿🌿🌿	🌿🌿🌿	🌿🌿	500	600+		Upright and large leaved

🌿 in leaf

Juncus
Rushes

True moisture lovers, Juncus species are happiest growing in water as emergents, or in permanently moist to wet soils. Most species are of little horticultural merit, but several make excellent, easy-care plants for the bog and water garden, and adapt well to life in pots.

Most are upright, with the stems taking over photosynthetic duties and leaves much reduced or entirely absent, and most are evergreen. The flowers of rushes are fairly inconspicuous, spiky brown spheres emerging part of the way up the stems.

A 'typical' rush, *Juncus effusus* has dark green, bolt-upright stems reaching 1m (39in), forming tight clumps to about the same spread. Hard rush, *J. inflexus* is similar at around 90cm, while the paler green stems of *J. pallidus* are around the same length but arch gracefully. *J.* 'Silver Spears' is silver green, with very thin stems to 60cm (24in).

Altogether different are two deciduous species with broad, flattened stems. *J. ensifolius*, the dagger rush, is mid-green and reaches 60cm (2ft) forming upright clumps. *J. xiphioides*, the iris leaved rush, is similar.

A common mutation in rushes is for the normally straight stems to become curled and twisted like corkscrews. Most of the forms are interesting rather than beautiful, but are not without their own odd merits, particularly shown off in a pot. The largest is *J. effusus* f. *spiralis*, the corkscrew rush, whose untidy dark green spirals can reach 30cm (12in) in length.

Juncus patens
'Carman's Gray'

Juncus xiphioides

Juncus decipiens 'Curly Wurly'

site	Moist to wet areas, or in standing water. Full sun to light shade
soil	Unfussy so long as moisture retentive or wet. Adapt well to containers
watering	Water these plants copiously as they are intolerant of drought for any length of time
general care	Amenable plants when kept moist enough. Benefit from regular thinning-out of older stems
pests & diseases	There are no real pest, disease or cultural problems, aside from dieback caused by dryness

	SPRING	SUMMER	AUTUMN	WINTER	height (cm)	spread (cm)	leaf colour	
Juncus balticus 'Spiralis'	in leaf	flowering	flowering/in leaf	in leaf	30	100		Similar to *J.effusus* f. *spiralis*
J. decipiens 'Curly Wurly'	in leaf	flowering	flowering/in leaf	in leaf	20	30		Small form with tight spirals
J. effusus	in leaf	flowering	flowering/in leaf	in leaf	100	100		Upright, happy as a marginal
J.effusus f. *spiralis*	in leaf	flowering	flowering/in leaf	in leaf	30	60		Largest spiral form
J. effusus 'Gold Strike'	in leaf	flowering	flowering/in leaf	in leaf	75	100		Unusual variegation
J. ensifolius	in leaf	flowering	in leaf		60	60		Flat, blade-like stems, deciduous
J. filiformis 'Spiralis'	in leaf	flowering	flowering/in leaf	in leaf	20	30		Small spiral form
J. inflexus	in leaf	flowering	flowering/in leaf	in leaf	90	90		Upright bog dweller
J. infexus 'Afro'	in leaf	flowering	flowering/in leaf	in leaf	30	60		Stands dryness better than other rushes
J. pallidus	in leaf	flowering	flowering/in leaf	in leaf	90	90		Arching habit unusual for a rush
J. patens 'Carman's Gray'	in leaf	flowering	flowering/in leaf	in leaf	60	60		Unusually free-flowering
J. 'Silver Spears'	in leaf	flowering	flowering/in leaf	in leaf	60	60		Thin, needle-like upright stems
J. xiphioides	in leaf	flowering	in leaf		60	60		Iris leaved rush, flat, broad stems, deciduous

in leaf · *flowering*

Koeleria
Blue hair grasses

A genus of fine-leaved small grasses native to the free-draining, alkaline soils of chalk and limestone areas, Koeleria species are pretty little plants resembling fescues in their narrow leaves and tight clumps, but have much more attractive, if short-lived, flowers than the rather weedy fescue panicles.

Koeleria glauca and *K. vallesiana* are broadly similar, and resemble *Festuca glauca* at first glance, with *K. glauca* perhaps marginally more blue. Their leaves are slightly broader than the rolled leaves that characterize the fescues, however. Both species form a dense mound of foliage up to 23cm (9in) tall and twice as broad, of a light silvery blue. From early to mid-summer, they produce striking fern-like, pointed white flowerheads which can reach 10cm (4in) long, held on thin, animated stalks above the foliage, that unfortunately do not last, shedding their seeds almost as soon as they are fully formed. Their neat mounds can look very striking planted *en masse* as a lawn alternative that never needs mowing, and

Koeleria glauca

site	Full sun preferred, can lose colouring even in semi-shade. Exposure tolerant
soil	Neutral to alkaline, and free draining. Will not grow on heavy, acidic soils
watering	Keep on the dry side, watering only during prolonged dry periods. Need dry feet in winter
general care	Given the right conditions, easy to care for and reliably hardy. Deadhead promptly to prevent self-seeding
pests & diseases	No real pest or disease problems. Culturally, winter wet the most likely cause of trouble

both species are reliably hardy and evergreen, although they prefer freer-draining soils, doing badly on acidic soils or ones that remain wet over the winter. In areas with acidic soils, they are probably best grown in pots of a loam-based (John Innes type) compost, with extra grit or sand added to improve drainage. Neither grow well in shade.

K. macrantha is relatively dull by comparison, a clump former with green leaves, though it does have the same attractively-shaped flowerheads.

	SPRING	SUMMER	AUTUMN	WINTER	height (cm)	spread (cm)	leaf colour	
Koeleria glauca	🍃🍃🍃	✸✸✸	🍃🍃🍃	🍃🍃🍃	23	45		Pretty small grass for alkaline soils
K. macrantha	🍃🍃🍃	✸✸✸	🍃🍃🍃	🍃🍃🍃	50	45		Native meadowland species
K. vallesiana	🍃🍃🍃	✸✸✸	🍃🍃🍃🍃	🍃🍃	30	45		Very similar to *K. glauca*

🍃 in leaf   ✸ flowering

85

Lagurus ovatus
Rabbit tail grass

Lagurus ovatus is another annual grass with an evocative and descriptive common name. It is grown for its flowers, which are densely hairy, forming teardrop-shaped 'pom poms' up to 5cm (2in) long. These are held well above the leaves on stems of up to 45cm (18in) in length, providing a dramatic effect.

The flowers are distinctly furry-looking, all the hairs pointing upright, and soft beige and white, exactly like the colouring in the tail of the rabbit, hence the common name.

The foliage of this plant is an unremarkable green, the leaves soft, fairly short but broad, and densely hairy, forming loose tufts or sprawling clumps rather than tussocks. As is common with many annual grasses, flowering is prolific, but once the seeds begin to mature in the seedheads and they lose their colouring, the foliage also begins to bleach off to straw. The flowers dry well, providing they are picked with some colour still in them.

A dwarf form is sometimes available, actually called 'Nanus' but sometimes sold as 'Bunny Tails', that grows to only 15cm (6in) but is otherwise a perfectly scaled-down replica of the species. It is a neat enough little plant to be used at the front of

Lagurus ovatus

Lagurus ovatus

borders as edging or even mixed with alpines, which it complements effectively.

Rabbit tail grass is fully hardy, unfussy as to soil type including poor and dry soils, and can either be sown in situ in autumn or spring where it is planned to flower, or raised in small pots or modules. Either way, its season of interest is relatively short, so it pehaps best looked on as a form of annual bedding and replaced once flowering has finished, or grown for cutting in parts of the garden not on permanent display.

site	Full sun preferred, but will take some shade and exposure
soil	Unfussy – will grow happily in most substrates including free-draining and poor soils
watering	Water moderately when in growth, and water less as flowering continues. Little else required
general care	Lagurus is late into leaf and flowering is usually over by the end of summer, so season of interest is short
pests & diseases	No real pest, disease or cultural problems as it is amenable to most cultural conditions

Luzula
Woodrushes

Woodrushes are one of the grass-like plants that tend to be lumped with the true grasses because their strap-shaped leaves look vaguely grass like. They are in fact members of the rush family, although they look completely different to Juncus.

anemones. Among the species and cultivars are plants to suit every size of garden, and few plants are as low maintenance or adaptable in cultivation. They make good edging plants, and are popular with gardeners favouring Oriental styles of garden, the smaller species being a useful alternative to Ophiopogon.

British native greater woodrush, *Luzula sylvatica*, sometimes sold as *L. maxima*, is perhaps the most shade tolerant and there are several selected forms, including some handsome variegated selections. It can be slightly invasive, so smaller species are perhaps a better choice in small gardens. It forms low clumps of arching leaves to 30cm

An increasing number of species is available, and while they cannot be said to be startlingly ornamental, they are extremely useful plants in that they will grow happily in deep shade that even sedges find too dark, whether conditions are wet and humid, or dry from the effects of thirsty tree roots.

Luzula are all evergreen, and spread by rhizomes, some of them quite quickly, producing small heads of open, sedge-like flowers in spring to early summer, and despite being shade adapted, most forms will also grow in full sun. Their broad leaves contrast well with finer leaved grasses and sedges, and they can form a good dark green backdrop for early spring bulbs such as snowdrops, crocus and wood

site	Succeeds everywhere from deep shade to full sun, and will take some exposure
soil	Will grow in all types from permanently damp to fairly dry soil
watering	Should need watering only in prolonged dry periods, although plants in full sun may need more
general care	Extremely easy, low maintenance plants. Benefit from spring haircut to remove dead leaves
pests & diseases	Few if any pest, disease or cultural problems – killing a woodrush is quite an achievement!

	SPRING	SUMMER	AUTUMN	WINTER	height (cm)	spread (cm)	leaf colour	
Luzula x *borreri* 'Botany Bay'					20	40		Colour changes from white through cream to green
L. canariensis					60	100		Broad leaves, white flowers; not the hardiest
L. lactea					80	120		Large and handsome, but not the hardiest
L. luzuloides					65	65		White-pink flowerheads
L. nivea					45	60		Leaves covered in white hairs, silvery appearance
L. pilosa					15	30		Lovely dwarf, carpeting plant
L. 'Ruby Stiletto'					40	60		Unusual new plant from the US

in leaf   *flowering*

L. x *borreri* 'Botany Bay' is very similar but only reaches half the size. *L. sylvatica* 'Marginata' is similar to the species, but has broader, hairy leaves edged thinly in white or cream. There is a variable cultivar sold as *L. sylvatica* 'Aurea', the best forms of which are a lovely pale yellow-green even in deep shade, growing to around 30cm (12in). A distinctive new introduction from the USA is *Luzula* 'Ruby Stiletto', which forms neat clumps of narrow, upright, grass-like leaves to 45cm (18in) long that flush red a short distance from the tips, rather like *Imperata cylindrica* 'Rubra'.

The most imposing species in cultivation is *L. lactea*, which reaches 80cm (28in) and has bright green, shiny, slightly curled leaves to 80cm (28in), and long, arching flower spikes with pure white flower from late spring. Similar but slightly smaller at 60cm (2ft), is broad leaved *L. canariensis* from the Canary Isles. Fully hardy is *Luzula luzuloides*, from Central and Southern Europe, which forms loose tufts to 60cm (2ft) with attractive white or pink flushed flowers.

The leaves of *L. nivea* are covered in conspicuous white hairs, giving the whole plant a silvery appearance. It grows to 45cm (18in) and also has white flowers.

L. ulophylla from New Zealand grows to only 10cm (4in) and has very dark green leaves folded down the middle into a V-shape, which displays their densely haired, silvery undersides. It has black flowers. Similarly dwarf is the hairy woodrush, *L. pilosa*, which is only 15cm (6in) tall in flower, but has relatively broad leaves, forming good, low ground cover.

(12in) long, bearing small clusters of light brown flowers in late spring. The flower stems continue growing as the seeds ripen, and can ultimately reach 90cm (3ft). There are several selections available. 'Hohe Tatra' has an upright, spiky habit unique among woodrushes, while 'Tauernpass' is slightly smaller than the species at 25cm (10in), with broader leaves that twist slightly at their tips.

More ornamental are the coloured leaved selections. 'Taggart's Cream' has leaves that emerge an unearthly white, turning cream then gradually flushing light green by midsummer, and dark green by autumn. It can reach 45cm (18in), and goes beautifully with the marbled leaves of *Arum italicum* subsp. *italicum* 'Marmoratum' ('Pictum').

	SPRING	SUMMER	AUTUMN	WINTER	height (cm)	spread (cm)	leaf colour	
L. sylvatica					45	120		Very shade tolerant but can spread rapidly
L. sylvatica 'Aurea'					30	60		Colour can vary between individual plants
L. sylvatica 'Hohe Tatra'					60	100		Upright growth pattern
L. sylvatica 'Marginata'					45	100		Thinly striped variegation
L. sylvatica 'Taggart's Cream'					45	100		Like a larger version of 'Botany Bay'
L. sylvatica 'Tauernpass'					25	60		Broad leaves with twisted tips
L. ulophylla					15	30		Dwarf species from New Zealand

⌀ in leaf ✳ flowering

Melica
Melics

Melica contains some species and forms of real horticultural merit that have a long flowering season for deciduous grasses. They are one of the relatively few grasses traditionally grown in mixed borders, where their rather lax habit can be propped up by the surrounding foliage to imprve their stature in the garden.

Melica altissima 'Atropurpurea'

Melica tend to form loose tufts of soft, upright foliage to around 60cm (2ft), but their flower spikes can be double this height and are much used by flower arrangers for their showy florets, in a range of colours from pure white to distinctly purple, maturing into seed like rice grains. They tend to be plants of woodland margins and hedgerows, will take full sun or partial shade, and are unfussy about soil types.

Melica altissima, Siberian melic, is the most commonly grown, with pale fawn to white, fairly large, downward pointing, overlapping florets, however its cultivar 'Atropurpurea' is much more popular, which has mauve-purple flowerheads and seeds that mature to shiny black, the flowerheads lasting well into autumn. It looks particularly good combined with purple-leaved plants or contrasted with silver-leaved perennials and other grasses. *M. penicillaris* is very similar in size and structure, but its flowers are pure white. There is

a purple form of a smaller species, *M. transsilvanica* 'Atropurpurea.

M. ciliata is smaller, usually forming clumps only around 45cm (18in) tall. It is relatively slow growing and is sometimes used as a backdrop in alpine plantings as it enjoys free-draining conditions. Its cylindrical flowers of white or off white are pretty. *M. nutans* is similar but rarely tops 30cm (12in), with graceful, arching flowerheads. Even smaller is *M. uniflora* 'Variegata', a striped form of wood melic that reaches only 15cm (6in).

site	Any site from full sun to partial shade, stands some exposure
soil	Unfussy, disliking only extremes of dryness and wet
watering	Evenly moist watering is ideal, but relatively drought tolerant once it has become established
general care	Easy care deciduous grasses. Cut dead leaves of clumps back hard in autumn or spring
pests & diseases	Relatively trouble free as no real pest or disease problems. Dislike long periods of winter wet

Bamboos & Grasses

	SPRING	SUMMER	AUTUMN	WINTER	height (cm)	spread (cm)	leaf colour	
Melica altissima	🍃🍃	✻ ✻ ✻ ✻ ✻	✻ ✻		120	100		Good border grass
M. altissima 'Atropurpurea'	🍃🍃	✻ ✻ ✻ ✻ ✻	✻ ✻		120	100		Deep purple flowerheads
M. ciliata	🍃🍃	✻ ✻ ✻	🍃🍃		75	75		Good small grass
M. penicillaris	🍃🍃	✻ ✻ ✻ ✻ ✻	✻ ✻		120	100		Large white flowerheads
M. transsilvanica	🍃🍃	✻ ✻ ✻ ✻ ✻	✻ ✻		100	60		Smaller than M. altissima but similar
M. transsilvanica 'Atropurpurea'	🍃🍃	✻ ✻ ✻ ✻ ✻	✻ ✻		100	60		Purple flowered form similar to purple M. altissima
M. transsilvanica 'Red Spire'	🍃🍃	✻ ✻ ✻ ✻ ✻	✻ ✻		100	60		Rust red flowers
M. uniflora f. albida	🍃🍃🍃	✻ ✻ 🍃	🍃🍃		15	25		White flowered and shade tolerant
M. uniflora 'Variegata'	🍃🍃🍃	✻ ✻ 🍃	🍃🍃		15	25		Lovely miniature variegated woodland grass

🍃 *in leaf*   ✻ *flowering*

Milium effusum

The yellow form of this lovely grass, *Milium effusum* 'Aureum', goes by the name of Bowles' golden grass, after E. A. Bowles, a British plantsman and garden writer of the early 20th century, and is probably the most widely grown of the plain yellow, unvariegated grasses.

Not only is it beautiful in its own right, it mixes equally well with silver, green and blue grasses, its relatively broad leaves go well with sedges and woodrushes whether plain or variegated, and its yellow colouring picks up and further highlights gold-variegated plants from grasses to shrubs.

Like the species, it prefers a moist root run and grows well near water, but given enough moisture will cope happily with full sun, which helps keep its leaves the brightest. It forms loose clumps to around 30cm (12in) tall, larger near water, and around the same across. The leaves are soft and gently arching. Even the flower spikes and spikelets are yellow, although not particularly prominent, and produced from late spring to early summer. Bowles' golden grass tends to be at its brightest in spring, and fades through the summer

to a more limy, yellow-green, particularly in deep shade. Even then, however, it still provides a real splash of brightness.

It is semi-evergreen in temperate areas, but the leaves may bleach and die back after flowering, particularly in full sun. If it decides to take a mid-summer break, it soon reappears in autumn, however, and can be cut back anyway after flowering to produce a new flush of fresh young leaves. A relatively new introduction is *M. effusum* 'Yaffle', which grows to 75cm (30in) and has green leaves with a bold yellow stripe running down the centre of each. It is lovely, but tends to scorch in sun, so needs full to semi-shade.

The plain green species is much less commonly encountered, but nevertheless will make an attractive mound of bright green leaves up to 90cm (35in) in height. *M. effusum* var. *esthonicum* is a bone-hardy selection from the Moscow Botanic Garden that is even larger with broader leaves, and is one of the few grasses grown for scent – its leaves have a pleasant, sweet, cumin-like scent, especially when bruised.

Milium effusum 'Yaffle'

Milium effusum 'Aureum'

site	Full sun to deep shade; 'Yaffle' needs shade. Prefers sheltered spots
soil	Soil should be moisture retentive, particularly if the plant is placed in the sun
watering	Evenly moist, does not deal well with drought, particularly combined with high temperatures
general care	Easy to maintain and cultivate if kept moist enough, and an excellent foil for a wide range of plants
pests & diseases	No real pest and disease problems. Cultural problems usually linked to drying out

	SPRING	SUMMER	AUTUMN	WINTER	height (cm)	spread (cm)	leaf colour	
Milium effusum	🌿🌿 ● ● ●		🌿🌿	🌿🌿🌿	90	100		Has its own subtle charm
M. effusum 'Aureum'	🌿🌿 ● ● ●		🌿🌿	🌿🌿🌿	30	30		Perhaps the best gold leaved grass
M. effusum var. *esthonicum*	🌿🌿 ● ● ●	● ● ●	🌿🌿	🌿🌿🌿	100	120		Larger, scented-leaf variety
M. effusum 'Yaffle'	🌿🌿 ● ● 🌿		🌿🌿	🌿🌿🌿	75	100		Beautiful new variegated form, needs shade

🌿 in leaf   ● flowering

Miscanthus
Eulalia grasses

Miscanthus have become something of a phenomenon. Large, bold, long flowering, hardy, amenable in cultivation and drought tolerant, about the only feature they lack is evergreeness. However, even this they make up for with good autumn colour and both leaves and flower stems that remain standing through the worst winter weather, continuing to contribute to the winter garden.

Miscanthus sinensis 'Morning Light'

Miscanthus sinensis cultivar

One species in particular has been responsible for their recent meteoric rise in popularity – *Miscanthus sinensis*, a naturally variable species that has spawned a multitude of cultivars that vary in size, timing of flowering, flower colour and shape. Some of these are admittedly rather similar, but the best offer enough variety of size and form to suit them to all sizes of garden, from 3m (10ft) giants to true dwarfs little bigger than 30cm (12in).

Miscanthus are particularly loved by designers of Prairie style and the 'New European' style of expansive grass and perennial planting for their long flowering season, height and winter interest, acting as perfect foils to tall, late-flowering perennials such as Michaelmas daisies, Rudbeckia and Echinacea. Although tall, they do not run at the root, forming tight clumps that expand only slowly. Most of the newer cultivars were developed by German breeders from *M. sinensis* 'Gracillimus', and typically form a broad, upright clump of mid-green or glaucous, very narrow leaves up to 1.8m (6ft) high and slightly more across. The large flower stems rise well clear of the foliage and can be plume-like, or narrow-fingered, in the latter case either stiffly vertical or longer and arching. They are often sold under translations of their names into

Miscanthus sinensis cultivar

site	These plants prefer full sun but will take light shade if necessary
soil	Most soil types, from quite heavy clays and free-draining sands
watering	Keep newly planted moist. Once established, should need water only in extremely dry periods
general care	Cutback to ground level in early spring before new leaves emerge. Divide clumps every 5–6 years
pests & diseases	There are no major problems with pests and diseases. As near to indestructible as garden plants can be

M

Bamboos & Grasses

	SPRING	SUMMER	AUTUMN	WINTER	height (cm)	spread (cm)	leaf colour	
Miscanthus sinensis 'Ferner Osten'					150	180		'Far East'. Good autumn colour
M. sinensis 'Gearmella'					75	100		Semi-dwarf
M. sinensis 'Kaskade'					180	180		'Cascade'. Largest early flowerer
M. sinensis 'Kleine Fontane'					150	180		'Little Fountain' arching flowerheads
M. sinensis 'Malepartus'					150	180		Popular, with good autumn colour
M. sinensis 'Rotsilber'					150	180		'Red-silver', narrow leaves and red emerging flowers
M. sinensis 'Silberfeder'					150	180		'Silver Feather', pale flowered
M. sinensis 'Sirene'					120	120		Large flowers
M. sinensis 'Vorlaufer'					75	100		Semi dwarf, similar to 'Rotsilber'

in leaf   *flowering*

Miscanthus sinensis 'Zebrinus'

English, which are included where relevant.

There are now well over a hundred Miscanthus cultivars. The following are some of the best, including species other than *M. sinensis*, and for clarity's sake are grouped according to size and flowering time. Early flowering means from mid-summer onwards; mid-season, 4–6 weeks later. Cultivars that flower very late, which can be into mid-autumn, are indicated individually.

Early flowering group

Most of the early flowering cultivars were bred for continental Europe's hotter summers, but do equally well in more temperate conditions, and are fairly compact compared to some of the later cultivars. The following are all *M. sinensis* selections, their flower spikes reaching 1.5m (5ft) unless stated otherwise:

'Silberfeder' ('Silver Feather') was an early cultivar, and has been largely superceded by newer selections that are more reliable in their flowering. The pale, silvery white panicles are undeniably striking, however. 'Malepartus' has relatively broad, dark green leaves and flowerheads that emerge an attractive red-purple, opening white. It has good autumn colours of reds, yellows and purples.

'Ferner Osten' ('Far East') is similar to 'Malepartus' with thinner leaves and a slighly more open structure, and good red-purple initial flower colour.

'Rotsilber' ('Red-silver') is named for the silver stripe down the centre of each leaf and strong rust red of its emerging flowers.

'Vorlaufer' is very similar to 'Rotsilber', but only half the height, at 75cm (30in), making it ideal for smaller gardens.

'Gearmella' is another semi-dwarf, to 75cm (30in) with fairly broad leaves and flowers that emerge pure silver, opening clean white.

The above all produce upright panicles, opening to resemble feather dusters. More arching or downright pendulous, less fluffy, finger-like flowers are produced by 'Sirene', a large-flowered cultivar reaching 1.2m (4ft) and 'Kaskade' ('Cascade'), a substantial plant reaching 1.8m (6ft). It has broader leaves with a white midrib, and flowers that emerge red, opening out into arching, white-cream fingers.

'Kleine Fontane' ('Little Fountain') is similar but a little smaller at 1.5m (5ft).

Mid-season flowering, large and medium group

The following tend to flower in late summer, 2–4 weeks after the previous group (depending on conditions):

'Grosse Fontane' ('Big Fountain') can top 1.8m (6ft), and has broad, attractive mid-green leaves with silver midribs. The flowers emerge silver flushed with red, opening out into thin fingered, weeping panicles that age more silvery.

'Graziella' is a similar size to 'Big Fountain', with large flowers that emerge silvery, ageing to pure white.

'Roland' is a lovely if slightly lax and floppy cultivar up to 2.1m (7ft) tall and more

	SPRING	SUMMER	AUTUMN	WINTER	height (cm)	spread (cm)	leaf colour	
M. sinensis 'Graziella'		in leaf	flowering	flowering	180	180		Large silver flowers
M. sinensis 'Grosse Fontane'		in leaf	flowering	flowering	180	180		Broad leaves, weeping flowers
M. sinensis 'Roland'		in leaf	flowering	flowering	210	210		Floppy silver plume-like flowers
M. sinensis 'Undine'		in leaf	flowering	flowering	140	160		Coppery pink flowers ageing paler

🍃 in leaf •🌸 flowering

Miscanthus sinensis 'Gracillimus'

Miscanthus sacchariflorus

across, producing large, rich silver plumes that are slightly weeping.

'Undine' is similar to 'Graziella' but smaller, around 1.4m (5ft), producing flowers that are coppery pink, ageing to buff.

Mid-season flowering, small group

This group contains some of the best Miscanthus for growing in smaller gardens and pots, that are the easiest to integrate in to planting with species of average vigour. They grow to 1.2m (4ft) unless otherwise stated.

'Silberspinne' ('Silver Spider') is unusual in that its leaves are held horizontally out from its stems, rather than arching up and over like most miscanthus, giving it an angular, spiky appearance. The flowers emerge reddish, opening out into long, thin, silver, hanging fingers.

'Kleine Silberspinne' ('Little Silver Spider') is as its name implies a smaller version, with even narrower leaves and relatively large flowers, reaching only 90cm (3ft).

'Nippon' contrasts with all the other smaller cultivars in this group in that its

flowers are narrow and upright, never really fluffing out. It is often planted to contrast with other selections.

'China' is a lovely small Miscanthus with narrow, olive green leaves and long stemmed, plume-like flowers that also has brilliant orange and scarlet autumn colour.

Dwarf, 'Adagio' group

This contains several species and cultivars that have taxed the taxonomists, but whose stature makes them perfect for the smallest gardens and for growing in pots. 'Adagio' itself is generally accepted as one of the best small *Miscanthus sinensis* cultivars; it is free flowering, early and barely reaches 30cm (12in), with good autumn colour and does well in a pot. 'Yakushima Dwarf' which reaches 1.2m (4ft) and bears large, oatmeal plumes has sometimes been given species status and sold as *M. yakushimensis*, but it appears it does belong with *M. sinensis*, which is a variable species in the wild. However, confusingly this species name was also applied to an even smaller plant that barely tops 30cm (12in), also sold as 'Yaku-jima', which appears identical to another well-known dwarf cultivar, 'Little Kitten'. At present, both 'Yaku-jima' and 'Little Kitten' are accepted as *M. sinensis* cultivars, but they may well prove to be the same plant.

Similar squabbles resulted over a dwarf *M. oligostachys* cultivar, 'Nanus Variegatus', an attractively cream-striped plant reaching

	SPRING	SUMMER	AUTUMN	WINTER	height (cm)	spread (cm)	leaf colour	
M. sinensis 'China'	in leaf	in leaf in leaf	flowering flowering flowering	flowering	120	100		Large late flowers and good autumn colour
M. sinensis 'Kleine Silberspinne'	in leaf	in leaf in leaf	flowering flowering flowering	flowering	90	90		'Small Silver Spider', narrow leaves held horizontally
M. sinensis 'Nippon'	in leaf	in leaf in leaf	flowering flowering flowering	flowering	120	120		Narrow, upright silvery plumes.
M. sinensis 'Silberspinne'	in leaf	in leaf in leaf	flowering flowering flowering	flowering	120	120		Weeping silver flowers and horizontal leaves
M. sinensis 'Adagio'	in leaf	in leaf in leaf	flowering flowering flowering	flowering	90	90		Free flowering, good autumn colour
M. sinensis 'Little Kitten'	in leaf	in leaf in leaf	flowering flowering flowering	flowering	30	30		Lovely tiny cultivar. May be same as 'Yaku-jima'
M. nepalensis	in leaf	in leaf in leaf	flowering flowering flowering	flowering	30	30		Light brown flowers, on the tender side
M. oligostachys 'Nanus Variegatus'	in leaf	in leaf in leaf	flowering flowering flowering	flowering	75	75		Rust red flowers on emergence, open tawny
M. transmorrisoniensis	in leaf	in leaf in leaf	flowering flowering flowering	flowering	120	180		Pale brown flowers
M. sinensis 'Yaku-jima'	in leaf	in leaf in leaf	flowering flowering flowering	flowering	30	30		Very similar to 'Little Kitten'
M. sinensis 'Yakushima Dwarf'	in leaf	in leaf in leaf	flowering flowering flowering	flowering	120	120		Narrow leaves and oatmeal flowers

 in leaf   flowering

Miscanthus sinensis 'Little Kitten'

Bamboos & Grasses

Miscanthus oligostachys
'Nanus Variegatus'

Variegated group

There are two major types of variegation within *Miscanthus sinensis*, the 'normal' type with stripes of white or cream running the length of the leaves, and a much more unusual type where horizontal bands of creamy yellow stripe the leaves, predictably enough given the common name zebra grasses. The largest in the former group is a selection of *M. sinensis* var. *condensatus*, 'Cosmopolitan', which can reach 2.4m (8ft), with very wide leaves margined and striped in white. 'Cabaret' is similarly handsome, with green margined leaves striped white down the centre. *M. sinensis* 'Variegatus' is smaller, making an arching clump to 1.5m (5ft) with even white stripes, and two dwarfer forms, 'Rigoletto' and 'Dixieland' are essentially similar, to 90cm (3ft) and 1.2m (4ft) respectively.

Very different is 'Morning Light', which has really narrow leaves margined in white, the whole plant appearing silver from a distance. It makes a mushroom shaped clump to 1.5m (5ft).

The original zebra grass, *M. sinensis* 'Zebrinus', makes loose arching clumps to 1.8m (6ft) in fresh green, with 5 or 6 horizontal bands crossing each leaf in light yellow, making the whole clump look spotted from a distance. The banding is temperature

only 75cm (18in) with rust red flowers opening to light brown. Some argue it is so similar to *M. transmorrisoniensis*, a small species from the orient it resembles far more closely than *M. oligostachys*, it should be transferred to it, but at present both names are valid.

A recently introduced species, *M. nepalensis*, is another tiny one, reaching 30cm (12in), producing unusual tawny-gold plumes, but is unfortunately proving on the tender side, although it can be grown in a pot and protected.

	SPRING	SUMMER	AUTUMN	WINTER	height (cm)	spread (cm)	leaf colour	
M. floridulus					270	120		Tall and upright, can be shy to flower
M. oligostachys					120	120		Superb autumn colour
M. oligostachys 'Afrika'					90	120		Red and orange autumn colour; late flowering
M. 'Purpurascens'					120	120		Flowers emerge purplish, red autumn colour
M. sacchariflorus					300	200+		Large, can prove invasive and shy to flower
M. s. var. *condensatus* 'Cosmo Revert'					210	120		Probably largest Miscanthus; sold under several names
M. sinensis var. *condensatus* 'Cabaret'					270	120		Leaves with white centres and green margins
M. s. var. *condensatus* 'Cosmopolitan'					300	210		Large flowered and white striped leaves
M. sinensis 'Dixieland'					120	120		New US cultivar; prefers warmer climates
M. sinensis 'Giraffe'					150	75		New zebra grass cultivar; horizontal variegation
M. sinensis 'Morning Light'					150	120		Very narrow, variegated leaves
M. sinensis 'Rigoletto'					90	100		Lovely dwarf variegated selection
M. sinensis 'Strictus'					180	75		Densely clumping zebra grass
M. sinensis 'Variegatus'					150	100		Well marked, medium sized variegated cultivar
M. sinensis 'Zebrinus'					240	120		The original zebra grass, horizontally striped

in leaf   flowering

Miscanthus sinensis 'Roland'

Miscanthus sinensis 'Roland'

dependant, only usually appearing after mid-summer in temperate conditions, and the bands are prone to scorch in full sun, making these cultivars best grown in light shade. It can run at the root. 'Strictus' is much more densely clumping, to 1.8m (6ft), as is a newer smaller cultivar, 'Giraffe'. Several more dwarf zebra grasses have been developed, but few are widely available as yet.

Tall growing Miscanthus and other species

One of the largest Miscanthus cultivars came from the variegated 'Cosmopolitan', and is correctly named *M. sinensis* var. *condensatus*

Miscanthus sinensis 'Strictus'

'Cosmo Revert', although often sold as 'Emerald Giant', 'Central Park' or even *M. giganteus*. It reaches 3m (10ft), rivalling pampass grass in scale but with fresher green leaves producing huge flower plumes. *M. sacchariflorus* is similarly imposing, with a more arching, running habit, while *M. floridulus* forms upright dense clumps to 2.7m (8ft). Neither of these species are as reliable to flower in temperate areas as *M. sinensis* selections, preferring hotter summers,

For autumn colour within Miscanthus, few can compete with *M. oligostachys*, a Japanese species similar to *M. sinensis* known as flame grass which will take more shade. The species reaches around 1.2m (4ft), with a more open habit than *M. sinensis*, producing upright flowers early. 'Purpurascens' has leaves tinged reddish, the colour intensifying through the season to become intensely red-purple in autumn, in contrast to its white panicles. 'Afrika' is slightly smaller, around 90cm (3ft), with even more intense red and orange autumn colour, and is late flowering.

M

Molinia
Moor grasses

There are two suspecies of *Molinia caerulea* in cultivation, each with several cultivars. *M. caerulea* subsp. *arundinacea*, tall moor grass and subsp. *caerulea*, purple moor grass. Both will grow in most garden soils but prefer those on the damper side, the former growing typically 1.8–2.1m (6–7ft) tall, the latter less than half that.

M. c. s. arundinacea 'Karl Foerster'

M. c. subsp. arundinacea 'Fontane'

They are unusual in being entirely deciduous, shedding their dead leaves in autumn unlike most grasses which retain them, and also can take a year or two to establish and grow away strongly, so are best planted as fairly large plants.

The tall moor grasses have fine leaves, moving in the slightest breeze, and an upright shape unless they are wet, which causes them to arch, springing up again as they dry. 'Zuneigung', a German selection whose name translates as 'Affection' is fairly typical, forming broad, slightly arching clumps whose mid-summer flowers reach 1.8m (6ft), topped with dense panicles of light green flowers ageing to golden brown. Its autumn colour is good, first yellow then cinnamon. 'Fontane' ('Fountain') and 'Windspiel' ('Windplay') are broadly similar, pehaps a little more weeping but with less showy flowers. The movement of these arching cultivars is best appreciated when they are planted alone or with much smaller grasses for company rather than in a block, where the clumps tend to merge together.

More erect selections can look fantastic planted in groups, however. 'Karl Foerster' is an old cultivar reaching 1.5m (5ft) with broad flower panicles that is still well worth growing. A more recent American cultivar, 'Skyracer', can top 2.4m (8ft), while 1.8m (6ft) tall 'Bergfreund' is also upright but has showy flowers tinted a gorgeous purple.

Purple moor grasses are smaller, with better autumn colour and green flushed purple flower colour. Largest is *M. caerulea* subsp. *caerulea* 'Heidebraut' ('Heatherbride') at 1.5m (5ft).

site	Full sun is preferred, or light shade. These plants are exposure tolerant
soil	Relatively moist, acid soils ideal. Will tolerate drier soil, but not alkaline
watering	Evenly moist is preferable. Water during dry periods, especially if taking their time to establish
general care	Easy to grow if slow to establish, and as leaves are shed don't need a spring tidy up
pests & diseases	No real pest or disease problems. Culturally, only extended drought causes major problems

	SPRING	SUMMER	AUTUMN	WINTER	height (cm)	spread (cm)	leaf colour	
M. c. subsp. *arundinacea* 'Bergfreund'	in leaf	flowering	flowering	flowering	180	120		Handsome tall grass, narrow clumps
M. c. subsp. *arundinacea* 'Fontane'	in leaf	flowering	flowering	flowering	180	120		'Fountain', more arching cultivar
M. c. s. arundinacea 'Karl Foerster'	in leaf	flowering	flowering	flowering	150	100		Smaller upright cultivar
M. c. subsp. *arundinacea* 'Skyracer'	in leaf	flowering	flowering	flowering	240	120		Tall and very narrow clumps
M. c. subsp. *arundinacea* 'Windspiel'	in leaf	flowering	flowering	flowering	180	120		'Windplay'
M. c. subsp. *arundinacea* 'Zuneigung'	in leaf	flowering	flowering	flowering	180	120		'Affection', arching
M. c. subsp. *caerulea* 'Carmarthen'	in leaf	flowering	flowering		30	60		Small, yellow striped leaves, tall purplish flowers
M. caerulea subsp. *caerulea* 'Claerwen'	in leaf	flowering	flowering		30	60		Small, yellow striped leaves, tall purplish flowers
M. c. subsp. *caerulea* 'Edith Dudszus'	in leaf	flowering	flowering	flowering	60	60		Purple flowers
M. c. subsp. *caerulea* 'Heidebraut'	in leaf	flowering	flowering	flowering	150	100		'Heather Bride', tall for susbp. *caerulea*
M. c. subsp. *caerulea* 'Moorhexe'	in leaf	flowering	flowering	flowering	60	60		'Bog Witch', small and elegant
M. c. subsp. *caerulea* 'Strahlenquelle'	in leaf	flowering	flowering	flowering	90	100		'Fountain Spray', arching
M. c. subsp. *caerulea* 'Variegatus'	in leaf	flowering	flowering		30	60		Yellow variegated, taller flowers

🌿 in leaf   ✺ flowering

Muhlenbergia japonica 'Variegata'

Striped muhly grass

Only a single cultivar of muhly grass is in general cultivation, and predictably enough it is a striped cultivar with the imaginative name of 'Variegata', or striped muhly grass. It is a singularly attractive grass, however, spreading slowly by underground rhizomes without ever becoming invasive and making a useful low groundcover in full sun or semi-shade.

It begins the year in mid-spring, with erect new culms (stems) no more than 20cm (7in) tall emerging. As these lengthen through summer, they become more and more prostrate, trailing along the ground until by the end of the season they can be 60cm (2ft) long. Unusually, they also often form roots at the nodes where they are in contact with the soil, providing a secondary means of spread, which makes the plant simplicity itself to propagate.

Muhlenbergia japonica 'Variegata'

The leaves are tapering and elegant, seldom more than 7.5cm (3in) long, each narrowly margined in white and with several thin white stripes down the centre of each leaf. Flowering begins in late summer, carrying on until mid-autumn, but can be somewhat erratic, as this plant is used to Japanese summers, which tend to be warmer, wetter and less unpredictable. In warmer summers, flowers appear at the end of each stem in small panicles, white with an attractive purplish cast, but unless produced en masse, they are less than showy. The first frosts of mid-

Muhlenbergia japonica 'Variegata'

autumn usually cause early bleaching and widespread dieback.

Striped muhly grass also makes an unusual subject for a pot, where its sprawling stems will cascade over the sides and become genuinely weeping

Other species of Muhlenbergia are beginning to enter cultivation from the USA, but the North American species tend to be from even warmer parts of that continent than conditions in Southern Japan, so their hardiness and flowering ability remain questionable.

Muhlenbergia japonica 'Variegata'

site	Anything from full sun to semi shade, prefers sheltered conditions
soil	Moisture retentive but not wet, and neutral to acid – dislikes lime
watering	Keep evenly moist, and ideally relatively humid, too. Little else is required for this plant
general care	Easy to grow in conditions it likes, and good, unusual pot subject. Not the longest season of interest
pests & diseases	Only extended dryness or alkaline soil likely to be problematical. No pest or disease problems

M

Bamboos & Grasses

Nasella

Nasella trichotoma was formerly placed within the Stipa genus, and looks similar to fine leaved *Stipa arundinacea*. It is one of a very few grasses from the Andes in cultivation in Europe and has fine, bright evergreen jade green leaves at first upright but becoming more arching as they lengthen, making a rounded clump up to 30cm (12in) high and around 45cm (18in) across.

Nasella trichotoma

Bamboos & Grasses

The flowers are airy in the extreme, broadly pyramidal with many tiny spikelets held on the thinnest of stems, appearing in early summer and in such numbers that the foliage is almost obscured by what looks like a pinky mauve, dense, hairy haze. As the seeds mature, they create tiny dark droplets within this haze, giving an attractive speckled effect. The flower stems themselves are quite weak, and often the outermost ones bend over to ground level, bringing the cloud down into a 'skirt' around the main clump, looking almost like a fibre-optic lamp. However, they belie their fragile appearance by lasting well into winter.

Nasella trichotoma is happy in most soils, if anything preferring life on the dry side, its fresh greenness an interesting contrast to silver and blue grasses like

Festuca, or more broad-leaved sedges and grasses like Milium, and variegated plants of all kinds. It also makes a good subject for a pot, arching down over the sides. Its airy flowerheads even make a good foil for the more upright plumes of some of the Miscanthus cultivars, and its relatively small stature can be used to great effect at the front of mixed borders, particularly those with a preponderance of yellow or purple leaves and flowers.

Nasella cernua, nodding needlegrass, is native to California but seems reasonably hardy. It is larger than *N. trichotoma*, with a different, coarser flower structure as the spikelets are larger each with a conspicuous hair (awn). Neither is the foliage such a fresh green, though equally narrow as that of *N. trichotoma*.

site	This plant prefers sunny sites, but will cope with light shade
soil	Happy in most soils but for extremes of wet and dryness
watering	Keep evenly moist, but should only require extra water in extended dry spells. Little else required
general care	Dislike prolonged winter wet. Benefit from a cutting back to remove dead leaves in spring
pests & diseases	No real pest or disease problems. Hardiness in colder northern areas unproven

	SPRING	SUMMER	AUTUMN	WINTER	height (cm)	spread (cm)	leaf colour	
Nasella cernua	🌿 🌿	✺	✺ ✺ ✺	✺ ✺ ✺	🌿 🌿 🌿	60	90		Large, spiky-looking flowerheads
N. trichotoma	🌿 🌿	✺ ✺ ✺	✺ ✺ ✺	✺ ✺ ✺	🌿	30	45		Makes a compact mound with airy, long-lasting flowerheads

🌿 in leaf   ● flowering

Ophiopogon
Mondo grass

Again I must admit to some bias, but the mondo grasses, neither grasses nor sedges but diminutive, evergreen members of the _Convallariaceae_, the convolvulus family, are some of the best small grass-like plants for shady groundcover or use in pots.

Ophiopogon wallichianus

O. p. 'Nigrescens'

So-called black grass, _Ophiopogon planiscapus_ 'Nigrescens' is the best known, and one of the few genuinely black-leaved plants available. Several other species and forms are becoming available. As they rarely grow above 15cm (6in) tall, they are excellent partners for planting around the base of larger specimen grasses, providing a dark base from which pale leaves and variegated selections in particular look good. All make excellent, undemanding pot plants.

O. planiscapus has relatively broad, strap-like leaves in dark green and reaches 15cm (6in), with small, star-shaped mauve flowers. Its cultivar 'Nigrescens' is much more widely grown, sometimes sold as 'Black Dragon' or 'Ebony Knight'. When the black leaves are wet, they shine as if polished, and the flowers are followed by

shiny jet-black berries. It looks gorgeous teamed with blue fescues, Japanese blood grass, the broader leaves of smaller hostas, or variegated plants of all kinds.

O. intermedius forms low tufts of dark green foliage, and spreads by underground stems (stolons), forming fairly extensive carpets. It also reaches 15cm (6in), with mauve flowers turning into attractive purple berries. _O. wallichianus_ is a variable species, but similar to _O. intermedius_.

site	Full sun to quite deep shade, will cope with some exposure
soil	These plants are unfussy if soil is neutral to acid but they dislike lime
watering	These plants prefer even moisture, but are surprisingly drought tolerant
general care	Easy to grow evergreens, neat and good foils for other plants if relatively slow growing
pests & diseases	No real pest or disease problems. Culturally, only wet winters on heavy soils can be problematical

Ophiopogon japonicus

	SPRING	SUMMER	AUTUMN	WINTER	height (cm)	spread (cm)	leaf colour	
Ophiopogon bodinieri					15	30+		More vigorous than other species
O. intermedius					15	30+		Drought tolerant lawn alternative
O. japonicus					15	30+		Narrow leaves
O. japonicus 'Compactus'					5	20+		Tiny, only 5cm (2in) high
O. japonicus 'Kigimafukiduma'					15	30+		Variegated, narrow leaved
O. japonicus 'Minor'					5	20+		Another tiny cultivar
O. japonicus 'Nippon'					10	30+		Semi-dwarf
O. japonicus 'Variegatus'					15	30+		Leaves with single broad white stripe
O. planiscapus					15	30+		Broadest leaved species
O. planiscapus 'Little Tabby'					15	30+		Cream variegation
O. planiscapus 'Nigrescens'					15	30+		Perhaps the blackest leaves of any cultivated plant
O. wallichianus					15	30+		Similar to _O. japonicus_

🌿 in leaf   ✹ flowering

Panicum
Switch grasses

Panicum is a fairly large grass genus containing annual and perennial species. Only a few are in cultivation, but these have many selected forms and are extremely good garden plants, associating well with a wide range of herbaceous plants and other grasses.

Panicum virgatum 'Cloud Nine'

Most are clump-forming and medium sized, rarely topping 1.2m (4ft) in flower. They are important components of North American prairies, preferring sharp drainage and full sun, and are often found in alkaline areas, so are good grasses for gardens on chalk and limestone.

The most widely grown is *Panicum virgatum*, switch grass, a deciduous perennial species forming narrowly upright clumps, its blue or purple tinged stems bearing flat, linear, mid-green leaves each up to 60cm (2ft) long. From the end of summer and through the autumn, it produces an abundance of diffuse, broad, weeping panicles made up of tiny purple-green spikelets that hover above the foliage, almost like a cloud of midges. In flower,

clumps can reach 1.2m (4ft) tall and 90cm (3ft) across. *P. virgatum*'s airy appearance makes an excellent contrast with the more compact flowers of two other prairie-type grasses, Calamagrostis and Pennisetum.

Selections from *P. virgatum* fall into two main groups, those with red and purple tinges to leaves, flowers and autumn colour, and those with a more bluish, glaucous hue.

site	These plants prefer sites with full sun, and are very exposure tolerant	
soil	Well drained and neutral to alkaline ideally, but succeed on most soils	
watering	These plants are drought tolerant when established, and they dislike winter wet. Little watering is needed	
general care	Flowers last well; cut dead clumps back in late autumn to help keep crowns of plants drier through winter	
pests & diseases	No real pest and disease problems. Culturally, acidic soils and winter wet cause the main problems	

	SPRING	SUMMER	AUTUMN	WINTER	height (cm)	spread (cm)	leaf colour	
Panicum clandestinum	in leaf	in leaf, flowering	flowering	flowering	90	90		Very broad leaves
P. miliaceum		in leaf, flowering	flowering		90	45		Annual millet
P. miliaceum 'Violaceum'		in leaf, flowering	flowering		90	45		Purple flowered millet
P. 'Squaw'	in leaf	in leaf	flowering	flowering	150	120		Distinctly purple tinges, good autumn colour
P. virgatum	in leaf	in leaf	flowering	flowering	100	75		Variable species, found from Florida to Canada
P. virgatum 'Cloud Nine'	in leaf	in leaf	flowering	flowering	180	150		Tall blue form
P. virgatum 'Dallas Blue'	in leaf	in leaf	flowering	flowering	120	75		Bluest foliage of all
P. virgatum 'Hanse Herms'	in leaf	in leaf	flowering	flowering	90	75		Red tinges to leaves, deep burgundy in autumn
P. virgatum 'Heavy Metal'	in leaf	in leaf	flowering	flowering	90	90		Upright and large flowered
P. virgatum 'Northwind'	in leaf	in leaf	flowering	flowering	120	90		Upright and blue foliage
P. virgatum 'Prairie Sky'	in leaf	in leaf	flowering	flowering	90	90		More arching than other named forms
P. virgatum 'Rehbraun'	in leaf	in leaf	flowering	flowering	90	90		Brilliant orange-red autumn colour
P. virgatum 'Rotstrahlbusch'	in leaf	in leaf	flowering	flowering	100	90		Like 'Rehbraun', slightly taller

in leaf ⚫ *flowering*

Panicum virgatum 'Dallas Blue'

lax, arching habit; and three particularly upright blue-leaved cultivars, 'Heavy Metal' (purple flowers reaching 90cm/3ft), 'Northwind' (blue-grey leaves and yellow orange autumn colour), and 'Strictum' (narrow clumps to 1.2m/4ft).

Most of the other switch grasses are from warmer parts of the world, so not many are reliably hardy outdoors, and flowering performance may not be wonderful in a typically cloudy, changeable British summer. The flowers of *P. clandestinum*, the deer tongue grass, are often lost within the foliage when it does flower in this country; however, it is primarily grown for its very broad, soft, arching leaves, which colour gold and purple in autumn. It needs a sheltered spot and good drainage.

The best known annual Panicum is more commonly encountered in bird cages than gardens, *P. miliaceum*, millet. Grown for its enormous flowers and copious seed production, it forms a lax clump up to 90cm (3ft) tall. More ornamental is its cultivar 'Violaceum', purple hog millet, where the flowers emerge purple-green but age to a strikingly deep, violet purple.

The red group includes 'Hanse Herms', a free-flowering older cultivar with burgundy autumn colour reaching around 90cm (3ft); 'Rehbraun', slightly taller, with orange-red autumn tones and the similar but taller again 'Rotstrahlbusch'; 'Rubrum', which is variable as several different plants are sold under this name but at its best is red-tinged in summer and purple in autumn; 'Squaw', an excellent American introduction with purple-green foliage, airy purple flowers and good dark autumn colour; and 'Shenandoah', similar to 'Squaw' but if anything even redder and colouring up earlier in autumn.

The blue-grey group includes statuesque 'Cloud Nine', which can reach 1.8m (6ft) and has good gold autumn colour; 'Warrior', only a little smaller at 1.5m (5ft) with huge purplish flowerheads; 'Dallas Blue', probably the bluest selection to date, smaller at 1.2m (4ft) and free flowering; 'Prairie Sky', notable for its much more

Panicum virgatum 'Strictum'

Panicum virgatum 'Hanse Herms'

	SPRING	SUMMER	AUTUMN	WINTER	height (cm)	spread (cm)	leaf colour	
P. virgatum 'Rubrum'		🌿 🌿 🌿	⚫ ⚫ ⚫	⚫ ⚫ ⚫	100	90		Variable, most forms red and purple tones
P. virgatum 'Shenandoah'		🌿 🌿 🌿	⚫ ⚫ ⚫	⚫ ⚫ ⚫	90	90		Dark red tinges in summer, rich burgundy in autumn
P. virgatum 'Strictum'		🌿 🌿 🌿	⚫ ⚫ ⚫	⚫ ⚫ ⚫	120	90		The original upright blue-leaved selection
P. virgatum 'Warrior'		🌿 🌿 🌿	⚫ ⚫ ⚫	⚫ ⚫ ⚫	150	120		Vigorous and free-flowering, needs space

🌿 in leaf　　⚫ flowering

Pennisetum

Fountain *or*
fox tail grasses

One of the most popular of all deciduous ornamental grasses, the fountain or fox tail grasses combine elegant, rounded mounds of fine, narrow leaves, usually broader than they are tall, with animated, dense flowerheads of brown or pink held on long, arching flower stems.

Pennisetum alopecuroides

Pennisetum alopecuroides 'Hameln'

Not all are reliable flowerers in temperate regions as many species are from areas with hotter, longer summers, but one species at least, *Pennisetum alopecuroides* and its many selections, revels in colder climates, doing well on most soil types and conditions. They also perform well in pots, and associate well with more upright grasses such as the smaller miscanthus and blue-leaved selections of Panicum.

P. alopecuroides forms rounded mounds of fine, mid-green leaves up to 75cm (30in) tall, and up to 90cm (3ft) across. The flowers appear from mid-summer, held well above the foliage on stems up to 1m (39in) tall, each stem topped by a dense, pink-brown hairy 'fox tail' or bottlebrush, arching out in all directions from the clump, giving the 'fountain' effect. There are several selections in a range of sizes and flower colours. The largest, 'Cassian's Choice',

reaches 1m (39in), and has notably good autumn colour in orange and red tints. 'Woodside' is similar to the species, but said to be a more reliable flowerer, as is German bred 'Weserbergland', whose flowers are greenish-white. *P. alopecuroides* f. *viridescens* has particularly bright emerald green foliage and brown flowers, and is

site	Unfussy, full sun or light shade, tender species sheltered spot
soil	This plant will succeed on most soils other than permanently wet
watering	Once they are established, they should only need watering in dry spells. Little else is required
general care	Several species not the hardiest, requiring winter protection and their flowering can be erratic
pests & diseases	No real pest and disease problems. Culturally, more tender species dislike frost and wet winters

P

Bamboos & Grasses

	SPRING	SUMMER	AUTUMN	WINTER	height (cm)	spread (cm)	leaf colour	
Pennisetum alopecuroides	in leaf	in leaf/flowering	flowering	flowering	75	90		The original fountain grass
P. alopecuroides 'Cassian's Choice'	in leaf	in leaf/flowering	flowering	flowering	100	90		Vigorous and good autumn colour
P. alopecuroides 'Hameln'	in leaf	in leaf/flowering	flowering	flowering	45	80		Semi-dwarf form
P. alopecuroides 'Little Bunny'	in leaf	in leaf/flowering	flowering	flowering	30	30		Dwarf form good for pots and edging
P. alopecuroides 'Little Honey'	in leaf	in leaf/flowering	flowering/in leaf	in leaf	30	30		Gorgeous variegated dwarf form, not the longest flowering
P. alopecuroides 'Moudry'	in leaf	in leaf/flowering	flowering		60	100		Very dark purple-black flowers
P. alopecuroides f. *viridescens*	in leaf	in leaf/flowering	flowering		60	90		Handsome bright green form
P. alopecuroides 'Weserbergland'	in leaf	in leaf/flowering	flowering	flowering	75	75		Green-white flowers
P. alopecuroides 'Woodside'	in leaf	in leaf/flowering	flowering	flowering	80	80		More reliable flowerer
P. incomptum	in leaf	in leaf/flowering	flowering/in leaf	in leaf	120	200+		Runs at root, good in pots
P. macrourum	in leaf	in leaf/flowering	flowering	flowering	120	45		Similar to *P. incomptum* but clump forming
P. orientale	in leaf	in leaf/flowering	flowering	flowering	90	90		Lovely but on the tender side
P. orientale 'Karley Rose'	in leaf	in leaf/flowering	flowering		90	90		Long pink white flowers

in leaf · *flowering*

Pennisetum alopecuroides 'Moudry'

Pennisetum setaceum 'Rubrum'

fountain grass, are both as decorative as *P. alopecuroides*, but not as reliably hardy, and although perennial are sometimes grown as annuals. *P. villosum* forms sprawling tussocks to 30cm (12in) high and 90cm (3ft) across, producing short, wide, furry white flowers all summer and autumn. *P. orientale* is slightly smaller, with long, thin mauve-pink flowerheads, even longer and pink-white in its cultivars 'Tall Tails', and long and pink in 'Karley Rose'. *P. setaceum* can reach 1m (3ft), and has the typical arching habit, with narrow foliage and long, reddish pink flowerheads, even redder in its dwarfer cultivar 'Rubrum'. It is not hardy, and perhaps best pot grown or lifted and pretected indoors for the winter.

Much more hardy are *P. incomptum*, meadow fountain grass, and *P. macrourum*, both of which have attractive grey-green leaves to 45cm (18in) and erect flower stems up to 1.2m (4ft), and are so similar that they are often confused. The former runs at the root, however, but is good in large shallow pots, while the latter is clump-forming. Both these species are white flowered.

semi-dwarf, at 60cm (2ft), a similar size to 'Moudry', a gorgeous cultivar with deep purple to near-black flowers, and 'Hameln', which is otherwise similar to the species. Smaller still are 'Little Bunny', which rarely makes 30cm (12in) even in flower, but whose flower stems are rather too upright to form the fountain effect, and 'Little Honey', around the same size, but with narrow green and white variegated foliage. Both make excellent front of border, edging or container plants, particularly combined with broader leaved grasses or *Ophiopogon p.* 'Nigrescens'.

P. orientale, oriental fountain grass, and *P. villosum*, Ethiopian

Pennisetum orientale 'Karley Rose'

	SPRING	SUMMER	AUTUMN	WINTER	height (cm)	spread (cm)	leaf colour	
P. orientale 'Tall Tails'		🌿🌿🌿🌿	⬡⬡⬡ ⬡⬡⬡	⬡⬡⬡	90	90		Long pink flowers
P. setaceum		🌿🌿🌿	⬡⬡⬡		100	30		Arching habit, not the hardiest
P. setaceum 'Rubrum'		🌿🌿🌿	⬡⬡⬡		60	30		Smaller red flowered form
P. villosum		🌿🌿🌿🌿	⬡⬡⬡ ⬡⬡⬡	⬡⬡⬡	60	100		White flowers, not the hardiest

🌿 *in leaf*　⬡ *flowering*

Phaenosperma globosa

Phaenosperma globosa is a grass grown primarily for its broad, strap-like leaves, to contrast with finer-leaved grass species and their cultivars

These are only around 30cm (12in) long, but up to 2.5cm (1in) wide, light green with prominent, much darker ribs, appearing almost pleated and with grey-green undersides partly displayed by their arching form. The leaves in fact look more like those of Phormium, New Zealand flax, or irises than those of a grass. In milder areas and through winters where the temperature never falls particularly low, it can remain evergreen, although leaves that have overwintered can begin to look tatty when the new spears emerge in spring, and are probably best removed.

P. globosa is happy in most soils and in sun or semi-shade, forming relatively low clumps up to 60cm (2ft) across, which throw up tall, thin flower stems up to 1.5m (5ft) tall, rising so far above the foliage they look like they should belong to a different plant. The flowerheads themselves are unusual rather than really decorative, forming wispy, pyramid-shaped panicles of tiny spikelets collected together into spheres looking almost like ball-bearings from a distance. They begin to appear in mid-summer and last well into autumn.

P. globosa's rounded shape and broad leaves contrast well with more upright grasses such as the smaller Miscanthus

site	Any sites from full sun to part shade, and will take some exposure
soil	This plant is fairly unfussy, disliking only extremes of wet or dry
watering	Once established should need watering only in extended dry periods. Little else is required
general care	Easy to look after, accommodating grass. Semi-evergreen in most areas
pests & diseases	No real pest or disease problems, and easy to please culturally. Dislikes extreme winter wet

cultivars, upright Panicum selections or even rushes and horsetails. Its mid-green leaves are a foil for more glaucous blue species and selections and also look good next to the more purple-red Panicum such as 'Rehbraun' and 'Hanse Herms', particularly as these assume their strong autumn colouring with P. globosa remaining green. Its broad leaves are also useful to link grass-dominated plantings with nearby borders containing herbaceous perennials.

Bamboos & Grasses

Phaenosperma globosa

Phalaris

Ribbon grass *or* gardener's garters

Another relatively broad-leaved grass that has long been a favourite of cottage gardeners despite its tendency to run at the roots, *Phalaris arundinacea* is rarely seen as a plain green species but nearly always encountered in one of several variegated forms, of which *P. arundinacea* var. *picta* is probably the most common.

All forms are deciduous, and produce a leaf mound 60–90cm (2–3ft) tall, each leaf to 30cm (12in) long and 1cm (⅓in) wide, unevenly striped green and white but with the white usually predominating. The flowers are small, narrow and white but have relatively little impact. Most soils including both permanently moist and moderately dry seem to suit them.

There are several named cultivars of var. *picta*, of which 'Feesey' is probably the pick. It is smaller than the type and less spreading, with cleaner white variegation, narrower green stripes and often tinged pink on emergence. This pink staining is more marked and persists longer on 'Tricolor'. 'Luteopicta' and 'Aureovariegata' have more

cream-yellow variegation and grow to around 75cm (30in), but are not to everyone's taste as they can look a little anaemic. 'Streamlined' is taller growing and narrower-leaved than the others, with more green in the leaves, and inevitably more vigour.

All forms of *P. arundinaceae* need careful siting or they can become invasive, and are perhaps best sited in mixed borders with vigorous shrubs as neighbours. Their strong variegation can fade as the summer goes on; if so, they can be cut back quite hard to encourage a new flush of fresh, bright foliage.

Phalaris arundinacea var. picta

site	Any from full sun to light shade. Variegation loses impact in too much shade
soil	This plant is fairly unfussy, from permanently moist to quite dry
watering	Should only need irrigating in prolonged dry spells. Keeping on the dry side reduces vigour
general care	Unfussy grasses with real variegated impact, accepting their tendency to run at the root
pests & diseases	Relatively trouble free from pest, disease or cultural problems. If anything, they are difficult to get rid of

	SPRING	SUMMER	AUTUMN	WINTER	height (cm)	spread (cm)	leaf colour	
Phalaris arundinacea					100	200+		Seldom seen, little ornamental value
P. arundinacea var. *picta*					100	200+		Commonest variegated form
P. a. var. *picta* 'Aureovariegata'					75	200+		Yellow-variegated on pale green
P. arundinacea var. *picta* 'Feesey'					90	200+		More compact and better coloured than type
P. arundinacea var. *picta* 'Picta'					100	200+		Indistinguishable from var. *picta*
P. arundinacea var. *picta* 'Luteopicta'					75	200+		Pale yellow stripes on green-yellow
P. arundinacea var. *picta* 'Streamlined'					110	200+		Taller growing than most, white stripes
P. arundinacea var. *picta* 'Tricolor'					80	200+		Pink flushing; most marked in full sun
P. canariensis					90	60		Annual usually grown for drying

 in leaf   ☀ flowering

P

Bamboos & Grasses

Phleum pratense

Timothy grass *or* cat's tail

A perennial deciduous British native grass, *Phleum pratense* forms relatively narrow, upright clumps of fine leaves up to 90cm (3ft) tall and 60cm (2ft) across. A naturally fast-growing species, it produces long, narrow, congested, furry cylindrical flowers. These are similar to those of Pennisetum, but they do not arch, measuring up to 15cm (6in) long and held on the ends of long stems up to 1.2m (4ft) tall.

The flowers emerge green, ageing to light brown like mini bullrushes. Timothy grass was formerly widely used in dried flower arrangements, but has been superseded by larger, showier imports, and is sometimes a constituent of meadow seed mixes. It is commonly added to fodder mixtures for cattle, and will grow on most soils but has a preference for damper areas, not tolerating drought well. It has never reached great popularity as a garden plant, as other species have more impact.

Tests on its pollen – which is produced copiously – have shown it can provoke allergic reactions in hay fever sufferers, so gardeners who suffer from this condition may be better avoiding it altogether. It is widespread in meadows, and self-seeds readily, so to avoid seedlings becoming a problem, deadhead before the spikes begin shedding their seed. Timothy grass has also become an introduced problem weed in much of North America, particularly in wetter areas where it can crowd out slower growing natives.

Nevertheless, it is a useful and attractive grass for meadows or wildlife gardens, not running excessively at the root and with relatively ornamental flowers. Its upright growth contrasts well with more arching grasses such as Panicum, or it can form a pleasing backdrop to the small blue fescues and variegated grasses of all types.

site	Unfussy, will grow in full sun or part shade and tolerates exposure
soil	This plant will succeed on most soils, other than very dry ones
watering	Prefers even moisture, dislikes prolonged drought so give additional water, especially during establishment
general care	Easy and undemanding native grass. Cut back to ground level in late autumn or early spring
pests & diseases	Relatively trouble free from pest or disease problems. Cultural difficulties usually drought related

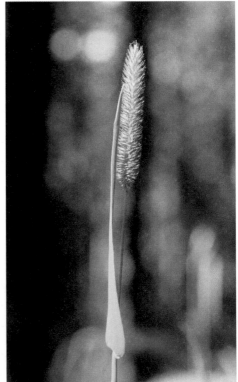

Phleum pratense

Phleum pratense

P

Bamboos & Grasses

Phragmites
Reeds

Phragmites australis, also known as **Norfolk reed**, is a **British** native ideal for colonizing the marshy banks of streams and watercourses. Indeed, this plant prefers to grow as an emergent with its roots submerged in water.

Phragmites australis 'Variegatus'

An aggressive colonizer of wet ground, spreading rapidly and persistently via its rhizomatous root system, it produces broad, iris like leaves that taper to a point and are held upright, reaching as much as 2.4m (8ft). *P. australis* subsp. *australis* (often sold as *P. australis giganteus*) is even more of a thug, reaching 3m (10ft) with similar wandering tendencies. Both plain green forms are really suited only to large informal pools and lakes, where they will form extensive marginal stands, unless restrained inside a large container. They produce attractive, shaggy, purple-brown drooping flowerheads in late summer and go well with other vigorous water plants like Typha, horse tails (Equisetum) and larger Juncus.

Fortunately, there are several much more ornamental and less vigorous variegated alternatives. The most common is probably *P. australis* subspecies *australis* var. *striatopictus* 'Variegatus' (usually understandably sold as plain 'Variegatus'), which has creamy-white variegation running the length of its leaves that reaches a more manageable 1.4m (4½ ft), and runs more slowly. Neither does it have to be grown in water, growing well in moist ordinary soils.

P. karka is a more recent introduction, slightly smaller and less vigorous than *P. australis*, with two beautiful variegated forms, *P. karka* 'Candy Stripe' and 'Variegatum', both of which rarely reach 1.2m (4ft), and have broader variegated stripes than *P. australis* 'Variegatus', plus attractive pink tinges. 'Candy Stripe' is a paler, mint-green with pronounced pink striping, while 'Variegatus' has, if anything, brighter white but slightly less pink on a darker green background. Both should still be grown in containers sunk into the pond or soil in smaller gardens, which will curtail their spread effectively.

site	Preferably place in or near water. Given moisture, exposure tolerant
soil	Moist to waterlogged soil is ideal for these plants. They are unfussy about pH
watering	Copiously if not grown as true emergents in standing water. Dislike drought for any length of time
general care	Easy to grow to the point of invasive unless container grown. Variegated cultivars will grow in moist soils
pests & diseases	Relatively trouble free from major pest or disease problems. Cultural problems only if dry

	SPRING	SUMMER	AUTUMN	WINTER	height (cm)	spread (cm)	leaf colour	
Phragmites australis	🌿🌿🌿	🌿	●●🌿	🌿🌿	240	200+	▢	Striking but invasive tendencies
P. australis subsp. *australis*	🌿🌿🌿	🌿	●●🌿	🌿🌿	300	200+	▢	Even more of a thug in cultivation
P. a. subsp. *a.* var. *striatopictus* 'Variegatus'	🌿🌿🌿	🌿	●🌿	🌿🌿	140	200+	▯	Green leaves broadly striped with white. Can revert
P. karka	🌿🌿🌿	🌿	●●●	●●	120	200+	▢	Slightly smaller species, longer flowering
P. karka 'Candy Stripe'	🌿🌿🌿	🌿	●●●	●●	120	200+	▯	Lovely green, white and pink striped foliage
P. karka 'Variegatum'	🌿🌿🌿	🌿	●●●	●●	120	200+	▯	Similar to Candy Stripe but whiter and less pink

🌿 *in leaf*   ● *flowering*

Phyllostachys

Phyllostachys is a genus temperate bamboo species from Northern lowland China that contains some of the best and most ornamental hardy bamboos.

Phyllostachys nigra

Phyllostachys aurea 'Koi'

These bamboos are bone-hardy, most down to at least -20°C (-6°F), and although technically their root systems are intermediate, in temperate climates they are reliably clump-forming, spreading slowly. In warmer areas like southern Europe, they can run at the root. They prefer full sun or only light shade, and some species are extremely exposure-tolerant. A deep groove, the sulcus, runs vertically up the culm (stem) above the branches, which usually appear in pairs from each node, and is characteristic of the genus. Many species and selections have beautiful culms in a range of colours that shine as if polished, and most have large, pointed leaves. The species and cultivars are organized below according to popularity, size and culm colour. Bear in mind the quoted heights are maximums achieved in the wild; in colder climates most species never make anything like this size, achieving 3–6m (10–20ft).

Black bamboo

Phyllostachys nigra, the black bamboo, is unique, the only bamboo to produce truly black culms, which contrast beautifully with the 9cm (3½in) dark green leaves. Slow

	site	Most prefer full sun but will take light shade. Some extremely exposure tolerant
	soil	Unfussy. Evenly moist preferred but relatively drought tolerant once established
	watering	Moist while establishing, particularly species preferring warmer summers. Never let potted plants dry out
	general care	Easy to grow bamboos. Will benefit from an annual thinning of weak, dead or congested culms
	pests & diseases	Largely pest and disease free, although aphids can attack some of the softer leaved species

	SPRING	SUMMER	AUTUMN	WINTER	height (cm)	spread (cm)	culm colour	
Phyllostachys bambusoides	🍃🍃🍃	🍃🍃🍃	🍃🍃🍃	🍃🍃🍃	2200	600+		Giant timber bamboo. Needs space
P. bambusoides 'Castillonis'	🍃🍃🍃	🍃🍃🍃	🍃🍃🍃	🍃🍃🍃	1000	400+		Popular and much smaller growing than species
P. bambusoides 'Castillonis Inversa'	🍃🍃🍃	🍃🍃🍃	🍃🍃🍃	🍃🍃🍃	1000	400+		Reverse variegation to 'Castillonis', rare
P. bambusoides 'Holochrysa'	🍃🍃🍃	🍃🍃🍃	🍃🍃🍃	🍃🍃🍃	1000	400+		Dark green leaves and rich gold culms
P. bambusoides 'Kawadana'	🍃🍃🍃	🍃🍃🍃	🍃🍃🍃	🍃🍃🍃	1000	400+		Fine variegation in yellow on both leaves and culms
P. bambusoides 'Marliacea'	🍃🍃🍃	🍃🍃🍃	🍃🍃🍃	🍃🍃🍃	1000	400+		Slow growing, culms ridged with prominent nodes
P. bambusoides 'Subvariegata'	🍃🍃🍃	🍃🍃🍃	🍃🍃🍃	🍃🍃🍃	1000	400+		Fine light green variegation on dark green leaves
P. bambusoides 'Tanakae'	🍃🍃🍃	🍃🍃🍃	🍃🍃🍃	🍃🍃🍃	1000	400+		Lovely cultivar but can be difficult to find
P. bambusoides 'Violascens'	🍃🍃🍃	🍃🍃🍃	🍃🍃🍃	🍃🍃🍃	1000	400+		Purple variegation more marked than on 'Tanakae'
P. dulcis	🍃🍃🍃	🍃🍃🍃	🍃🍃🍃	🍃🍃🍃	1200	600+		Vigorous and strong grower even in cooler areas
P. edulis	🍃🍃🍃	🍃🍃🍃	🍃🍃🍃	🍃🍃🍃	2000	600+		Prefers warmer climes
P. edulis 'Bicolor'	🍃🍃🍃	🍃🍃🍃	🍃🍃🍃	🍃🍃🍃	600	400+		Smaller and slower growing than species
P. nigra	🍃🍃🍃	🍃🍃🍃	🍃🍃🍃	🍃🍃🍃	1500	600+		Black colouring takes time to develop
P. nigra 'Boryana'	🍃🍃🍃	🍃🍃🍃	🍃🍃🍃	🍃🍃🍃	1500	600+		Leopard or snakeskin bamboo

Bamboos & Grasses

P

🍃 *in leaf*

Phyllostachys aurea

Phyllostachys aureosulcata

larger than the type and culms retain some green-brown; *P. nigra* 'Boryana', the snakeskin or leopard skin bamboo, vigorous, culms ageing green with large brown-black spots; 'Hale', one of the earliest to colour of the black culmed selections; 'Megurochiku', light orange-brown culms with black grooves; and 'Tosaensis', similar to 'Boryana' but with fewer, more elongated black-brown spots.

Large Phyllostachys

Some Phyllostachys are real giants, approaching the size of tropical bamboos, and are widely used for timber. They achieve nowhere near this size in temperate climates, but still make statuesque groves in gardens where there is space. Some of the selected cultivars are much smaller, however, and will adapt to cultivation in large containers. Despite their size and vigour in subtropical areas, short summers will tend to keep these large plants in check in both height and spread.

P. bambusoides can reach 22m (72ft) in the wild, with leaves 15cm (6in) long produced on long branches, but in cultivation rarely tops 10m (33ft). It has bright green culms and is widely grown for timber in the Orient, but prefers warm summers, although it is hardy to -15°C (5°F). The many cultivars do better in colder

growing and compact, it usually reaches 3–5m (10–16ft) in cultivation but can top 15m (50ft) in the wild. The culms emerge green-brown and turn black gradually, usually taking 12–18 months, more rapidly in full sun. Black bamboos make breathtaking specimen plants, grow well in large pots, and are ideally suited to both Japanese gardens and the sub-tropical gardening style.

There are several forms and cultivars, including: *P. nigra* f. *nigra*, slower growing and colouring early; f. *henonis*, rough green culms that do not turn black; f. *punctata*,

	SPRING	SUMMER	AUTUMN	WINTER	height (cm)	spread (cm)	culm colour	
P. nigra 'Hale'	🍃🍃🍃	🍃🍃🍃	🍃🍃🍃	🍃🍃🍃	600	400+	■	One of the earliest to colour, compact
P. nigra f. henonis	🍃🍃🍃	🍃🍃🍃	🍃🍃🍃	🍃🍃🍃	1500	600+	■	May actually be the 'wild', unmutated form
P. nigra 'Megurochiku'	🍃🍃🍃	🍃🍃🍃	🍃🍃🍃	🍃🍃🍃	600	400+	▥	Very attractive, smaller and slower growing than species
P. nigra f. nigra	🍃🍃🍃	🍃🍃🍃	🍃🍃🍃	🍃🍃🍃	1000	600+	■	Slower growing than species
P. nigra f. punctata	🍃🍃🍃	🍃🍃🍃	🍃🍃🍃	🍃🍃🍃	1500	600+	▨	Large and vigorous, culms never entirely black
P. nigra 'Tosaensis'	🍃🍃🍃	🍃🍃🍃	🍃🍃🍃	🍃🍃🍃	600	600+	▨	Similar to 'Boryana' but more compact, elongated spots
P. sulphurea	🍃🍃🍃	🍃🍃🍃	🍃🍃🍃	🍃🍃🍃	1500	600+	□	Large and cold tolerant
P. sulphurea 'Houzeau'	🍃🍃🍃	🍃🍃🍃	🍃🍃🍃	🍃🍃🍃	600	400+	▥	Hardy but needs sunny position
P. sulphurea 'Robert Young'	🍃🍃🍃	🍃🍃🍃	🍃🍃🍃	🍃🍃🍃	600	400+	▥	Warm yellow culms with a few green stripes in sun
P. sulphurea 'Viridis'	🍃🍃🍃	🍃🍃🍃	🍃🍃🍃	🍃🍃🍃	600	400+	□	Attractive soft green culms, rose culm sheaths
P. vivax	🍃🍃🍃	🍃🍃🍃	🍃🍃🍃	🍃🍃🍃	1500	600+	□	Fast growing and large even in cold areas
P. vivax f. aureocaulis	🍃🍃🍃	🍃🍃🍃	🍃🍃🍃	🍃🍃🍃	800	400+	▥	Rich yellow culms heavily striped green, needs space
P. vivax f. huanvenzhu	🍃🍃🍃	🍃🍃🍃	🍃🍃🍃	🍃🍃🍃	800	400+	▥	Bright green culms with yellow grooves

🍃 in leaf

climates and make good garden plants, rarely growing above 5m (16ft). They include 'Castillonis', a gorgeous yellow-culmed selection striped with green; 'Castillonis Inversa', green striped yellow; 'Holochrysa' (or 'Allgold'), dark green leaves and rich gold culms; 'Marliacea', a slow growing selection with ridged culms and prominent nodes; 'Tanakae', green culms prominently striped with purple-brown; and 'Violascens', green culms with a purple flush. There are also variegated cultivars, including 'Subvariegata', leaves striped with pale and dark green, and 'Kawadana', a lovely form with fine yellow stripes on both

Phyllostachys bambusoides 'Castillonis'

Phyllostachys bambusoides

leaves and culms.

P. vivax is similar to *P. bambusoides*, with thinner green culms and more arching foliage, but copes better with cooler conditions, so is a better choice for colder climates. Again, it will reach nowhere near its potential 15m (50ft). Two naturally-occuring forms are in cultivation (and sometimes sold as cultivars), f. *aureocaulis*, which has rich yellow culms heavily striped with green, and f. *huanvenzhu*, which has green culms and yellow grooves.

P. dulcis is a strong grower even in colder regions, growing up to 12m (40ft) with green culms and large leaves that can make a good windbreak but tends to run at the root. More ornamental is *P. edulis*, the source of culinary bamboo shoots, which has striking yellow-orange culms but can be slow to establish and really prefers hotter summers. It can make 20m (65ft) in the wild. 'Bicolor' is much smaller, with culms striped green. Better in cooler areas, though needing full sun, are selections of *P. sulphurea*, which

	SPRING	SUMMER	AUTUMN	WINTER	height (cm)	spread (cm)	culm colour	
Phyllostachys angusta	🍃🍃🍃	🍃🍃🍃	🍃🍃🍃	🍃🍃🍃	700	400+		Hardy and relatively small
P. arcana	🍃🍃🍃	🍃🍃🍃	🍃🍃🍃	🍃🍃🍃	800	400+		Unremarkable
P. arcana 'Luteosulcata'	🍃🍃🍃	🍃🍃🍃	🍃🍃🍃	🍃🍃🍃	800	400+		Much more ornamental than species
P. aurea	🍃🍃🍃	🍃🍃🍃	🍃🍃🍃	🍃🍃🍃	800	400+		Upright, good for hedging, leaves yellowish in sun
P. aurea 'Albovariegata'	🍃🍃🍃	🍃🍃🍃	🍃🍃🍃	🍃🍃🍃	600	400+		Leaves thinly white variegated, smaller than species
P. aurea 'Flavescens Inversa'	🍃🍃🍃	🍃🍃🍃	🍃🍃🍃	🍃🍃🍃	800	400+		More ornamental than species
P. aurea 'Holochrysa'	🍃🍃🍃	🍃🍃🍃	🍃🍃🍃	🍃🍃🍃	600	400+		Full sun for best culm colour
P. aurea 'Koi'	🍃🍃🍃	🍃🍃🍃	🍃🍃🍃	🍃🍃🍃	600	400+		Prefers semi-shade
P. aureosulcata	🍃🍃🍃	🍃🍃🍃	🍃🍃🍃	🍃🍃🍃	800	400+		Lower parts of culms often zig-zag. Popular in USA
P. aureosulcata f. *aureocaulis*	🍃🍃🍃	🍃🍃🍃	🍃🍃🍃	🍃🍃🍃	800	400+		Culms a rich golden yellow in sun
P. aureosulcata f. *spectabilis*	🍃🍃🍃	🍃🍃🍃	🍃🍃🍃	🍃🍃🍃	800	400+		Lovely form, but can be difficult to find
P. aureosulcata 'Harbin'	🍃🍃🍃	🍃🍃🍃	🍃🍃🍃	🍃🍃🍃	600	400+		Less vigorous than species and forms

🍃 *in leaf*

Phyllostachys bissetii

P. bambusoides 'Castillonis Inversa'

grows to 15m (50ft) in the wild but again much less in cultivation. 'Viridis' has soft green culms, those of 'Houzeau' have the grooves highlighted in yellow, while in 'Robert Young' the culms start green, ageing to yellow-green randomly striped with darker green.

Coloured culms

The basic phyllostachys culm colour is olive green; however, there are species and cultivars with a wide range of culm colours, that develop once the new shoots have emerged and lengthened. These can look extremely ornamental in the garden placed with other plants that subtly echo or contrast with them. Many growers remove the lower branches of their bamboos to emphasize the culms further and allow light into the clump, heightening the colour.

Yellow culms are produced by many phyllostachys. *P. aurea* culms emerge green but turn a clear yellow as they age, particularly in full sun, when the leaves can also take on a yellow tinge. It is an upright growing bamboo reaching a maximum 8m (26ft) but usually much smaller. Cultivars include 'Albovariegata', which has green and white leaf variegation and is smaller and slower growing than the species; 'Koi', which has green grooves on yellow culms; 'Flavescens Inversa', the opposite, green culms and yellow grooves; and 'Holochrysa', a vivid, shiny yellow-gold. *P. aureosulcata* is similar but with larger leaves and has the curious growth habit of the lower parts of its culms zig-zagging away from vertical. The species is green culmed, but both f. *aureocaulis* and f. *spectabilis* have rich golden culms, the latter's with green grooves. *P. aureosulcata* 'Harbin' is a lovely less vigorous selection with green and yellow striped culms, while 'Harbin Inversa' has gold culms thinly striped with green.

P. humilis reaches only 5m (16ft) with culms emerging dark purple to near black, ageing to a gorgeous orange yellow; it can run in conditions it likes. *P. rubromarginata* can reach 9.5m (30ft) with large leaves to 12cm (5in) long. It produces bright green

	SPRING	SUMMER	AUTUMN	WINTER	height (cm)	spread (cm)	culm colour	
P. aureosulcata 'Harbin Inversa'	🍃🍃	🍃🍃	🍃🍃	🍃🍃	600	400+		Perhaps even more ornamental than 'Harbin'; rare
P. bissetii	🍃🍃	🍃🍃	🍃🍃	🍃🍃	700	400+		Exposure tolerant, good for hedges and windbreaks
P. decora	🍃🍃	🍃🍃	🍃🍃	🍃🍃	700	400+		Arching form, heat and drought tolerant
P. flexuosa	🍃🍃	🍃🍃	🍃🍃	🍃🍃	1000	600+		Ages to attractive yellow-black mottling in sun, arching form
P. glauca	🍃🍃	🍃🍃	🍃🍃	🍃🍃	1100	400+		White mealy coating on culms
P. humilis	🍃🍃	🍃🍃	🍃🍃	🍃🍃	500	400+		Attractive, but can run at the root
P. iridescens	🍃🍃	🍃🍃	🍃🍃	🍃🍃	1200	600+		Culms age from green to brown-purplish mottling
P. nuda f. localis	🍃🍃	🍃🍃	🍃🍃	🍃🍃	750	400+		Extremely hardy, culms emerge very dark
P. praecox	🍃🍃	🍃🍃	🍃🍃	🍃🍃	1000	400+		Edible shoots, rare, white bloom in new culms
P. propinqua	🍃🍃	🍃🍃	🍃🍃	🍃🍃	750	400+		Unremarkable
P. rubromarginata	🍃🍃	🍃🍃	🍃🍃	🍃🍃	950	400+		Tall. Culm colour contrasts with red striped sheaths
P. violascens	🍃🍃	🍃🍃	🍃🍃	🍃🍃	1100	400+		Very attractive but can run. Similar to P. iridescens
P. viridiglaucescens	🍃🍃	🍃🍃	🍃🍃	🍃🍃	1000	600+		Other species and forms have more to recommend them

🍃 in leaf

culms that age to a greyish yellow, contrasting with the red-striping on its persistent sheaths, and is an excellent specimen bamboo where there is space.

Some of the most striking Phyllostachys are those with purplish culms, looking gorgeous teamed with other dark-leaved plants such as black elders, purple leaved smoke bush or cannas. Only a few species retain this colouring, including *P. violascens*, deep violet new culms ageing dull brown with brown-purple stripes (it can be invasive; some growers recommend cutting out all the older culms as the new culms leaf out, both to give the

best colour and curb its vigour); *P. iridescens*, similar to *P. violascens* but more clump-forming; and bone-hardy, slow spreading *P. nuda* f. *localis*, whose older culms are dark green blotched with purple black.

Greyish culms are produced by *P. angusta*, a large-leaved species up to 7m (23ft) tall but usually much less, and *P. bissetii*, a strong-growing, dark-leaved plant of about the same height that makes a good windbreak or hedge.

Green culmed Phyllostachys species include *P. decora*, which like *P. bissetii* is exposure and drought tolerant, making a good hedge and reaching 7m (23ft), but with a more weeping habit and white sheaths striped green; *P. arcana*, the species is unremarkable but its cultivar 'Luteosulcata' has contrasting yellow grooves and makes a good garden plant; *P. flexuosa*, which has glossy, sinuous culms and a weeping habit, staying compact; *P. glauca*, whose culms are covered in an attractive powdery white bloom, as are those of larger, edible-shooted *P. praecox*; and *P. propinqua* and *P. viridiglaucescens*, which are really plants for the bamboo collector, with little to recommend them above other species.

Pleioblastus

One of the larger bamboo genera, relatively few Pleioblastus are in cultivation as the majority have little to recommend them horticulturally, and are rampantly invasive. The whole genus has running (leptomorphic) rhizomes, but the smaller and daintier species can be controlled in all but the smallest gardens, or successfully confined in pots if they are repotted on a regular basis.

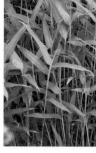

Pleioblastus pygmaeus

Most species are short for bamboos, rarely topping 5m (17ft) and are forest understory plants, so quite shade tolerant, with relatively large, broad leaves. They are extremely hardy, the larger species putting up with exposed conditions well enough to make good hedges and windbreaks, while the smaller species make excellent groundcover in sun or shade.

The most popular pleioblastus are both small and among the best variegated bamboos. *Pleioblastus variegatus*, often sold as *P. shibuyanus* 'Tsuboi' reaches 1.8m (6ft) but is usually much smaller, with broad leaves up to 15cm (6in) long of fresh, apple green marked with wide bands of broad cream. It can run, but not excessively so, and adapts well to life in a pot where it can look fetching teamed with plain green grasses. *P. viridistriatus* (often called *P. auricomus*) is arguably one of the best yellow-variegated of all garden plants, with rich gold leaves up to 17cm (7in) long, striped with green held on short, purple-green culms up to 1.5m (5ft) tall, but again, usually much smaller. It prefers a moist site and semi

Pleioblastus chino f. aureostriatus

site	Unfussy, full sun or part shade. Larger species are exposure tolerant
soil	Most soils. Smaller and variegated selections prefer moist conditions
watering	Evenly moist best for smaller plants. Larger species drought-tolerant once established
general care	Easy to care for bamboos, but take tendency to spread into account. Cut back old culms in spring
pests & diseases	No pest or disease problems. Can thrive in all but the driest or most waterlogged conditions

shade, and spreads more slowly. An all yellow cultivar, 'Chrysophyllus', is even slower growing and will scorch in full sun. *P. viridistriatus* 'Bracken Hill' is reputed to be taller than the species, but is otherwise very similar. Both *P. variegatus* and *P. viridistriatus* are often cut back hard to ground level in spring, as the new leaves are the most brightly-marked.

Two even smaller species are becoming more widely available, both also making excellent groundcover for small gardens. *P. argenteostriatus* 'Akebono' (often sold as

Bamboos & Grasses

	SPRING	SUMMER	AUTUMN	WINTER	height (cm)	spread (cm)	leaf colour	
P. argenteostriatus 'Akebono'	🌱🌱	🌱🌱	🌱🌱	🌱🌱	30	400+	▯	Beautiful, unusual variegation pattern, slow spreading
P. argenteostriatus f. *pumilus*	🌱🌱	🌱🌱	🌱🌱	🌱🌱	20	400+	▮	Even more compact
P. chino	🌱🌱	🌱🌱	🌱🌱	🌱🌱	400	400+	▮	Japanese species, can run
P. chino f. *aureostriatus*	🌱🌱	🌱🌱	🌱🌱	🌱🌱	200	400+	▯	Smaller and slower growing, delicate variegation
P. chino f. *elegantissimus*	🌱🌱	🌱🌱	🌱🌱	🌱🌱	180	400+	▯	Narrower leaves finely striped white, can still run
P. hindsii	🌱🌱	🌱🌱	🌱🌱	🌱🌱	500	400+	▮	Exposure tolerant and not that invasive
P. linearis	🌱🌱	🌱🌱	🌱🌱	🌱🌱	450	600+	▮	Narrow leaves, weeping form but runs
P. pygmaeus	🌱🌱	🌱🌱	🌱🌱	🌱🌱	60	400+	▮	Variable, from very dwarf to 60cm (2ft) and running

🌱 *in leaf*

Pleioblastus viridistriatus

P. akebono) is a gorgeous little bamboo, reaching only 30cm (12in) with leaves 6cm (2½in) long, each shading from green at the base to near-white at the tip. It is probably the least invasive of the genus, with an even dwarfer plain-leaved form, f. *pumilus. P. pygmaeus* is a naturally very variable species and clones are offered that grow anywhere between 60cm (2ft) to barely 10cm (4in). The leaves are held characteristically in rows either side of the branch, giving a herringbone or fern-like appearance. 'Distichus' is one of the larger clones and can be invasive, with *P. pygmaeus* var. *pygmaeus* 'Mini', to only 10cm (4in) one of the smallest. All make excellent pot plants if repotted regularly.

The other Pleioblastus species are larger, and not at all suitable for smaller gardens unless physically contained in large pots or rhizome barriers sunk into the ground. *P chino* is an attractive Japanese species reaching 4m (13ft), with large leaves to 20cm (8in) long. Two of its forms are more common in cultivation, f. *aureostriatus*, which is smaller and slower growing with thin white stripes on its leaves, and f. *elegantissimus*, with narrow leaves, white variegation and rarely topping 1.8m (6ft). All can prove invasive, but make good groundcover in wooded areas. *P. linearis* has an elegant, weeping form to 4.5m (15ft) and narrower leaves held on dull grey culms. It is good in shade, but also runs.

The two most exposure tolerant species that make good hedges and windbreaks are *P. hindsii* and *P. simonii*. Both can make 5m (16ft), with *P. hindsii* the more leafy and upright, and slightly less vigorous in habit. *P. simonii* has a less than ornamental variegated form, 'Variegatus', which tends to look rather piebald, as the white markings are anything but uniform.

Pleioblastus variegatus

	SPRING	SUMMER	AUTUMN	WINTER	height (cm)	spread (cm)	leaf colour	
P. pygmaeus 'Distichus'	🍃🍃🍃	🍃🍃🍃	🍃🍃🍃	🍃🍃🍃	60	200+	�largeblock	Small, but can prove invasive
P. pygmaeus var. *pygmaeus* 'Mini'	🍃🍃🍃	🍃🍃🍃	🍃🍃🍃	🍃🍃🍃	10	200+	▪	Smallest, least invasive form
P. simonii	🍃🍃🍃	🍃🍃🍃	🍃🍃🍃	🍃🍃🍃	500	400+	▪	Exposure tolerant; good hedge or windbreak but runs
P. simonii 'Variegatus'	🍃🍃🍃	🍃🍃🍃	🍃🍃🍃	🍃🍃🍃	400	400+	▯	Variegation is inconsistent – 'piebald' look
P. variegatus	🍃🍃🍃	🍃🍃🍃	🍃🍃🍃	🍃🍃🍃	200	400+	▯	One of the best small variegated bamboos
P. viridistriatus	🍃🍃🍃	🍃🍃🍃	🍃🍃🍃	🍃🍃🍃	150	400+	▯	Beautiful yellow variegated bamboo, slow spreader
P. viridistriatus 'Bracken Hill'	🍃🍃🍃	🍃🍃🍃	🍃🍃🍃	🍃🍃🍃	180	400+	▯	Very similar to species, said to be larger
P. viridistriatus 'Chrysophyllus'	🍃🍃🍃	🍃🍃🍃	🍃🍃🍃	🍃🍃🍃	100	200+	▫	All gold form. Scorches in sun, best in light shade

🍃 *in leaf*

Poa

The genus that lent the grass family, the Poaceae, its name may be expected to be common in cultivation but in fact relatively few of this largely evergreen, small-statured genus are widely grown. None are particularly large, reaching a maximum of around 90cm (3ft) in flower, and the flowers themselves are not particularly showy.

Poa colensoi

Poa labillardierei

Most species prefer nutrient poor, well drained soils in full sun, and adapt well to pot culture in free-draining composts.

The two largest species grown are *P. chaixii*, broad leaved meadow grass, which forms a clump up to 40cm (16in) tall and wide and flower stems up to 90cm (3ft), and *P. labillardierei*, a New Zealand grass whose tufts can reach 60cm (2ft), and 90cm (3ft) across, first upright then arching. *P. chaixii* copes with more shade than other poas, mixing well with Millium, Deschampsia and Luzula cultivars, forming substantial clumps of bright, evergreen leaves, with attractive if insubstantial purple-tinged flowerheads. *P. labillardierei* has narrower, blue-green evergreen foliage, going well with silver leaved grasses and other plants. It needs full sun, free drainage, and may not be reliably hardy in colder areas.

P. colensoi, also from New Zealand, has narrow, cylindrical blue leaves that rival the blueness of the better *Festuca glauca* cultivars, forming clumps 20cm (8in) high and about the same across, but unlike festucas it is evergreen (or everblue). *P. x jemtlandica* is an oddity whose embryos germinate early, while still attached to the parent, forming little plantlets rather than seed. In *P. x jemtlandica* the plantlets have an attractive red tinge. It forms low clumps of grey-green leaves only 10cm (4in) high, slightly broader, and is deciduous, preferring full sun. Finally, *P. alpina* is a true alpine, reaching only 4cm (1½in) in height and spreading to only 15cm (6in). The short, mid-green leaves are stiff and prickly. It needs free-drainage and full sun, associating better with other mat-forming alpine plants than other grasses.

site	Full sun. Cope well with exposure, except *P. chaixii*, part shade
soil	Poor and on the dry side preferred, not fussy about pH
watering	Should only require watering in extended dry periods, except *P. chaixii*, which likes even moisture
general care	Easy to grow and adaptable, largely evergreen grasses. Comb out and cut back dead leaves of clumps in spring
pests & diseases	Culturally, all bar *P. chaixii* do badly in prolonged winter wetness unless on very free draining soils

P Bamboos & Grasses

	SPRING	SUMMER	AUTUMN	WINTER	height (cm)	spread (cm)	leaf colour	
Poa alpina					10	15		Tiny alpine grass
P. chaixii					90	45		Broad leaved, good in shade
P. colensoi					20	20		Rivals *Festuca glauca* for blueness
P. x jemtlandica					10	15		Viviparous – produces plantlets rather than seed
P. labillardierei					90	90		Evergreen New Zealand grass; not the hardiest

🌿 in leaf   ❋ flowering

Polypogon monspeliensis

Annual beard grass

An annual grass species native to Britain and most of Europe usually grown for drying, *Polypogon monspeliensis* is an attractive, mid-green, clump forming species whose narrow leaf mound reaches some 50cm (20in) by 35cm (14in).

P. monspeliensis flowers copiously, like many annual grasses, producing dense, cylindrical, silky then bristly-looking yellow-green flower spikes like the mini-bulrushes of Timothy grass, up to 15cm (6in) long on upright, animated flower stems that can reach 75 cm (30in). It prefers an open position in full sun, but unlike many other annual species it does not bleach to straw as the seeds of the first flush of flowers mature, instead producing a succession of flowers through the summer, fading abruptly with the onset of shorter days in autumn. Flowers should be cut while still relatively young to dry well.

Polypogon monspeliensis

Polypogon monspeliensis

Annual beard grass is happy on most soils, but prefers more moisture and favours richer soils than many annual species. It is commonly added to annual meadow seed mixes, acting as a good foil to annual flowers such as poppies, cornflowers and Nigella (love-in-the-mist), and to grasses with more airy flowerheads such as Agrostis, Aria and Panicum. It can be raised in modules for planting out, but it is fully hardy, so can be sown in situ wherever it is to flower in autumn or early spring.

site	Site should be in full sun. This plant is both exposure- and salt-tolerant
soil	Moist preferred, and likes richer soils than most annual species
watering	Keep evenly moist, particularly at the seedling stage, Not as drought tolerant as most annual grasses
general care	Annual grass with a longer flowering season than most, but can self-seed unless dead-headed
pests & diseases	No real pest or disease problems. Culturally, only extended dryness causes difficulties

Polypogon monspeliensis

P. monspeliensis self-seeds widely, so deadhead it after flowering to avoid seedlings appearing the following year. This tendency has made it a relatively common non-native weed grass in North America, Australia and even Egypt, particularly in wet and marshy areas.

In its native regions, *P. monspeliensis* is most commonly found in coastal areas, so it is a good choice for seaside gardens that suffer from salt spray.

Bamboos & Grasses

Pseudosasa

A small bamboo genus with similarities to the better known Sasa, Pseudosasa are large leaved bamboos but fairly compact, usually producing a single branch at each node. They are running (leptomorphic) species like Sasa and Indocalamus, but much less invasive than either of these genera, and better suited to use as screens or hedges in average sized gardens.

Pseudosasa japonica var. pleioblastoides

Pseudosasa japonica 'Tsutsumiana'

These bamboos will also do well in shade, and without being forefront specimen plants, their large leaves and evergreen nature add an instant sub-tropical note.

The best known species is *Pseudosasa japonica*, reliably hardy to -23°C (-10°F) and reaching a maximum 4m (13ft), although usually considerably less, with broad leaves up to 30cm (12in) long. Even though it is fully hardy, its leaves can brown in cold snaps, so it is not to be recommended for the coldest areas. Two attractive variegated cultivars are available – 'Akebonosuji', which has leaves boldly striped with bright yellow, and 'Akebono', in which each leaf grades from green at the base to yellow-white at the tip, probably selected from it. *P. japonica* 'Tsutsumiana' has swollen, elongated internodes on its mature culms; however, as the culm sheaths of Pseudosasa are persistent and do not shed, these are masked unless deliberately exposed. All three cultivars are smaller and slower growing than the species. *P.japonica* var. *pleioblastoides*, previously classed as a separate species, is very similar, reaching 4.5m (15ft), but more upright with smaller, narrower leaves. It is just as exposure tolerant.

site	From full sun to quite deep shade, exposure tolerant, some species extremely so
soil	Unfussy, prefer permanently moist but drought tolerant when established
watering	Watering is only necessary during establishment or in extended dry spells to avoid leaf browning
general care	Low maintenance bamboos. Run a little at the roots, but much less so than other large leaved bamboos
pests & diseases	No real pest or disease problems. Cuturally, only likely to suffer on very dry, exposed sites

Pseudosasa amabilis is much larger, to 13m (43ft) with leaves to 30cm (12in), requiring a warm spot and temperatures no lower than -10°C (14°F). The culms are upright, ageing yellow, and branchless in their lower parts. It is extensively grown for garden canes in parts of China. At the other extreme, *P. owatarii* is an extremely ornamental dwarf bamboo, sadly rare as yet, reaching a maximum 1m (39in) but usually half that, and leaves to 8cm (3in). It is superficially similar to *Pleioblastus pygmaeus*, but better behaved, spreading so slowly that it can grace the smallest gardens, also taking clipping to shape well.

	SPRING	SUMMER	AUTUMN	WINTER	height (cm)	spread (cm)	culm colour	
Pseudosasa amabilis	leaf	leaf	leaf	leaf	130	600+		Large, handsome bamboo but not hardiest
P. japonica	leaf	leaf	leaf	leaf	400	400+		Tough and hardy, good hedge or windbreak
P. japonica 'Akebonosuji'	leaf	leaf	leaf	leaf	300	400+		Divide frequently, discarding all-green culms
P. japonica 'Akebono'	leaf	leaf	leaf	leaf	300	400+		Leaf shades from green at base to yellow-white at tips. Rare
P. japonica var. *pleioblastoides*	leaf	leaf	leaf	leaf	450	400+		Similiar to *P. japonica*; more upright and smaller leaves
P. japonica 'Tsutsumiana'	leaf	leaf	leaf	leaf	300	400+		Swollen nodes, difficult to see beneath culm sheaths
P. owatarii	leaf	leaf	leaf	leaf	100	400+		Lovely dwarf bamboo, slow spreader. Rare

in leaf

Saccharum
Ravenna grasses

Ravenna grasses are large, statuesque and imposing grasses built along similar lines to pampass grasses. Unfortunately, they are one of the grass genera that prefer longer, hotter summers than the temperate climate typically offers. This preference extends to the point where their growth seemingly does not have time to fully 'ripen' and is often badly affected by early autumn cold snaps, making these grasses less than reliable outside the warmest areas.

The most widely cultivated species is *Saccharum officinarum*, sugar cane, one of the world's most important food crops, but this is a sub-tropical species seldom grown outdoors in temperate regions.

In the USA, *S. ravennae* produces huge flower plumes up to 3.6m (12ft) tall, looking like elongated, silvery pampass grass plumes, the flowerheads themselves up to 60cm (2ft) long, appearing in early autumn and lasting well into winter. These rise from substantial clumps of arching, dark green leaves that produce shades of orange and purple as they die back in autumn. Even in warmer temperate regions, ravenna grass usually betrays its unhappiness by growing to only 90cm (3ft), and if flowers are produced at all they are slender, rarely above 1.5m (5ft), and often break in strong winds. It can grow well in the warmest, most sheltered parts of temperate regions, particularly placed at the foot of a south-facing wall, and is undeniably spectacular in full flower, but may be a grass for the future if global warming does raise summer temperatures.

S. brevibarbe var. *contortum*, bent awn plume grass, is considerably smaller, reaching around 60cm (2ft) with upright, silky, elongated flowerheads with conspicuously bent hairs (awns) tipping each individual flower and seed. It prefers moist to wet soils and full sun, but as a native to a swathe of the southern United States, it also seems to need warmer summers than ours to thrive and flower well and its hardiness is questionable.

Saccharum ravennae

site	Sites should be as sheltered and warm as possible for these plants
soil	*S. ravennae* prefers free-draining soils, *S. brevibarbe* var. *contortum*, moisture
watering	Evenly moist in summer, and drier in winter is the ideal. Little else is required regarding watering
general care	Not reliably hardy in most temperate areas, needing long hot summers to flower well
pests & diseases	Relatively trouble free from pest or disease problems. Culturally, winter cold and wet can prove fatal

	SPRING	SUMMER	AUTUMN	WINTER	height (cm)	spread (cm)	leaf colour	
S. brevibarbe var. *contortum*		in leaf	flowering		90	90		Attractive but less than hardy
S. ravennae		in leaf	flowering		150	120		Spectacular in warmer climes

⬿ *in leaf*   ✺ *flowering*

Bamboos & Grasses

Sasa

Sasa is perhaps the genus that gave bamboos their reputation for invasiveness in the West. Much planted in Victorian and Edwardian times, they are large leaved, tropical-looking, hardy and relatively short plants.

Sasa veitchii

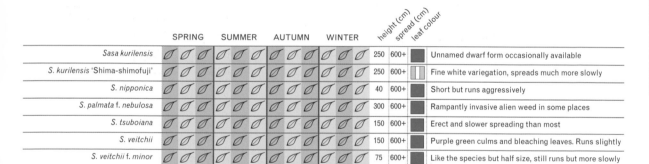

Sasa palmata f. nebulosa

Often slow to establish, once they do, their growth is best described as 'rampant'. These are not bamboos for the open garden, unless the space is large and a jungly grove is the desired effect. They can be constrained in large containers or isolated beds, but rhizome barriers need to be stout and deep to hold back these plants' seemingly telescopic root systems.

The most useful Sasa are small, but even these can run to excess. *S. nipponica* reaches only 40cm (16in) with leaves up to 15cm (6in), but can still be invasive and is best used as ground cover under trees or confined to a pot. *Sasa veitchii* reaches 1.5m (5ft) with leaves to 25cm (10in), the margins of which bleach prominently to a parchment colour in winter. It is probably the slowest spreader in the genus, though still should be planted with care. A dwarf version, f. *minor*, is around half the size and slower spreading *Sasa tsuboiana* is of similar size and vigour, but more erect growing with less prominent leaf bleaching.

The real thugs of the genus are *Sasa palmata*, capable of 3m (10ft) and nearly always encountered as f. *nebulosa*, named for the cloud like patterning of brown on older culms. The species has leapt the fence of several Victorian gardens and is 'naturalized' (invading) in some areas. A plant that should come with a health warning, it can no longer be recommended for garden use.

Sasa kurilensis, the most northerly growing of all bamboos, reaches 2.5m (8ft) and has attractive yellow culms but is nearly as rampant as *S. palmata*. A lovely variegated cultivar, 'Shima-shimofuji', its leaves generously banded with fine white stripes, can grow as large as the species but is much less invasive.

site	Full sun to part shade preferred, fairly exposure tolerant and very hardy
soil	Do well on all soils other than waterlogged or extremely dry
watering	Like moisture, but drought tolerant. Restricting watering and thinning out older culms slows spread
general care	Can be slow to settle, but once established run rapidly over large areas. Site with care or physically constrain
pests & diseases	Relatively trouble free as there are not usually any problems in terms of pests and diseases

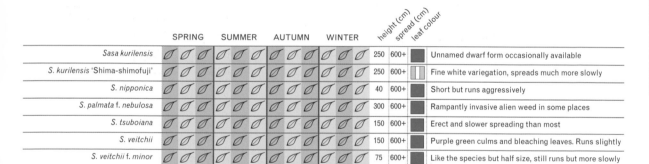

	SPRING	SUMMER	AUTUMN	WINTER	height (cm)	spread (cm)	leaf colour	
Sasa kurilensis	🍃🍃🍃	🍃🍃🍃	🍃🍃🍃	🍃🍃🍃	250	600+		Unnamed dwarf form occasionally available
S. kurilensis 'Shima-shimofuji'	🍃🍃🍃	🍃🍃🍃	🍃🍃🍃	🍃🍃🍃	250	600+		Fine white variegation, spreads much more slowly
S. nipponica	🍃🍃🍃	🍃🍃🍃	🍃🍃🍃	🍃🍃🍃	40	600+		Short but runs aggressively
S. palmata f. *nebulosa*	🍃🍃🍃	🍃🍃🍃	🍃🍃🍃	🍃🍃🍃	300	600+		Rampantly invasive alien weed in some places
S. tsuboiana	🍃🍃🍃	🍃🍃🍃	🍃🍃🍃	🍃🍃🍃	150	600+		Erect and slower spreading than most
S. veitchii	🍃🍃🍃	🍃🍃🍃	🍃🍃🍃	🍃🍃🍃	150	600+		Purple green culms and bleaching leaves. Runs slightly
S. veitchii f. *minor*	🍃🍃🍃	🍃🍃🍃	🍃🍃🍃	🍃🍃🍃	75	600+		Like the species but half size, still runs but more slowly

🍃 *in leaf*

Sasaella

Members of this genus are so similar to Sasa species that even bamboo experts can find it difficult to distinguish between them. The leaves tend to be smaller than those of Sasa and more narrow, but their leptomorphic (running) rhizomes are just as invasive and best physically constrained in large pots or behind rhizome barriers, and only planted out where space is available and rapid ground cover wanted.

Sasaella masamuneana 'Albostriata'

Sasaella masamuneana f. *aureostriata*

The culms of *Sasaella masamuneana* grow to 1m (39in), with leaves to 18cm (7in), but the plain green species is so invasive that it is rarely seen in cultivation. Its two variegated forms spread a little more slowly, making them perhaps semi-rampant. 'Albostriata' has irregular bold white striping on newly emerged leaves that fade to a more yellowy colour as they age and is undeniably ornamental. Forma *aureostriata* is less vigorous, and less ornamental, with larger leaves and dull yellow stripes that fade back to near-green over the growing season; these are inconstant, many leaves being plain green.

The only other widely cultivated species is *S. ramosa*, a native of Japan which is

site	Any site from full sun to part shade, as they are exposure tolerant
soil	These plants are generally unfussy, and will grow in all but the driest spots
watering	Evenly moist is preferred but it is fairly drought tolerant once established. Little else is required
general care	Rampantly invasive running bamboos that will grow almost anywhere. Site with care
pests & diseases	Relatively trouble free, as there are not usually any problems in terms of pests and diseases

around the same height as *S. masamuneana*, with smaller, narrower leaves held in distinctive and attractive palm-like fan shapes. It is a lovely plant, but has been described even by bamboo enthusiasts as 'probably the most invasive bamboo in cultivation, and not a species to introduce into any garden'. Even extensive flowering during the 1980s, which can cause dieback and even death in many bamboo species, seems not to have checked its vigour. However attractive and compact some of the resulting seedling plants may prove, like *Sasa palmata*, they should be sold with a health warning given their potential to establish as an exotic weed in the wider countryside.

Sasaella masamuneana 'Albostriata'

S

Bamboos & Grasses

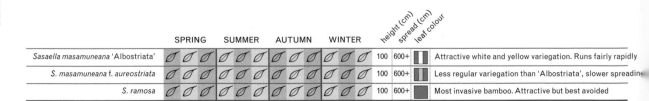

	SPRING	SUMMER	AUTUMN	WINTER	height (cm)	spread (cm)	leaf colour	
Sasaella masamuneana 'Albostriata'	🌿🌿🌿	🌿🌿🌿	🌿🌿🌿	🌿🌿🌿	100	600+		Attractive white and yellow variegation. Runs fairly rapidly
S. masamuneana f. aureostriata	🌿🌿🌿	🌿🌿🌿	🌿🌿🌿	🌿🌿🌿	100	600+		Less regular variegation than 'Albostriata', slower spreading
S. ramosa	🌿🌿🌿	🌿🌿🌿	🌿🌿🌿	🌿🌿🌿	100	600+		Most invasive bamboo. Attractive but best avoided

🌿 *in leaf*

Schoenoplectus

Bulrushes *or*
clubrushes

Confusingly, the true bulrushes, Schoenoplectus, are members of the sedge family, the Cyperacea. It comes as a surprise that they are not instead from the rush family, Juncaceae, but like them they are adapted for life as aquatic emergents.

Schoenoplectus tabernaemontani 'Albescens'

Although they are smaller and (arguably) more attractive than Phragmites, common reeds, they do spread at the root, if more slowly than the reeds, so are best grown in pots in smaller ponds. What look like ramrod-straight leaves are actually hollow stems that have taken over photosynthetic duties, with the true leaves reduced to small sheaths, much as in horsetails.

The true bulrush, *S. lacustris*, has grey-green stems and used to be a familiar sight in the British countryside around ponds, watercourses and drainage ditches. It reaches 1.5m (5ft), spreading to about 1.8m (6ft) clumps, and produces brown flowers in late summer. The flowers appear to be produced around three quarters of the way up the stem but are actually held at the tip; the end of the 'stem' is actually surmounted by two green bracts that extend it. It is an excellent plant for wildlife ponds and larger bog gardens, but much more ornamental for garden ponds are two variegated selections of *S. lacustris* subsp. *tabernaemontani*, 'Albescens' and 'Zebrinus'. 'Albescens' reaches to 1.8m (6ft) in flower, forming clumps of vertical, white-striped stems that

are more white than green, while 'Zebrinus' is unusually striped with horizontal bands. Both spread relatively slowly, forming clumps to a maximum of 1.2m (4ft) across.

Bulrushes should be grown with no more than 10cm (3in) of water over their rootballs, and can be acclimatized to bog gardens but suffer badly in droughts; this applies particularly to the less vigorous variegated selections. They mix well with other upright semi-aquatics like reeds, reedmaces (Typha), and horsetails. The variegated forms can pick up the highlights of coloured-leaved and variegated sedges, while their strong vertical lines contrast nicely with the fine foliage of ferns and broadleaved herbaceous perennial moisture lovers such as hostas and Ligularia.

site	Full sun and permanently wet, ideally in water as emergents
soil	Unfussy about pH and texture as long as permanently waterlogged
watering	As emergents, rootball should always be below the water. In bog gardens, keep permanently wet
general care	Easy to grow and reliably hardy. Cut out older, damaged leaves and dead flower stems in spring
pests & diseases	Relatively trouble free from pest and disease problems. Culturally, they react badly to drying out

	SPRING	SUMMER	AUTUMN	WINTER	height (cm)	spread (cm)	flower colour	
Schoenoplectus lacustris		⚘⚘⚘⚘	⚘⚘		150	180		UK native bulrush
S. l. s. tabernaemontani 'Albescens'		⚘⚘⚘⚘	⚘⚘		150	120		Lovely vertically striped variegated form
S. l. s. tabernaemontani 'Zebrinus'		⚘⚘⚘⚘	⚘⚘		150	120		Unusual horizontally-banded variegation

🖉 *in leaf*   ⚘ *flowering*

Bamboos & Grasses

Schoenus pauciflorus

Schoenus pauciflorus is a beautiful sedge from New Zealand that does a very passable imitation of being a rush. What look like the leaves are actually stems; the leaves themselves are reduced to sheath-like structures wrapped around the lower part of each stem. These are coloured red and are thus particularly attractive set against the stems that they envelop.

The stems are green in their lower parts, but increasingly maroon-brown towards the tip, giving the whole plant a reddish-brown tinge from a distance. The stems can reach 90cm (3ft) in boggy ground, forming clumps to 60cm (2ft) across, but it needs full sun to produce the best red colouring.

This plant is virtually evergreen, the stems lasting well through the winter and only looking tatty in early spring, when they can be cut back to allow the fresh, well-coloured new growth to come through.

Unlike the rushes it resembles, *S. pauciflorus* will grow happily in moist soils that never get too dry, although the drier the conditions, the shorter the plant. It does flower reliably, in spring to early summer, but these are small and dull even for a sedge, and often unnoticed. Its compact nature and slow growth rate make it an excellent choice for growing in a pot.

Schoenus pauciflorus

S. pauciflorus' dark leaves make it an excellent foil for smaller, lighter-coloured sedges placed in front of it, such as yellow *Carex aurea* and *Carex elata* 'Aurea', smaller yellow hosta cultivars, blue toned sedges like *Carex trifida* 'Chatham Blue' or *Poa colensoi*. The brown leaved New Zealand sedges like

Schoenus pauciflorus

Carex comans and *C. buchananii* harmonize well with it, being essentially similar in colouring but in lighter shades. Virtually any small variegated plant placed in front of *S. pauciflorus*' unusual background colouring

Schoenus pauciflorus

will be thrown into high relief. *Carex morrowii* 'Variegata' or *C. oshimensis* 'Evergold' are obvious choices, and *Imperata cylindrica* 'Rubra', Japanese bloodgrass, is a stunning companion with contrasting colour.

In its native New Zealand, particularly the North Island, *Schoenus pauciflorus* is a pioneer species, often among the first plants to colonise bare or disturbed ground, and is popular with gardeners and environmental managers for its value to wildlife.

site	This plant colours best in full sun, and it copes well with exposure
soil	More tolerant of dry soils than many sedges, but gets largest on wet soils
watering	Keep evenly moist, particularly during initial establishment; otherwise, little else is required
general care	Easy to grow and care for. A low-maintenance sedge needing only an annual spring spruce-up
pests & diseases	Relatively free from real pest or disease problems, and cultural problems only in prolonged dry periods

Semiarundinaria

Semiarundinaria is an odd bamboo genus; several experts consider its 'species' are actually sterile hybrids between various Phyllostachys and Pleioblastus, since its characteristics are a mixture of the two.

Semiarundinaria yashadake

Semiarundinaria have leptomorphic (running) rhizomes, but like Phyllostachys, few run to excess and are reliably clumping in habit. They are fairly tall, and tolerant enough of exposure to make good windbreaks and hedges.

Semiarundinaria fastuosa is the best known species, reaching up to 8m (26ft), but nearer 5m (16ft) in colder climates, spreading slowly. The culms emerge green, but age to a beautiful red-purple in sun. The leaves are fairly large at up to 15cm (6in) and quite narrow. Its green-culmed variety *viridis* is larger, reaching 12m (40ft). *S. kagamiana* is similar, growing up to 10m (33ft), nearer 4m (13ft) in temperate areas with thinner purplish culms and smaller leaves. Even newer to garden cultivation is *S. makinoi*, again similar to *S. fastuosa*, reaching 10m (33ft) in the wild, shorter here, with an arching, umbrella-like habit, and spreads relatively rapidly.

Semiarundinaria kagamiana

S. yashadake has leaves to 15cm (6in), and is dark green in both culms and leaves, usually making 3–5m (10–16ft), and is a stately plant good in both sun and semi-shade. *S. yashadake* f. *kimmei* has yellow culms striped green, often emerging pink-tinged, and leaves striped with fine, creamy-yellow variegation, reaching around 2.5m (8ft). It spreads, but not excessively. *S. lubrica* is similar to *S. yashadake*, with dark green leaves and culms. Similarly rare is *S. okuboi*, with green culms ageing an attractive yellow green and leaves clustered at the ends of the branches.

S. yamadorii is probably the fastest-spreading Semiarundinaria, but is still nowhere near as invasive as most running species. It grows to 7m (23ft), usually less, and the weight of the leaves makes the culms arch gracefully, which is unusual in such an upright genus.

site	Any site from full sun to semi-shade, and relatively exposure tolerant
soil	Happy in most soil types and pH, dislikes extremes of dryness and waterlogging
watering	Evenly moist preferred, but relatively drought tolerant once established, so little irrigation should be needed
general care	Easy to grow and not too invasive. Cut out dead and thin culms annually. Not suited to small gardens
pests & diseases	No pest or disease problems. Culturally, only prolonged sogginess or drought detrimental

	SPRING	SUMMER	AUTUMN	WINTER	height (cm)	spread (cm)	culm colour	
Semiarundinaria fastuosa	in leaf	in leaf	in leaf	in leaf	800	400+		One of the best specimen bamboos
S. fastuosa var. *viridis*	in leaf	in leaf	in leaf	in leaf	1200	400+		More vigorous form whose culms stay green
S. kagamiana	in leaf	in leaf	in leaf	in leaf	1000	600+		Similar to *S. fastuosa*
S. lubrica	in leaf	in leaf	in leaf	in leaf	800	400+		Dark and brooding
S. makinoi	in leaf	in leaf	in leaf	in leaf	1000	600+		Can run at the roots; relatively rare
S. okuboi	in leaf	in leaf	in leaf	in leaf	700	400+		Leaves clustered at ends of branches; distinctive but rare
S. yamadorii	in leaf	in leaf	in leaf	in leaf	700	400+		Elegant arching habit; zig-zag older culms
S. yamadorii 'Brimscombe'	in leaf	in leaf	in leaf	in leaf	500	400+		Less vigorous variegated form
S. yashadake	in leaf	in leaf	in leaf	in leaf	800	400+		Another dark and brooding looking species
S. yashadake f. *kimmei*	in leaf	in leaf	in leaf	in leaf	500	400+		Yellow culms striped green, contrast with dark green leaves

in leaf

Sesleria
Moor grasses

Sesleria, the moor grasses, are hardy, adaptable and useful plants for full sun or light shade that deserve to be more widely grown. They are for the most part evergreen, though overwintered foliage can look tatty and is best cut back before the new growth comes through, mixing well with other compact grass species such as Festuca and Panicum, or even making good alternative, evergreen lawns planted in blocks.

These grasses tend to have the most impact placed in groups of at least three or five rather than as single specimens. *Sesleria autumnalis*, autumn moor grass, usually begins flowering in mid-summer and lasts well into autumn; however, it can begin to bloom as early as spring, producing fat, purplish black spikes up to 15cm (6in) long on long stalks that open silvery. These contrast nicely with the bright, yellow-green leaves that form bold evergreen clumps up to 45cm (18in) tall. *S. heufleriana*, green moor grass, is smaller, to 30cm (12in), with dark brown flower spikes in early spring. These are held on stems to 75cm (30in) above the mid-green leaves that arch, showing their silvery undersides. It is a lovely plant to mix with similarly early flowering bulbs and shrubs. *S. sadleriana* also has a two-tone effect, its broad, fresh green leaves having pale silver undersides, forming clumps to 40cm (15in) high and across.

S. caerulea, blue moor grass, reaches only 15cm (6in) and also has the two-tone effect, the upper leaf surfaces being an attractive matt blue-green and the undersides a deep shiny green. It is a British native and also flowers early, late spring to early summer, but produces dense little violet to silver grey 'pom-poms' at the tips of short stems. *S. nitida* is bigger and bluer, producing arching clumps of leaves that are blue on both surfaces up to 60cm (2ft) tall. It flowers around the same time as *S. caerulea* producing pale grey, cigar shaped flowerheads on stems to 90cm (3ft).

Sesleria autumnalis

site	This plant is fairly unfussy; will take full sun and exposure as well as shade
soil	Happy in most soils with no marked preference for pH, including poor and dry soils
watering	Prefers evenly moist, though it is generally drought tolerant once established
general care	Easy to grow, amenable grasses that do not run or self-seed to excess. Little is required
pests & diseases	Relatively trouble free as there are usually no problems in terms of pests and diseases

	SPRING	SUMMER	AUTUMN	WINTER	height (cm)	spread (cm)	leaf colour	
Sesleria autumnalis					45	60		Attractive and underrated evergreen grass
S. caerulea					15	30		Compact and mat-forming blue grass
S. heufleriana					75	60		Green leaves and silvery undersides
S. nitida					90	90		One of the better blue-leaved grasses
S. sadleriana					40	60		Green leaves with silver undersides

in leaf   flowering

Setaria
Foxtail millets

Perhaps the showiest of all the annual grasses, there are several species of Setaria that go by the same common name of foxtail millet. They are tall-growing for annual grasses, 90cm (3ft) not being uncommon, with broad, relatively coarse leaves forming loose clumps.

The flowers of these grasses are spectacular, looking like vivid green, conspicuously hairy caterpillars, the long hairs (awns) often beautifully purple tinged. Their sheer size and weight causes the stems to arch over characteristically, so that the flowerhead often droops to touch the leaves. Foxtail millets are so unusual looking that they can be difficult to place in the garden. They need full sun and appreciate sheltered conditions, and although they do combine well with other annual and perennial grasses, their conspicuous flowers tend to steal the show.

Setaria macrostachya is the species most frequently encountered. It is late to emerge, the seedlings not appearing above ground until late spring or early summer, but then grows rapidly to 90cm (3ft), forming a narrow clump to 30cm (12in) across of fresh green leaves. Flowering begins in mid-summer and lasts well into autumn, when the seeds are shed and the plant bleaches to straw and dies back. The flowerheads dry well if cut before the seeds begin to be shed,

Setaria macrostachya

site	Sites with full sun and that are sheltered are preferred by this plant
soil	Happy in most soils except permanently wet or very free draining
watering	Evenly moist, but avoid overwatering, particularly in cooler springs. Little else is required
general care	Amenable grasses with spectacular flowering performance. Flowers last well for annuals
pests & diseases	Relatively free from real pest or disease problems. Culturally, dislike late frosts and waterlogging

but when hung upside drown to dry, they usually straighten out, losing the characteristic arching shape. Also worth growing if you can locate a seed supplier is *S. viridis*, yellow bristle grass, which is similar in most respects to *S. macrostachya* but actually has greyish green foliage and yellow tinged flowers with a reddish rather than purple tinge to the awns.

Setaria are best sown where they are to flower in spring; keep an eye out for emerging seedlings and protect them from any unseasonably late frosts. They can be raised indoors, but need high light levels.

Setaria macrostachya

	SPRING	SUMMER	AUTUMN	WINTER	height (cm)	spread (cm)	leaf colour	
Setaria macrostachya		🌱 ● ● ● ●	● ●		90	30		One of the showiest annual grasses
S. viridis		🌱 ● ● ● ●	● ●		90	30		Similar but more yellow-red flowerheads

🌱 in leaf   ● flowering

Shibataea

Again, I have to admit to some personal bias, but Shibataea are compact, non-invasive and supremely elegant small bamboos that rarely top 60cm (2ft), and are underused and underappreciated in the West.

Shibataea kumasaca

They form dense little thickets with short, wide leaves only 8cm (3in) long, the distance between the nodes on their slender culms being very short, as are the branches. The tips of the leaves often bleach in the winter, giving an attractive variegated effect. Hailing from Japan and China, they are some of the best small bamboos for Japanese gardens and also look good planted in gravel gardens or large pots, or as foreground plants in front of larger bamboos. They will take full sun, but excel in semi-shade. Perhaps their only negative point is that they require an acid soil and hate lime, so on chalk or limestone soils are best grown in a pot of loam-based (John Innes-type) ericaceous compost.

The best known species is *Shibataea kumasaca*. It can reach 1.8m (6ft) in Japan, but in colder climates rarely makes half that and more usually forms a dense clump to 60cm (2ft) tall. The leaves emerge mid-green but age to an attractive yellow-green, and there are usually only one or two leaves per branch. Some

Shibataea kumasaca

growers prefer to thin out all the older culms as the leaves emerge from the new shoots, but this is not strictly necessary. *S. kumasaca* evolved to enjoy the warm, wet summers of Japan and although it is reliably hardy, it may not do so well in cooler northern climes. It dislikes being droughted, so may need watering regularly during dry spells, particularly if grown in full sun. A lovely variegated form, f. *aureostriata*, with bold, creamy variegation is occasionally offered for sale but is even slower growing than the species.

S. chinensis is the only other species commonly encountered, though there may be more introductions to come. It is very similar to *S. kumasaca*, but even smaller, reaching only 1m (39in), less in cultivation. The leaves are more oval, and usefully it is

site	Prefers shelter and part shade, though will take full sun and some exposure
soil	Evenly moist soil and lime free soil is ideal for *S. kumasaca*
watering	These plants need to be kept moist to give their best, particularly in sun, but amenable in cultivation
general care	Easy to grow, neat little bamboos that are very slow spreaders. Culms can be thinned annually
pests & diseases	No real pest or disease problems. Poor growth usually due to lack of water or limy soils

	SPRING	SUMMER	AUTUMN	WINTER	height (cm)	spread (cm)	leaf colour	
Shibataea kumasaca	🍃🍃🍃	🍃🍃🍃	🍃🍃🍃	🍃🍃🍃	180	200+		Usually only 60cm tall in cultivation
S. kumasaca f. *aureostriata*	🍃🍃🍃	🍃🍃🍃	🍃🍃🍃	🍃🍃🍃	90	200+		Also to 60cm, slow growing
S. chinensis	🍃🍃🍃	🍃🍃🍃	🍃🍃🍃	🍃🍃🍃	100	200+		Even more compact in cultivation, 60cm max

🍃 in leaf

Sorghastrum nutans

Indian grass

A blue-foliaged grass that forms a major constituent of the US tall-grass prairies, *Sorghastrum nutans* or Indian grass is lovely used as a specimen in its own right, or does well mixed with other grasses such as Stipa and Miscanthus and tall perennials like Rudbeckia, Echinacea and Asters in the New European or prairie planting style.

It is particularly striking planted in groups or drifts with silver-leaved or purple neighbours. Like some other American grasses, although fully hardy it performs better in the hotter summers of continental climates, not growing anything like as large in a temperate climate. It does however flower more reliably than other warm-season grasses.

In the USA, *Sorghastrum nutans* varies from grey green to almost blue, taking on yellow and orange autumn colours and can grow as tall as 3m (10ft). In colder climates, it tends to be greener and reaches only 90cm (3ft) in flower, occasionally up to 1.5m (5ft), forming dense clumps up to 1m (39in) across. It flowers in late summer or early autumn, producing coppery-tan, densely branched panicles up to 15cm (6in) long and 7.5cm (3in) across held on stiff, yellowish stems. The whole plant turns bright yellow in late autumn, its structure and flowerheads lasting well into winter, although tending to collapse in spring. It is happy in most soils, including those that are fairly dry, but needs full sun to flower well. Several selections

Sorghastrum nutans

are becoming available, but only 'Indian Steel' is at present easy to find. This has bluer foliage than the species, also reaching 90cm (3ft) or so, with more reddish flowerheads, and has better autumn colour including purple and red shades.

Sorghastrum nutans

site	This plant needs sites with full sun to flower well but copes with exposure
soil	Unfussy, from fairly moist to dry and free draining. Tolerates lime
watering	Evenly moist is preferred, but the plant is fairly drought tolerant once established
general care	Easy to grow and amenable grass, though never reaches the stature of its home range in colder climates
pests & diseases	No real pest or disease problems. Not as sensitive to winter wet as many warm-climate grass species

Spartina pectinata

Prairie cord grass

Prairie cord grass is a fairly large North American species that forms arching clumps of dark green, narrow leaves up to 1.2m (4ft) long, reaching up and outwards to form clumps to 90cm (3ft) across. The leaves of this plant are unusually animated even for a grass, shifting easily in the slightest of breezes.

Spartina pectinata 'Aureomarginata'

It grows well in wetter soils, where it will spread at the root, but not excessively so, performing well in all but the driest of soils once established. The flower stems are up to 1.5m (5ft) tall, holding unusual green, comb-like spikelets upon which hang conspicuous purple anthers, from which the pollen is shed. The spikelets turn an attractive reddish brown as they age and seed is produced. This is well picked at any stage, even the anthers holding their colour fairly well. In autumn, the whole plant turns a rich butter-yellow, then pale fawn, lasting well through the winter.

The plain green form is less common in cultivation than *Spartina pectinata* 'Aureomarginata', which is an attractive variegated form of only marginally less vigour than the species. It has thin margins of a rich gold colour, obvious close up but making the plant look greyish-green from a distance. Variegated prairie cord grass looks good grouped with other moisture lovers such as horsetails and Phragmites, and the variegated forms of Schoenoplectus (bulrushes), or yellow-foliaged sedges such as *Carex aurea* and *Carex elata* 'Aurea', but is equally happy in ordinary garden soil that does not get too dry, where it can be contrasted with more upright grasses such as Stipa and the smaller Miscanthus cultivars. It can also be successfully grown in a pot provided it is never allowed to dry out completely.

site	Unfussy, any site from full sun to part shade. Tolerates some exposure
soil	From quite wet to normal garden soil, dislikes only extremes of dryness
watering	Evenly moist is preferred, but this plant is relatively drought tolerant once it has been established
general care	Easy to maintain and cultivate – an attractive deciduous grass with a long season of interest
pests & diseases	No real pest or disease problems. Cultural problems only on dry, exposed sites

Spodiopogon sibiricus

Another North American species of grass found over much of the Southern States, *Spodiopogon sibiricus* is a stiffly upright deciduous grass growing to 1.2m (4ft) and spreading nearly as far, with relatively broad, mid-green leaves held out horizontally or slightly below the horizontal, giving it a distinctive, almost bamboo-like outline.

Spodiopogon sibiricus produces attractive flowers in late summer and early autumn, forming fairly large, oval shaped panicles made up of green, grey and purple spikelets. These are merely the forerunner for its main seasonal show, however. From late summer onwards, the tips of the leaves take on a rich burgundy or purple hue that slowly seeps like a stain down each leaf blade. By mid-autumn, brighter tones of red and yellow

Spodiopogon sibiricus

also develop so that in a good autumn, it almost rivals the leaf colours of some maple species.

Spodiopogon is happy on most soils, with a preference for the more moisture retentive, and semi-shade, though it will grow happily enough in full sun if it does not go short of water. It also makes a good

site	Partial shade preferred, but will take full sun and some exposure kept moist
soil	This plant does best in permanently moist soils, but they can be of any pH
watering	Evenly moist is preferred; be prepared to water this plant very regularly, particularly those in pots
general care	Easy to maintain and cultivate, and amenable in cultivation, exceptional autumn colour
pests & diseases	Reltively trouble free from pest, disease or cultural problems. Reacts badly to droughting

Spodiopogon sibiricus

container plant if kept well watered. It is as yet relatively little known in cultivation and deserves to be more widely grown. It would combine well with other plants grown for their autumn effect, such as Michaelmas daisies (*Aster novi-belgii* and cultivars), Japanese anemones (*Anemone hupehensis* var. *japonica* and *Anemone* x *hybrida*, and cultivars) or *Sedum spectabile*, all of which should still be in flower as Spodiopogon's autumn colour develops. Other autumn interest grasses it comines well with are the purple forms of *Miscanthus sinensis*, which turn similar colours but have a contrasting weeping habit, *Molinia caerulea*, which turns first yellow then more amber, and *Panicum virgatum* 'Strictum', whose upright habit and butter yellow colouring contrast beautifully.

One evocative common name for this plant, graybeard grass, derives from the scientific name: 'spodios' is Greek for 'ashen' and 'pogon' means 'beard' – quite descriptive of the plant's hairy, open flowerheads that do appear greyish from a distance. If you squint.

Stenotapharum secundatum 'Variegatum'

Striped St Augustine grass

An unusual tender variegated grass that can be bedded out for the summer or grown permanently indoors, striped St Augustine grass is one of a rare breed – the indoor grasses.

It is a vigorous grower, spreading by horizontal stems (stolons) that creep fairly rapidly over the surface, throwing up short, broad leaves heavily striped with cream. It can be used for ground cover under the staging of heated greenhouses and makes an interesting, unusual subject for growing in hanging baskets, its stems trailing over the sides of the basket and cascading down the sides. The alternate, fairly broad, blunt-ended leaves make a plant grown in this way look more like a spider plant than a grass. Its bright variegated colouring and trailing habit make a pot of it an excellent contrast to plain green-leaved houseplants such as weeping figs and yuccas, though its vigour makes it unsuitable for planting in the same pot in houseplant arrangements.

Stenotapharum secundatum 'Variegatum'

S. secundatum 'Variegatum' prefers good light, tending to lose the vividness of its variegation indoors during the winter, and given its vigour is a greedy plant, requiring a rich, moist substrate and regular liquid feeds. It will not stand any degree of frost, but divisions can be bedded out in early summer if hardened off well and will quickly spread to form attractive, unusual tender ground cover or edging to similarly tender bedding plant displays. To overwinter, lift clumps before the first autumn frosts, pot up and cut back hard to within just over a thumb's width of the main crown of the plant. Keep on the dry side and in as light a position as possible over winter, and by the following spring lifted plants should have recovered their vigour and be growing away well.

Stenotapharum secundatum 'Variegatum'

site	Heated greenhouses and conservatories preferred. Grows outdoors in summer
soil	This plant likes even moisture, and a rich soil or compost
watering	Keep evenly moist. Reacts badly to drought, but keeping on the dry side can curb its vigour
general care	Tender species that will not tolerate frost but which need high light levels should it be kept indoors
pests & diseases	Indoors, red spider mite and aphids can be a problem. Treat with an appropriate pesticide

Stipa
Oat grasses

Together with Miscanthus, species and selections of Stipa were arguably the plants that established the use of grasses as ornamental garden plants in their own right during the latter part of the 20th century. While mostly deciduous, Stipa have great garden presence, forming clumps of attractive, often narrow leaves and flowering abundantly for long periods.

Stipa tenuissima

Stipa calamagrostis

Stipa can be divided into two groups, feather grasses, with airy, finely haired flowerheads that often persist for months like *Stipa tenuissima*, and needle grasses, which have long, sharp, needle-like awns (hairs). Stipa are native to prairies and Steppes, and do best in full sun on free-draining, dry soils. They are extremely free flowering, excellent in drifts and in prairie-style plantings, but as a group do not perform well in pots. After seed-set, several species can dieback completely and will look a mess in the garden if not cleared away.

Stipa gigantea is evergreen and unmistakeable, with dark green leaf mounds to around 75cm (30in). In late spring, huge, 1.8m (6ft) panicles of large, loose, oat-like spikelets appear, first gold, ageing golden brown and persisting well into winter. It is tough, drought resistant, relishes full sun and is spectacular in drifts. 'Gold Fontaene' ('Gold Fountain') has even larger, showier panicles. *S. grandis* is similar but smaller,

site	Full sun preferred, do not cope well with shade, but are exposure tolerant
soil	Free-draining to downright dry and low in nutrients preferred
watering	Once established should need watering only in extremely dry periods, very drought tolerant
general care	Easy to grow, accommodating and rewarding grasses. Can grow lax and floppy on overly rich soils
pests & diseases	No real pest and disease problems, Cultural problems usually associated with winter wet

with flowers to 1m (39in), as is *S. splendens*, slightly taller and broader-leaved than *S. grandis* at up to 1.3m (4.5ft), flowering later, in mid-summer.

Feather grasses

Among fine-leaved, feathery-flowered grasses, stipas reign supreme. The two most widely grown are *S. calamagrostis*, producing rounded mounds of narrow, arching foliage up to 90cm (3ft) high and across, and from early summer cloaked in

	SPRING	SUMMER	AUTUMN	WINTER	height (cm)	spread (cm)	leaf colour	
S. arundinacea (Anemanthele lessoniana)					100	100		Unusual colour, from New Zealand
S. barbata					45	45		Can go dormant after flowering
S. barbata 'Silver Feather'					45	45		Larger, more silvery flowers
S. calamagrostis					90	100		Long flowering season, reliable
S. capillata					90	60		Like a mini S. gigantea
S. extremiorientalis					120	100		Broad, yellowish leaves
S. gigantea					180	180		Evergreen; one of the showiest of all hardy grasses
S. gigantea 'Gold Fontaene'					180	180		Larger and more yellow-gold flowers

in leaf   *flowering*

Stipa arundinacea (Anemanthele lessoniana)

soft, feathery, greenish-white flower plumes held just above the foliage that gradually turn beige. These are produced throughout the summer right up until the first frosts. *Stipa tenuissima* is more upright, its leaves and flowers arching out in a 'shaving brush' effect. It produces similarly fine flower stems from late spring onwards and if anything is even more free-flowering.

Stipa barbata is smaller, forming a leaf mound to 45cm (18in), with white, wispy-awned flowerheads as much as 25cm (10in) long, even longer in the cultivar 'Silver Feather'. It flowers in mid-summer, and can die back and go dormant once seeds have set (collecting and sowing some seeds can be prudent). *S. pennata* is similar, if a little smaller, with more blue-green leaves reaching 75cm (30in) in flower.

Needle grasses

The needle grasses have sharper, spikier hairs (awns) than the silky, feathery appendages of the feather grass stipas. *S. capillata* is fairly typical, looking rather like a mini-version of *S. gigantea*, and better suited to smaller gardens. Its flower stems are up to 90cm (3ft) high, carrying long, thin spikelets above low-growing, desnse clumps of thin green leaves. *S. extremiorientalis* and *S. turkestanica* both have exceptionally long 'needles'. *S. extremiorientalis* can reach 1.2m (4ft) in flower, forming a rather yellow-green leaved clump spreading to 1m (39in), while *S. turkestanica* is darker and makes around 90cm (3ft) in height and spread. *S. lessingiana*, Steppe needle grass, is much smaller and blue-green in leaf, making compact clumps 60cm (2ft) high and 30cm (12in) across.

Completely atypical is a New Zealand grass still widely sold as *S. arundinacea* but correctly named *Anemanthele lessoniana*, which has chocolate brown new leaves, ageing to olive-green with bronzy overtones. It flowers in autumn with relatively small, lax, needle-type panicles and has good reddish autumn colour.

Stipa gigantea

	SPRING	SUMMER	AUTUMN	WINTER	height (cm)	spread (cm)	flower/leaf colour	
Stipa grandis					100	100		Handsome larger grass
S. lessingiana					60	30		Steppe needle grass, similar to *S. tenuissima*
S. offneri					100	60		Similar to *S. capillata*
S. pennata					45	45		Attractive blue hue, unusual in Stipa
S. pulcherrima					80	60		Silvery flower spikes, slow-growing
S. pulcherrima 'Windfeder'					80	60		Said to be freer-flowering and more silvery
S. splendens					130	100		Also like smaller version of *S. gigantea*
S. tenuifolia					45	45		Jade green leaves and beige flowers
S. tenuissima					75	60		One of the most popular grasses, arching shape
S. tenuissima 'Pony Tails'					75	60		Larger, lighter flowers than species
S. turkestanica					90	75		Good alternative to *S. gigantea* for small gardens

🍃 in leaf   ✹ flowering

Thamnocalamus

One of the most ornamental, graceful and underrated of bamboo genera, Thamnocalamus species have yet to gain widespread popularity. Most species are from relatively high altitudes in the Himalayas, with waxy culms, many branches and small leaves, and are reliably clump-forming (pachymorphic).

Thamnocalamus crassinodus 'Merlyn'

They will take full sun, although light shade is the ideal. In the wild, Thamnocalamus are often deciduous at higher altitudes, and in an exposed position may drop their leaves for the winter – don't despair, they will leaf out again in spring.

Thamnocalamus crassinodus is the most widely available species. Its culms reach 8m (26ft) in the wild, but are usually around 4m (13ft) in cultivation. It is naturally very variable, with small leaves (maximum 6cm/2.5in) and many branches. The culms have characteristic swellings above each node, emerging with a blue bloom, ageing to an attractive brownish-red. There are several named selections, the pick of which is 'Kew Beauty', with powder blue new culms ageing through green to a rich, deep red in sun, a colour that unusually also develops on the branches. The culms of 'Lang Tang' also emerge blue, ageing green, the leaves even smaller at barely an inch. It rarely tops 3.5m (11ft). 'Merlyn' has relatively thick culms, also emerging the attractive blue but ageing to a rich straw yellow, as are the branches.

T. spathiflorus produces thin-walled culms that emerge rich green, ageing to an unusual pinkish brown. Its leaves are much larger than those of *T. crassinodus*, at up to 12cm (5in). It can top 10m (33ft) in the wild but is usually less than half this in cultivation, around 4m (13ft). It can spread to cover substantial areas, albeit relatively slowly. The cultivar 'Aristatus' is similar to the species, but with old culms an attractive yellow-green. *T. aristatus* is rare, but a beautiful plant with slightly pendent foliage hanging from thick, yellow-green canes that develop a pale orange-red tint in sun. It makes around 3.5m (10ft) in cultivation.

Thamnocalamus crassinodus 'Lang Tang'

			site	Sites in full sun to part shade are preferred; some shelter is required

site	Sites in full sun to part shade are preferred; some shelter is required
soil	Generally unfussy, most soil types tolerated, evenly moist preferred
watering	Likes to be kept moist, water in dry spells although will cope with some dryness once established
general care	Easy to grow and attractive bamboos making good specimen plants. Thin old, weak and dead culms out
pests & diseases	No real pest or disease problems. Can drop leaves in cold, exposed sites, but leaf out again in spring

	SPRING	SUMMER	AUTUMN	WINTER	height (cm)	spread (cm)	culm colour	
Thamnocalamus aristatus	▱▱▱	▱▱▱	▱▱▱	▱▱▱	700	400+		Delicate looking but hardy, slightly pendent foliage
T. crassinodus	▱▱▱	▱▱▱	▱▱▱	▱▱▱	800	400+		Small leaved and elegant species
T. crassinodus 'Kew Beauty'	▱▱▱	▱▱▱	▱▱▱	▱▱▱	800	400+		Gorgeous cultivar, culms age from blue to green to red
T. crassinodus 'Lang Tang'	▱▱▱	▱▱▱	▱▱▱	▱▱▱	800	400+		Even smaller leaves, blue culms ageing green
T. crassinodus 'Merlyn'	▱▱▱	▱▱▱	▱▱▱	▱▱▱	800	400+		More leafy than other selections, yellow green culms
T. spathiflorus	▱▱▱	▱▱▱	▱▱▱	▱▱▱	1000	600+		Culms emerge green, age to unusual pinkish brown
T. spathiflorus 'Aristatus'	▱▱▱	▱▱▱	▱▱▱	▱▱▱	1000	600+		Like the species, more wind tolerant than most

▱ in leaf

Bamboos & Grasses

Typha
Reed maces

Typha are often called bulrushes in the vernacular, for their cigar-shaped brown flowers (in fact the true bulrush is *Schoenoplectus lacustris*, see p121). However, they are also known as reed maces or cats' tails, and are placed in their own family, the Typhaceae. Out-and-out moisture lovers, they grow best as emergents with their roots constantly submerged in water.

Typha laxmannii

Typha latifolia

All species run at the root, so unless space is available are probably best grown in pots sunk into ponds or pools, and the largest are too vigorous for smaller ponds and water features.

Typha latifolia, often called the bulrush, is an undeniably handsome British native, but can reach 3m (10ft). Its architectural ramrod-straight stems hold flat, blue-green leaves arching out to either side. Its flowers are like fat, brown cigars up to 30cm (12in) long and as much as 5cm (2in) thick, appearing in mid-summer and lasting well into winter, finally disintegrating into wispy parachutes that disperse the seeds. The rest of the plant turns yellow then brown in autumn, often collapsing, at which point the leaves should be cut back and discarded to avoid them decaying in the pond. It is not a plant for small gardens, but looks great with the similarly upright rushes, reeds and horsetails, or contrasted with lower, more arching sedges. Its variegated selection, 'Variegata', is striped with creamy white and is much less vigorous, reaching only 1.2m (4ft), but also has its parents' wandering root system.

Better choices for smaller ponds and the soggiest of bog gardens are *T. angustifolia*, lesser reed mace, essentially a smaller version of *T. latifolia* and also a British native, but growing to a more manageable 1.5m (5ft) at most. *T. minima* reaches only 60cm (2ft), with narrow, upright, grass-like foliage topped with shortened, more ball-like than cigar shaped flowers that emerge green ageing to brown. *T. laxmannii* has the same habit and flower structure but is larger, at up to 1.2m (4ft).

site	Best in ponds as emergents in full sun, smaller species will grow in bog gardens
soil	Generally unfussy, so long as permanently wet or waterlogged
watering	Water copiously at all times, as these plants react extremely badly to drought. Do not let them dry out
general care	Easy to maintain and cultivate to the point of invasive, but all species are best grown in containers
pests & diseases	Relatively trouble free from pest or disease problems. Culturally, dislike only dry conditions

	SPRING	SUMMER	AUTUMN	WINTER	height (cm)	spread (cm)	leaf colour	
Typha angustifolia					120	200+		Handsome but a bit of a thug – invasive!
T. latifolia					300	200+		More manageable, but still runs
T. latifolia 'Variegata'					120	200+		Attractively striped leaves
T. laxmannii					120	200+		Shortened, near-spherical flowers
T. minima					60	200+		Best choice for smaller ponds

in leaf   *flowering*

Uncinia
New Zealand hook sedges

The hook sedges are aptly named, as each seed has a stout, curved, distinctly hook-like spur designed to catch the fur (or clothes) of passing animals to aid seed dispersal. The hooks are small and sharp enough to catch in skin too, so handle these plants with care while they are in flower.

Uncinia uncinata rubra

Uncinia uncinata rubra

Uncinia are true sedges, members of the Cyperaceae, and from a distance look rather like the bronze-leaved New Zealand Carex species like *C. buchananii* and *C. uncifolia*. They prefer a partially shaded site that is at least permanently moist, but somewhat wetter than that would be ideal, and are evergreen. Well-coloured examples can rival the redness of *Imperata cylindrica* 'Rubra', Japanese blood grass, although their leathery matt evergreen leaves lack the translucent qualities of blood grass.

Close up, the differences between Carex and Uncinia are obvious. Uncinia have considerably broader, distinctly keeled leaves, as well as the hooked seedheads, and both species in common cultivation are much more richly coloured than the dull bronze and browns of New Zealand carex. *Uncinia uncinata rubra*, red or mahogany hook sedge (often sold as simply *U. rubra*), has leaves that are much more red than brown, growing to around 30cm (12in) tall and up to 90cm (3ft) across,

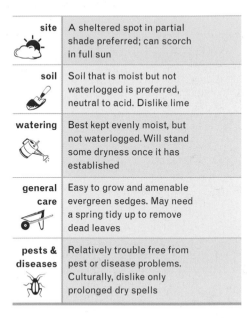

site	A sheltered spot in partial shade preferred; can scorch in full sun
soil	Soil that is moist but not waterlogged is preferred, neutral to acid. Dislike lime
watering	Best kept evenly moist, but not waterlogged. Will stand some dryness once it has established
general care	Easy to grow and amenable evergreen sedges. May need a spring tidy up to remove dead leaves
pests & diseases	Relatively trouble free from pest or disease problems. Culturally, dislike only prolonged dry spells

making an unusual splash of colour in shade and looking magnificent teamed with other coloured leaf sedges such as *Carex elata* 'Aurea' (Bowles' golden sedge) or even silvery-white *C. pendula* 'Moonraker', as well as plain green shade lovers like Luzula.

Uncinia egmontiana, orange hook sedge, is a more recent introduction, with a more upright growth pattern than *U. uncinata rubra*, with brighter, orange-red to downright crimson leaves. It grows to a similar size and has arresting black flowers and seedheads. These two hook sedges look good when grown together, subtly highlighting each others' leaf shades. Of the two, red hook sedge has the longer lasting flowers, which will often persist well into winter.

Bamboos & Grasses

	SPRING	SUMMER	AUTUMN	WINTER	height (cm)	spread (cm)	leaf colour	
Uncinia egmontiana	🌿🌿🌿	🌿●●	●●●	🌿🌿🌿	30	90		Orange hook sedge, unusual black flowers
U. uncinata rubra	🌿🌿🌿	🌿●●	●●●	🌿🌿🌿	30	90		Red hook sedge, easier to find

🌿 in leaf   ● flowering

Yushania

Yushania are bamboos that are technically clump-forming (pachymorphic) but can actually behave more like running species, though they are nowhere near as invasive as species of Sasa and Pleioblastus, and can be controlled with rhizome barriers or by snapping off emerging culms that wander too far from the main clump

Yushania anceps

Yushania maculata

These are tall, graceful, arching plants with relatively small leaves, making beautiful specimen bamboos for Oriental style gardens, and good, fine-leaved backgrounds for species such as bananas, cannas and tree ferns in the sub-tropical planting style. Given their tendency to wander, however, they are probably best avoided in small gardens and their root systems do not adapt well to container cultivation.

Yushania anceps is native to India and was introduced to the West as early as 1865. Depending on growing conditions, it can reach 4m (13ft) with leaves to 10cm (4in), but is often considerably smaller. Short growing plants are upright, but the weight of foliage causes taller culms to arch over gracefully, a characteristic of a particularly vigorous selection called 'Pitt White', after the garden in the English county of Devon

where it grows. All forms make fine hedges or screens, and have glossy green culms. *Y. maling* is rarer and looks very similar to *Y. anceps*, but can grow taller, reaching 10m (33ft) in the wild. The main differences are in culm colour, those of *Y. maling* being a grey-green, and culm texture, those of *Y. maling* being roughened and ridged while those of *Y. anceps* are smooth and shiny.

Y. maculata is relatively rare, reaching around 3.5m (12ft), with attractive blue-grey new culms ageing to dark green. The culm sheaths are persistent, and a striking brick-red colour. A relatively new introduction, this plant is proving at least as hardy and exposure tolerant as *Y. anceps*, although it is less leafy, and it could also be used for hedging and windbreaks.

site	Any sites in full sun to light shade, and it will stand some exposure
soil	Unfussy, though grow largest on rich, moisture-retentive soils
watering	Prefer evenly moist, disliking extremes of wet and dry. Keep well watered during establishment
general care	Easy to grow, useful bamboos that can wander but are relatively easily controlled
pests & diseases	No real pest or disease problems. Dislike winter waterlogging and extremes of summer heat

Bamboos & Grasses

	SPRING	SUMMER	AUTUMN	WINTER	height (cm)	spread (cm)	culm colour	
Yushania anceps	🍃🍃🍃	🍃🍃🍃	🍃🍃🍃	🍃🍃🍃	400	400+		Handsome, arching specimen bamboo
Y. anceps 'Pitt White'	🍃🍃🍃	🍃🍃🍃	🍃🍃🍃	🍃🍃🍃	900	400+		More vigorous selection
Y. maculata	🍃🍃🍃	🍃🍃🍃	🍃🍃🍃	🍃🍃🍃	350	400+		Blue-grey new culms, red sheaths
Y. maling	🍃🍃🍃	🍃🍃🍃	🍃🍃🍃	🍃🍃🍃	1000	400+		Similar to *Y. anceps*

🍃 *in leaf*

Zea mays

Maize *or* sweetcorn

Zea mays, Indian corn, maize or sweetcorn, needs warmer, longer summers than those of the temperate regions to produce good 'cobs', however there are several cultivars grown as ornamentals, making bold, statuesque, broad-leaved and upright plants capable of reaching 2.4m (8ft) in the warmest parts – very tall for an annual.

The leaves of plain green cultivars and *Zea mays* itself can be as much as 90cm (3ft) long and 11cm (4.5in) across, arching out in pairs either side of the stout central stem (culm). Male flowers or tassels appear at the top of the stems, forming attractive curving fingers like the flowers of some miscanthus, while the female flowers or silks appear at the sides of the stems, forming masses of threads protruding from leafy sheaths that enclose the actual flowers.

Nowhere near hardy, all cultivars are best germinated and grown on in good light indoors or in a glasshouse, and only planted out once all risk of frost has passed, usually in late spring to early summer. They may take a couple of weeks to settle, but once they have their roots down their rate of growth can be astonishing.

Groups of sweetcorn look immediately exotic and can be used in subtropical garden styles, or placed singly as the centrepiece of mixed grass plantings or annual bedding schemes.

The variegated cultivars tend to be smaller growing than plain-leaved maize. *Z. mays* var. *japonica* is dwarf, growing to only 1.2m (4ft), and has the same broad white leaf striping as *Z. mays* 'Variegata', while 'Harlequin' has green leaves striped with red, and produces red cobs. 'Quadricolor' is a gaudy mix of green, white, yellow and pink stripes. 'Amoro' and 'Multicolor' have plain green leaves, but produce cobs with an attractive random mixture of white, yellow, orange, red, blue and brown kernels good for drying.

Zea mays 'Quadricolor'

site	As warm and sheltered a spot as possible, but preferably in full sun	
soil	These plants are generally unfussy, but not too dry or waterlogged	
watering	Water copiously while in growth and during fruit set; however, little else is required regarding watering	
general care	Easy to grow if kept frost free, potted on before becoming pot bound and hardened off well	
pests & diseases	Aphids can be a problem and slugs can defoliate young plants. Treat with appropriate pesticides	

	SPRING	SUMMER	AUTUMN	WINTER	height (cm)	spread (cm)	leaf colour	
Zea mays		🌿🌿	●●●●		240	100		Statuesque annual grass
Z. mays 'Amoro'		🌿🌿	●●●●		180	100		Cultivar with kernels of mixed colours
Z. mays 'Harlequin'		🌿🌿	●●●●		180	100		Red striped leaves and cobs
Z. mays 'Multicolor'		🌿🌿	●●●●		180	100		Mixed kernel colours like 'Amoro'
Z. mays 'Quadricolor'		🌿🌿	●●●●		180	100		Gaudy variegation, not to everyone's taste
Z. mays 'Variegata'		🌿🌿	●●●●		180	100		Green leaves striped with broad white bands
Z. mays var. *japonica*		🌿🌿	●●●●		120	90		Dwarf, white variegated

🌿 in leaf   ● flowering

Bamboos & Grasses

Troubleshooting

The following charts summarise the main problems gardeners may encounter in growing the species and cultivars covered by this book. They are separated into a chart for grasses, sedges and the other grass-like plants, and another for bamboos. Start with the symptoms, and by answering successive questions 'yes' [✓] or 'no' [✗] you should quickly arrive at the probable cause. These are covered in more depth, including remedies or suggested treatments, in the list of pests and diseases that follows.

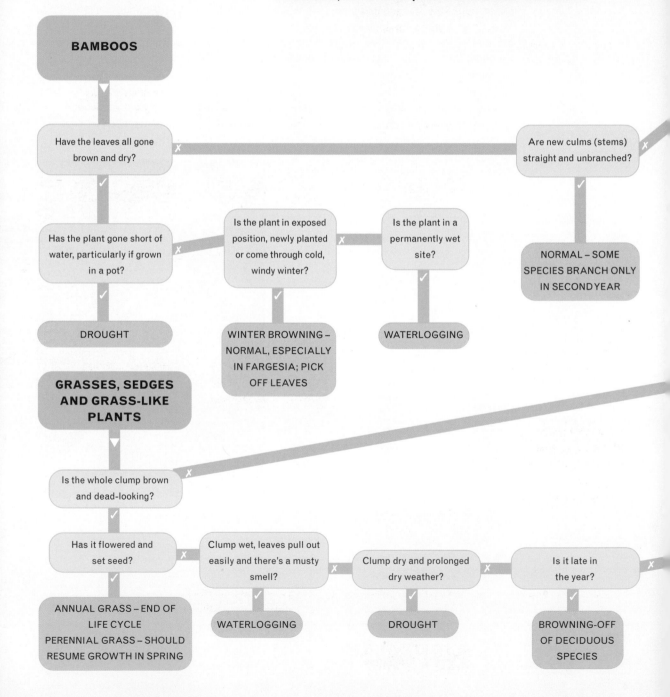

BAMBOOS

Have the leaves all gone brown and dry?

Are new culms (stems) straight and unbranched?

Has the plant gone short of water, particularly if grown in a pot?

Is the plant in exposed position, newly planted or come through cold, windy winter?

Is the plant in a permanently wet site?

NORMAL – SOME SPECIES BRANCH ONLY IN SECOND YEAR

DROUGHT

WINTER BROWNING – NORMAL, ESPECIALLY IN FARGESIA; PICK OFF LEAVES

WATERLOGGING

GRASSES, SEDGES AND GRASS-LIKE PLANTS

Is the whole clump brown and dead-looking?

Has it flowered and set seed?

Clump wet, leaves pull out easily and there's a musty smell?

Clump dry and prolonged dry weather?

Is it late in the year?

ANNUAL GRASS – END OF LIFE CYCLE PERENNIAL GRASS – SHOULD RESUME GROWTH IN SPRING

WATERLOGGING

DROUGHT

BROWNING-OFF OF DECIDUOUS SPECIES

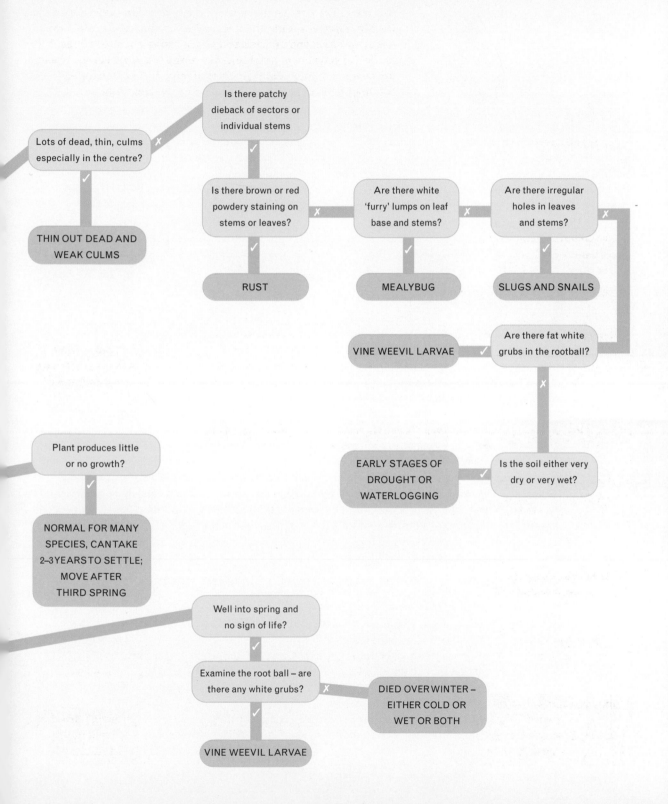

Lots of dead, thin, culms especially in the centre?

Is there patchy dieback of sectors or individual stems

THIN OUT DEAD AND WEAK CULMS

Is there brown or red powdery staining on stems or leaves?

Are there white 'furry' lumps on leaf base and stems?

Are there irregular holes in leaves and stems?

RUST

MEALYBUG

SLUGS AND SNAILS

VINE WEEVIL LARVAE

Are there fat white grubs in the rootball?

EARLY STAGES OF DROUGHT OR WATERLOGGING

Is the soil either very dry or very wet?

Plant produces little or no growth?

NORMAL FOR MANY SPECIES, CAN TAKE 2–3 YEARS TO SETTLE; MOVE AFTER THIRD SPRING

Well into spring and no sign of life?

Examine the root ball – are there any white grubs?

DIED OVER WINTER – EITHER COLD OR WET OR BOTH

VINE WEEVIL LARVAE

Pests, Diseases & Cultural Problems

While they cannot be called trouble free, the grasses, bamboos and grass-like plants covered in this book are for the most part extremely amenable in cultivation, and compared to many other plant groups are attacked by relatively few pests or diseases.

The major problems likely to be encountered are usually related to the gardener trying to grow the wrong plant in the wrong place, in conditions that do not suit it, or through climatic extremes of drought or waterlogging. Rectifying the former may simply be a matter of moving an unhappy specimen elsewhere in the garden where conditions may suit it better.

Excesses of drought or waterlogging are probably the single biggest causes of failure with grasses and bamboos. They can cause similar-looking symptoms – dead, bleached or brown leaves and stems – but it is usually easy to see which was to blame, and in the early stages remedial action can be taken.

Unfortunately, by the time severe symptoms of distress are noticed, it may be already too late for the plant, and this is particularly so with deciduous grass species over the winter.

The first sign a gardener may have that a grass has succumbed to winter wet or frost (more often a combination of the two) may be when its dead clump of leaves fail to re-shoot in the spring.

Either replant with a more moisture-tolerant selection, or work plenty of sand and grit into the soil to improve drainage and try the same grass again.

Problems

Drought

Plants can suffer from drought at any time of year, but the problem is more pronounced during hot, windy and dry spells in summer. The main symptoms are browning, dying leaves (usually beginning at the tips) and stems. This should not be confused with the habit of many grasses, the annual species in particular (but not exclusively), or natural dieback following flowering and seed set.

For many grass species, an early autumn is quite natural as following seed set, the plant has done its job for the year. To avoid problems with drought, keep an eye on how moist the garden is, and do not assume a light summer shower will give plants enough water, particularly if the weather is windy. Plants in pots need to be watched particularly carefully.

Drought is probably the only Achilles' heel of bamboos. Once established, most bamboos should only need watering in the driest of periods, but young plants, those that are newly planted and those grown in pots particularly can react extremely badly to lack of water. Unfortunately, leaf browning is often delayed, so the plant only appears to react 'after the event'. Bamboos that have suffered from drought can look to all intents and purpose dead, with every leaf brown and crisped, but will often recover, though it may take a while for them to regain full vigour.

Waterlogging

Some of the emergents and aquatics in this book like rushes, horse tails and some of the sedges positively thrive on waterlogging, but for many grasses, the combination of winter cold and wet can be fatal. The symptoms are similar to those of the early stages of drought, browning leaves and stems, but a waterlogged grass plant can be a sorry sight when the entire clump has browned and begun to fall apart.

There is often a smell of rot, and the leaves and stems pull easily away from the clump, which is usually soft and sodden. Various bacterial and fungal rots are to blame, but these tend only to invade a dead or dying grass root system on the point of drowning anyway.

Caught in its early stages, many grasses will revive from waterlogging if moved to a drier site (or into a pot with free-draining compost), otherwise replant with an alternative species better suited to damper conditions such as a sedge.

Pests

Aphids

Aphids or greenfly (though some species are red or black) can affect grasses, generally the thinner, softer leaved species, particularly early in the growing season before numbers of their predators have had a chance to build up. They can be disfiguring, distorting shoot growth, but do the plant little real harm. For the non-squeamish, drawing the thumb and forefinger along each stem and leaf squashes the majority (wear gloves for sharp-edged grass species), or they can be blasted off with a strong jet of water from a hose. Use pesticides with caution and check the label says they are suitable for use on grasses.

Mealybugs

These unpleasant cousins of the aphid secrete a white, waxy coating as protection from predators, making them look like flecks of cotton wool. They usually infest the lowest parts of the stems of grasses, down inside the clump, so can be difficult to spot. If the stems of an otherwise healthy looking grass are being shed for no apparent reason, there may be mealybugs feasting on the juicy lower part of the grass culm. Their coating protects them from many insecticides. Wipe each insect with a cotton bud or soft brush dipped in surgical spirits. Effective, if tedious.

Slugs and snails

Both categories of these voracious molluscs seem to have little taste for many of the species included in this book. However, they do attack many sedges, particularly broad leaved *Carex siderosticha*, and soft leaved grasses such as *Milium effusum*. Irregular holes and slices are taken out of the leaves, which will probably also show the tell-tale slimy trails. Surrounding affected plants with grit, broken eggshells or a mulch of bark chippings or cocoa shells, beer-filled traps or hand-picking at night by torchlight are several more ecologically-sound options than chemical slug pellets.

Vine weevil

Although the adult weevils seem to steer clear of grasses and bamboos, the larvae of this pest are voracious consumers of the root system of a range of plants, including grasses and sedges. The symptoms – browning foliage and dieback – can look like other problems so to confirm the diagnosis, uproot the affected plants and examine the rootball. If you encounter fat, white grubs up to 15mm (⅝in) long, vine weevils are to blame. They are particularly dangerous to pot-grown specimens, which they can kill outright. A biological remedy contains microscopic worms or nematodes that parasitise the larvae. A new chemical, imidacloprid, was recently licensed for use against vine weevil. Vine weevil activity tends to peak in late summer, so keep an eye out for plants looking sickly for no obvious reason.

Diseases

Rust

Rust is a term for a group of fungi that can attack all sorts of plants. Its most obvious symptom is the reddish or brown nodules or spots (spores) on the surface of the leaves. Rust tends to be encouraged by moist weather and can overwinter on dead leaves, so cutting the plants hard back in autumn and disposing of (not composting) the leaves can help, as does improving air circulation around the plants. Wettable (powdered) sulphur, applied to the surrounding soil, can be an effective control method if repeated several times during the growing season. Rusts tend to be more unsightly and reduce a plant's vigour than be life-threatening.

Index

Acknowledgements

The majority of the photographs in this book were taken by Tim Sandall, with the assistance of David Sarton. The image on page 104 was supplied by John Feltwell/Garden Matters.

The publishers would like to thank Coolings Nurseries for their cooperation and assistance with the photography in this book, including the loan of tools and much specialist equipment. Special thanks go to: Sandra Gratwick. Coolings Nurseries Ltd., Rushmore Hill, Knockholt, Kent, TN14 7NN. Tel: 00 44 1959 532269; Email: coolings@coolings.co.uk; Website: www.coolings.co.uk.